REMEMBERING

REJUVENATION

REUNION

RESTORYING

THE SOULISTIC JOURNEY

A PILGRIMAGE TO THE SOURCE OF YOUR BEING

GENEVIEVE BOAST & LORNA HOWARTH

PANACEA

BOOKS THAT REIMAGINE
THE WORLD

Published by Panacea Books, 2020

ISBN 978-1-8382866-0-6

With gratitude and love to Beth Lewis for the book interior and cover
design; to Natasha Griss for the Soulistic Wheel illustration and website
design; to Becky Rui for the photograph of the authors under the apple tree
and to Donna Byatt for co-hosting the Soulistic Retreats
at Elements of Avebury.

www.beyondhumanstories.com/soulistic-journey

ACKNOWLEDGEMENTS

This book would not have come into being were it not for the courage of the Wisdom Weavers, the first women to undertake the Soulistic Journey. We are indebted to their honesty, tenacity, humour and love. And so, this book is dedicated to them – to Alexis, Amy, Daniela, Donna, Julie, Kelsey and Teri – and to all who follow the path of the Soul.

"WE DON'T SEE THINGS
AS THEY ARE.
WE SEE THEM AS WE ARE."
- ANAIS NIN

DEDICATIONS

GENEVIEVE BOAST:

This book would not have come into being, were it not for the lessons taught to me by my family. My mother and father who birthed me from a place beyond the stars. My two sisters, eternal playmates who are the first to my side whenever there is trouble or celebrations to be handled with loving care. My husband, Euan, without whom I would never have developed the courage to show up real and raw in this crazy yet exquisite world; without whom I would never have known what love beyond love is. All the 'littles' in the form of step-kids, nieces and nephews – my greatest teachers and allies. My soul family, many of whom feature in these pages. And Lorna, you are a sacred sister and joyous co-creator – for you my heart swells with gratitude. Of course, I give thanks to all the more than human beings who are also my family. The mountains of my birth, the bird tribes and animal communities who walk with me. The angels, star nations and beings of light who sit with me in council. Because of you all, I am who I am, and this book has now begun its journey.

LORNA HOWARTH:

As I started to write my Dedications, I realised I feel immense gratitude to every entity on this beautiful planet: every bird that has delighted me, every flower that has enchanted me, every being that has fed me, every loving friend who has supported me… I am grateful to my colleagues who, over the years, have taught me so much – Satish Kumar, Sophie Poklewski Koziell, John Moat, Lynn Batten, David Cadman, Kenny Young, and to my niece, the brilliant designer, Beth Lewis. I feel blessed beyond measure to have met Genevieve Boast and to work with her co-creatively on this book and others. Gen, you are truly inspirational. For the unconditional love of my incredible family who have been there when times really did get tough, I thank you with all my heart. But my gratitude knows no bounds for my partner of thirty years, Rob Swan, who is the kindest, funniest, most talented and loving person you could ever hope to meet. Rob, if not for you…

GIFTING

The meeting had been scheduled for quite a while and there was a long Agenda of things to discuss – like, who should publish this book, and how should it be promoted – but it was a beautifully sunny early Autumn day and the call of the wild drew Genevieve and Lorna out of the office and into the woods.

They leaned against the twisted ancient trunk of the beautiful hornbeam tree known as Sophia and she seemed to say to them in the susurration of her leaves, "Let Nature be your guide." And then, as they sat on the banks of the river, gazing into its sparkling depths, Genevieve asked her divining rods yet more questions; and the answers were astounding. The Agenda was no more, irrelevant, as the flow found its own direction.

That night Lorna had a dreamlike remembrance of a story she'd once heard her friend Satish Kumar tell. In the story, Mother Apple said, "When it is time to bear fruit, I gift my apples to all beings without discrimination. Humans savour my tasty apples and throw the core in the hedge or the compost bin; blackbirds peck away at my ripe fruit until it is no more and the seeds find their way back into the dark earth; badgers gnaw on any of my windfalls they find upon their path; and wasps and butterflies enjoy the sweet juices of my fruit that has rolled away and settled in the long grass. In this way, I ensure the regeneration of my kind – through kindness."

The following day, as Genevieve and Lorna walked through the valley to the sea, discussing the Mother Apple story and how the revelations of the last few days might come to pass, they stumbled across a beautiful ancient apple tree, dripping with ripe fruit. They knew their compass was set.

In The Soulistic Journey, we take our cues from Nature and aspire to learn from Nature's intelligence. Therefore, reflecting Mother Apple's wisdom, we are gifting 200 copies of this book to our friends, family and colleagues in the hope that you will enjoy what you read in these pages. And if, as you read, you think of others who may enjoy this book, we ask that you consider gifting them a copy too. In this way, The Soulistic Journey will bear fruit, finding its way to the people who will enjoy it most; and seeds of joyful transformation will proliferate and germinate across the world.

With thanks and love – Genevieve Boast and Lorna Howarth

Love is the primary energy in the Universe. It is the beginning and the ending of all that is. Loving unconditionally is the ultimate adventure.

CONTENTS

THE PRACTICE

NORTH

NORTH QUARTER MEDITATION

NOVEMBER

DECEMBER

SOUTH

THE SOLAR AND LUNAR ARCHETYPES OVERVIEW

INTRODUCTION

THE SOULISTIC ADVENTURE

There can come a time in life when you face a crossroads, when it feels as if your existing patterns of behaviour or your lifestyle choices no longer serve you, but you don't know which way to turn. You may be experiencing illness, divorce, death of a loved one, exhaustion, redundancy, depression, or even a loss of faith in life itself. It is at these times as you begin to question 'what it's all about' – times of crisis and yet of opportunity too – when *The Soulistic Journey* takes you by the hand and offers a new way of being; a path less travelled to the source of your being.

Conversely, all may be well with your life and work, but you may simply feel, 'there has to be more to life than this'. That is a signal to you that exploration and adventure beckon. Whatever has brought you to this point in your life – where you are reading these pages – you now have an opportunity to dive deeply into your unique story and to reweave all the threads into a new blueprint.

Lorna Howarth, co-author of this book, was a participant on the first guided Soulistic Journey course. She explains why she chose to walk this path:

> *"I was running a successful literary agency when I was diagnosed with cancer for the second time, which came as a complete shock – I thought I'd 'been there and done that.' But looking back, I can see it was a kind of 'cosmic nudge' to drop the prioritisation of work over everything else, including my own health, and begin to explore other ways of being.*

However, whilst I could see that my illness had brought me to a crossroads in my life, all the signposts were blank, with no clear direction ahead. All I had was an awareness that the path I was on, which I thought was serving the greater good, no longer served me.

Then, by a series of wonderful synchronicities, the Soulistic Journey came into my life and I felt absolutely ready to participate in this adventure, as I really had no idea what was next for me. I felt like an empty vessel waiting to be filled up with something new and inspiring. I've never felt particularly adventurous before, but that is the quality that defines this journey for me. It's an inner journey, an inner adventure and I was more than ready for the experience."

Many people are now beginning to question the prevailing narrative of contemporary culture – that of 'Work, Buy, Consume, Repeat' – and are looking for a deeper connection with life's mysteries, beyond the human stories we tell ourselves about who we are and what we should do with our lives. These stories are rooted in our own history and culture and are influenced by the lives and experiences of our ancestors, yet they have begun to feel limited, even irrelevant in the current, fast-transforming social and environmental ecosystems of our planet.

We are bombarded by advertising and social media which indoctrinate us to look a certain way, buy particular brands of goods and aspire to have more money and more things – and yet in our hearts, this way of life feels meaningless and empty and… what is that word…? Oh yes, soulless.

The deeper connections we yearn for, but perhaps cannot yet imagine, can still be found in timeless wisdom traditions, in the magic and majesty of the natural world, in synchronicity and mindfulness, in constellations of like-minded friendships, and also, in 're-storying' our lives to harmonise with our Soul Purpose: that yearning, that deep knowing that we were born to experience more than this.

The Soulistic Journey itself sprang 'through' the imaginal realms into the day world where it stalked and romanced us – Genevieve and Lorna – over the period of a year until we both stopped to listen and align to its energetic gifts. In 2018, the first ever Soulistic Journey was catalysed, and the essence of the work shared with you in these pages has been growing, evolving and shapeshifting ever since.

This book accompanies travellers like you on a year and a day-long 'walk'; a path of self-discovery and transformation. The walk itself is 'meta-physical' which means you don't actually have to go anywhere, except inside your being; the walk is an inner journey of adventure and all that you experience will unfold from within you. This is a process of inside out change, that will challenge you to mine your authentic depths of wisdom and courage. That is the wonderful thing – your Soul Purpose already resides within you – it just needs to be awakened and remembered.

The journey can be undertaken alone, with this book as your guide, or you may like to join a group of adventurers, facilitated by the authors of this book, and dive into the online/onlife Soulistic Journey Mentoring Programme.[1] (See page 325 for more details.) Whichever way you choose to walk the Soulistic Journey, you will find your life will be irrevocably transformed, because you will be able to see more clearly your heart's desire, your true calling and your reason for incarnation in your body at this time – your Soul Purpose. You are asked to slow down to the pace of Nature, letting go of your opinions and judgements about how things should be, and to trust instead in the wisdom of the other-than-human realms. The Soulistic Journey is, as they say in Permaculture[2], 'the perfect meandering' – because meandering allows for time, Nature, wisdom and courage to percolate and create their magic!

But first, we must sound a note of caution. The Soulistic Journey is not for the faint-hearted. It asks quite a lot of you because it is an initiation. If you suffer with uncertainty about your mental health, or if you are fearful of change or struggle with anxiety, then we would advise that you always have supportive friends, family or therapists who you can turn to as you undertake this path. We offer online guidance, but you may also need other trusted support networks as you undertake the practices. They are not dangerous in any way, but they

YOU ARE THE
ARCHITECT OF
YOUR REALITY

are challenging. They are not designed to replace any health approaches that you may already be taking, but they can complement them. So, make sure you feel grounded and mentally buoyant before embarking on this journey.

The Soulistic Journey will move you beyond your comfort zones into the realms of the imagination, working with archetypal energies, and calling upon mentors and guides to light your way. As you walk the path of your unique Soulistic Journey, you will find that deeper layers of reality open up for you so that you are able to make life-enhancing choices that ensure you are truly the architect of your reality.

Are you feeling the call of the pilgrimage of purpose?

Do you have the courage to step into who you were born to be?

Are you ready to say 'Yes!' to rewriting your story?

Good – then let's begin walking a new path together.

Authors' Note: A key aspect of the Soulistic Journey is about slowing down to the pace of Nature and taking our cues from what is happening in the natural world. We appreciate that many of our readers will live in towns and cities where experiencing the gifts of Nature on a daily basis is not easy. You may not live near a park or river or have a garden or window box. Finding a reconnection to Nature may be challenging, but even if all you can do is buy a houseplant and look out of your window at the weather, that is a start. Slowly, just by making this first tenuous reconnection, Nature will find its way back into your life.

The authors of this book live in the Northern Hemisphere and our Earth observations are based on the four seasons experienced here. If you are reading this book in the Southern Hemisphere or any country where the flora, fauna and seasons differ, feel free to interpret the seasonal fluctuations and energies as appropriate to you. We have a friend in Tasmania who relishes the fact that our Summer Solstice is her Winter Solstice, and that when we are planting tomato seeds, she is harvesting hers. Be flexible about the seasonal observations; for on any given moment on Earth it is both summer and winter, autumn and spring, day and night. Time is not linear, and neither is this book. Dive in and swim into the flow that is right for you.

THE CHALLENGE

CHALLENGE IS A PRECURSOR TO EVOLUTION

Whilst this book is designed to be enjoyable and thought-provoking, it may also be disconcerting and downright challenging – after all, you are being invited to make some fundamental life shifts, and change can often be unsettling. Rather than judge these emotions as good or bad, we ask that you sit with them and try and tune-in to the guidance they are bringing you. This can be hard; you may feel unsupported in your journey by friends and family; you may doubt the veracity of what you are experiencing; you may feel like quitting – but that's okay. All these feelings are valid and offer you a starting point to work with. Remember e-motions are simply 'energy in motion'. If we allow ourselves to move with and through our various emotional states then we are by the very nature of life, transforming.

Everyone has doubts, in fact doubt is often the flipside of truth. If you can determine why you are doubtful, this can be the precursor to epiphany. As you progress further into your Soulistic Journey you will find that your doubt starts to transform into discernment. You may be invited to participate in practices that you are uncomfortable with – that's fine! Don't do them – or do a version of them that you are comfortable with. Or perhaps recognise that your resistance stems from an inner desire to protect old habits that thus far have kept you safe in the confines of your story. However, often what you need or yearn for is not found in your comfort zone; it is beyond that, in a place of potential and creativity that you may rarely visit. So, if you are feeling uncomfortable, perhaps ask yourself why, and explore that feeling.

You can participate in the Soulistic Journey however you like; you can dip in and out of this book at will, interpreting it in whatever way is meaningful to you at the time. Or you may follow it to the letter for a year and a day, and then start all over again, as many of our past participants have done – because they want to deepen what they have experienced. It's entirely your choice. This book is designed to accompany your journeying and to be a support system for your transformation over months, years and even decades. As co-creators and authors of this experience, we have found that the journey expands and becomes more powerful each time it is repeated. Indeed, it is a lifetime(s) quest.

DOUBT WILL
TRANSFORM
INTO
DISCERNMENT

THE AUTHORS

The authors of this book – Genevieve Boast and Lorna Howarth – first worked together on *Tough Bliss*, a book that unflinchingly describes Genevieve's personal journey to restory her life. Between them they have lifetimes of experience in the fields of personal development, life coaching and mentoring, sustainability, environmental ethics, environmental activism, book and magazine publishing and writing.

LORNA'S STORY

For 18 years, I worked as a writer and editor for various publications, including *Positive News*, *Living Lightly* and *Resurgence*, the UK's leading magazine on ecology, spirituality and the arts. During this time, I interviewed many inspirational teachers who helped shape my thinking, including Jonathon Porritt,

James Lovelock, Deepak Chopra, Vandana Shiva, John Seymour, Anita Roddick and others, although perhaps my foremost teacher was Satish Kumar, Editor Emeritus of *Resurgence*, and a Gandhian philosopher and peace activist.

Then, in 2008, I joined my friend and colleague, the musician and activist Kenny Young, to work as Development Director for the NGO Artists Project Earth. We funded over 350 climate change mitigation projects around the world, as well as supplying emergency funding for disaster relief. During this time, I was fortunate to attend the international COP Climate Conferences in Copenhagen, Cancun and Durban, seeing first-hand the impenetrable barrier between inter-governmental decision-making and civil society activism.

In 2012, I set up my publishing agency, The Write Factor, inspired by the words of my good friend and writer, John Moat, who said, "Your story is imperative to the completion of the all-important Universe Story." My aim was to help people who fell between the gaps in the traditional publishing industry to tell their stories. At this time, I helped edit, design and publish over 60 books.

In 2020 after participating in the Soulistic Journey, I honed my publishing agency into the imprint, Panacea Books, which specialises in publishing books that 're-imagine the world'. I am also beginning to write my own stories and facilitate the path of others as they walk the Soulistic Journey.

GENEVIEVE'S STORY

Born in Colorado USA, I spent the first years of my life running wild in the mountains, with the rocks, plants, animals and stars as my friends and teachers. My parents were archaeologists and my grandparents were embedded in the world of business and education, flavoured with a healthy dose of mysticism. As a result, I grew up rooted in the past whilst simultaneously having my vision trained on the horizon of human potential.

Then when I was six years old, my family moved to England and thus began a period of feeling like an alien in a strange land. My adolescence was turbulent and rebellious, creating frequent confusion and crisis. Synchronicity then led me through arrest, near death experiences and a powerful whistleblowing encounter into another storytelling realm, finding a career in media and entertainment. I progressed through a series of roles within the fields of continuous improvement, cultural change and corporate social responsibility, becoming an experienced coach, facilitator and public speaker. I also trained in NLP, Reiki and Sustainability.

Yet for all the glamour of the media, I found myself sinking deeply into a 'dark night of the soul' in my late twenties, when suddenly, all my human stories stopped making sense. In the space of a year, I got divorced, changed jobs, moved away from family and friends and slowly began to rebuild my physical, emotional and mental health. I had lived through a breakdown and a breakthrough and had begun my metamorphosis towards the 'butterfly' of my true story.

In 2010, I was drawn by the call of inner adventure to strike out on my own and found my first business, Emergency Happiness. I worked with individuals and organisations towards cultural change and transformation. Later, I also completed an MSc in Responsible Sustainable Business to delve deeper into the ecology of sustainable human living systems. In 2013 on a Vision Quest in the canyons of Utah, I received a vision that would see me re-story my work into the organisation, Beyond Human Stories. Since that moment, I have been dedicated to making and telling stories that unite rather than separate us and that allow us to choose our narrative in this exciting time to be alive.

OUR WRITING STYLE

This book is written using the first-person pronouns 'I' or 'we' – but in most of the book, we do not determine which of the two authors is writing. This is because we want the book to be a weave of our combined experiences. What one writes, the other concurs with; and writing in this way frees us to express our own experiences through a unified voice.

We have also chosen this format because we support a more general shift from, 'Me to We' – a shorthand formula for acknowledging that we are all connected and that our words and actions create profound inter-actions: that what I do has repercussions for you, and vice versa. So, we ask that you do not try to differentiate between who wrote which section – but accept that we have woven in and out of each other's stories like the warp and weft of a loom, creating a picture that is multi-dimensional. Where, for the sake of clarity, it is necessary to establish which one of us is narrating, then we will include our name in brackets.

As you are reading this, we believe your wise soul has brought you to this place, much like Dorothy at the beginning of the yellow brick road, or Lucy, taking her first steps into Narnia. Where you go from here is up to you (and your soul). The path you take will be full of twists and turns and you will find guardians and tricksters awaiting you – but that is the nature of any real quest. There has to be challenge as a precursor to evolution. There has to be the mystery leading you forwards into unknown territory. And you always have within you the necessary strength to overcome any obstacle – you just have to begin the journey and see where it takes you.

Are you ready?

No one really ever is.

Are you willing to learn and grow?

That's all that is needed.

Take our hands.

Let us guide you on your first steps of the Soulistic Journey's wheel of life.

HOW TO USE THIS BOOK

THIS BOOK IS PRESENTED IN FOUR PARTS:

THE FOUNDATIONS

A GENTLE UNFOLDMENT OF TRANSFORMATION

The first part of the book sets out the context of the journey. This section demystifies the language and terminology that is used in this book; it explains the Core Practices, including how to create your altar and the art of seeing with 'mythic eyes'. It illuminates the importance of keeping a daily journal and explores the principles of alchemy and the trusted guides of Synchronicity and Intuition. It is a section that you will refer to time and again as you walk the Soulistic Journey for a year and a day – a Shamanic timeframe that allows for a gentle unfoldment of your transformation and gives space for reflection, contemplation and celebration along the way.

THE SOULISTIC ARCHETYPES

THE KEY TO A DEEPER UNDERSTANDING OF YOURSELF

The Soulistic Archetypes are unique to this journey. They are a distillation of the Solar (masculine) and Lunar (feminine) energetic qualities that imbue our world with story, form and meaning, and in each month we delve into how these dynamic energies may affect you and how the unification of their qualities offers a key that can unlock and shift some self-limiting behaviour patterns.

There is a Mystery (shadow element) and a Wisdom (gift element) to each of the archetypes to give you a deeper connection with how they may show up in your life. The Soulistic Archetypes underpin the practices that you are invited to play with each month, offering an energetic and symbolic way into a deeper understanding of yourself. However, in reality, these archetypal qualities are omnipresent so you may feel any one or more of their energies at any time. This is natural and nothing to be concerned about. The very fact that you are able to ascertain a particular quality resonating in your life is a good thing, as it will allow you to open the door to the wisdom and narrative that it offers.

THE PRACTICE

THE POWER OF CHOICE LIES WITH YOU

In the third section of the book, you will begin your journey via the seven directions of the Soulistic Wheel – North, East, South, West, Above, Below and Within (otherwise known as the 'Heart Centre'). These seven directions drawn from the indigenous traditions of many cultures across the world, relate to the months of the year and specific practices that are undertaken in each direction. So, for example, as you walk in the North Quarter of the Soulistic Wheel, from November through December to January, each month you will explore the energetic qualities of the natural world at that time and the cosmological and archetypal qualities that weave above, below and within you.

You can begin your journey at any point in time that feels right for you. Although the book starts in the North Quarter of November, you can still step on the wheel in the South Quarter of July if that is when you naturally connect with the Soulistic Journey. All directions ultimately lead to the 'Heart Centre' of your unique Soulistic Wheel, a personal place you will come to know and visit often.

Within 'The Practice' section, you will also see our monthly 'Storyhacks' which offer insights designed to help you re-imagine, or 're-story' your life. In essence the storyhacks cut through your personal mythology, asking deep questions that can help you to see more clearly how you may be self-sabotaging or choosing a comfort-zone existence. The storyhacks dive deeply into what makes you uniquely human, but also invite you to step-up to become a wiser, multifaceted being: a challenge that can change your whole life each time you jump outside of the boundaries of your previous narrative. The power of choice to do this lies with you.

In this journey, there are no rules, but there is a slowing down to a pace that allows time for the miraculous to occur; you will be creating space for adventuring and curious exploration of your inner and outer landscapes and you are encouraged to follow your intuition and spontaneity in how you interpret the practices. They have to be meaningful for you. As we have mentioned already, you are the architect of your reality, so ultimately, how you decipher and experience the wisdom that lies within the practices, is up to you.

The Soulistic Journey is not only the adventure of a year and a day, but is also your inner sanctum, your power place, the container for your unique life quest. The guidance offered in this book is there to assist your journey, but the path reveals itself in unexpected ways because deep magic is beyond words and all life's answers exist in the imaginal realm. Be childlike in your adventuring and enjoy the ride!

THE SOULISTIC LIBRARY

The fourth section of this book is The Soulistic Library, where we have included information that can deepen and enrich your journey.

On the Bookshelf, you will find details of many of our favourite books and authors providing a wellspring of mind-expanding wisdom for you to dive into. In the Library you will also find links to the recorded versions of the 'Quarterly Meditations' – as most people find guided meditations easier to listen to than to read. You will also find descriptions of the Solar, Lunar and Unification Soulistic Archetypes for each month, making the information easily accessible from the Library at any time.

Ideally, you will use the pages entitled 'My Insights and Illuminations' in this section to record and build your own library of resources as you travel your unique Soulistic Journey. These insights are likely to come from the books, recordings, web links, snippets of information and teachers that you come across as you move through your adventure. Again, this isn't about the authors giving you a reading list that you must consume to the letter. This is about us sowing the seeds of magic within you, so that you can curate your own library of inspiration that enables you to navigate your unique path to the source of your being.

Visit the Soulistic Library often and be curious for great wisdom resides there, leading you to adventures beyond your wildest imaginings!

THE
FOUNDATIONS

THE CALL OF THE SOUL

SOUL ADVENTURES BECKON US WITH THE LURE OF MYSTERY

What does the word 'soul' mean to you? It's a word that's hard to define because it means something different to everyone: some people explain it as a familiar feeling, a sense of ease, altered perception or yearning. It is worth taking some time to ponder the question: 'What does 'soul' mean to me?'

Recently, as I (Genevieve) was facilitating one of the Soulistic Journey circles, I was struck with a realisation: it was a deeper understanding of the role and meaning of soul in my life that hadn't come to me in quite this way before, but which has revolutionised the way I now see my own growth and evolution.

Often when I ask people what their soul feels like, the response is, 'a feeling like coming home,' a 'sense of peace within,' of 'knowingness,' or of 'love'. I totally agree with each of these in the context of tuning-in to a higher place of inner wisdom that sits beyond the realm of human form or stories. However, as I started to reflect on my own experiences of soul, I realised that my soul often comes into my life to disrupt habits, to stretch comfort zones and generally break me out of my patterns of security. Therefore, when I invite my soul to take the driving seat, things tend to get more than a little crazy! In fact, they get positively uncomfortable (and exciting).

Let me explain. There is a story my NLP teacher told me almost 15 years ago. It has stayed with me ever since and serves as a reminder of the role of soul in encouraging me to evolve and forge into unknown territory. It goes something like this (and forgive me if I embellish it with elements of my own story):

> There was once a woman who focussed her whole life on creating 'success'. She worked super hard in her career and got promoted several times. She had a good salary, a loving husband who

SOUL OFTEN COMES INTO MY LIFE TO DISRUPT HABITS

worshiped the ground she walked on, and she lived in a reason-ably-sized house in the city. She had savings, she had a company car and she had a pension. A life of relative luxury, you might say.

But inside she was secretly crying because she had lost any sense of who she really was beyond the mask of a businesswoman. In the dark hours of the night, she would wake with fear pulsing in her chest. The fear was called mediocrity. The pulsing was called soul.

Then one day, as she was cooking dinner, she heard a knock on the front door. Curious, as her husband was already home, she put down her spoon and, she went to see who was at the door. Opening it, she was surprised to see two huge angels waiting for her.

Smiling, they said, "Are you ready? Let's go," and turned to escort her to an unknown destination.

"But… but, I have a life. I have a job…" she stammered.

"Exactly! That's precisely why it's time to go," the angels replied and without further ado, extended their wings to embrace and welcome her to her new Soul Adventure.

I never did find out if the woman said 'yes' or 'no' to her adventure. In my own experience of it, I turned around at the door and was able, for the first time, to acknowledge that the safe, tight confines of the story I had painstakingly built up around me, no longer fitted me. I had suffocated my soul and it was pulsing louder each and every day until I was finally ready to take the hands of the angels and leave my old skin behind.

So, that's what I did, almost 11 years ago now. And although the first year of my new adventure was scary, challenging and required massive amounts of courage to embark upon, I have since lived some of the best years of any life I have ever experienced.

WHAT WE DO
TO THE EARTH,
WE DO TO
OURSELVES

Soul adventures call you out of your comfort zones and beckon you with the lure of mystery. They come to you when you least expect them and most need them, in order to lead you to new beginnings, down unexpected roads, to surprise meetings with people who will love you into a whole new sense of yourself.

What if you simply allow your comfort zones to melt in favour of the mystery? What if you are brave enough to acknowledge that there is a reason the angels have come to escort you to a new path and a new reality? If you do, you follow the pulse of your soul evolution. You become a savvy cosmic adventurer.

As you travel for a year-and-a-day on the Soulistic Journey there will be plenty of opportunities to reconnect with your Soul Purpose – by which we mean, your highest potential; the reason why you chose to be here now. Many people, through no fault of their own, are unable to hear the quiet inner voice that speaks of another way, distracted as they are by the demands of modern life: of raising children, holding down a stressful job, paying the mortgage… But eventually, that voice begins to get louder, and more demanding. It asks questions of you: 'What is the point of this? Am I happy with my life? What do I really want?'

It is worth paying attention to this wise voice or inner knowing, because it is the voice of your soul; it comes from your subconscious (or superconscious), a part of your being that remains connected to the great etheric web of inter-being, also known as the Cosmic Hologram[3] or in ancient wisdom traditions, Indra's Net. Your soul, in fact your entire being, of which your soul is a part – your corporeal body, your etheric body, your conscious and subconscious mind, your multidimensional spirit – is inextricably linked to every other being in the Universe, human and other-than-human. What an incredible thought that is – everything is connected…

Indigenous peoples have always known this, which is why many elders from traditional cultures express such consternation for the disrespectful way that society now treats the Earth; as if she is just a 'resource' to be bought and sold. For those who have ears to hear, the words attributed to Chief Seattle, leader of the Duwamish people, still resonate profoundly today, well over a century after he spoke them: 'What we do to the Earth, we do to ourselves.' We are so interconnected and interdependent that any act of ruination perpetrated upon the being of our Mother Earth – whether it be destruction of the rainforests, or coal mining, or oceans plastic – eventually brings about our own downfall. How can it not? We are part of Gaia; we are sustained by her, so when we subjugate her, we subjugate ourselves.

Sadly, we have become so disconnected from the natural world that many people in over-developed countries now live in the illusion of 'Perpetual Summer'; we have eschewed the wisdom of the seasons. As Genevieve's sister, Kelsey Boast, explained in one of the Soulistic Retreats, "For decades humanity has sought to live in the light of perpetual summer. We are constantly active, always consuming, partying, celebrating and burning the candle at both ends; we yearn for holidays in the sun and groan about the rain and colder months; we fly-in summer fruits like strawberries and peaches at all times thinking that it is our right to have whatever we want all year round; we are only happy when it is hot and sunny and we are busy accumulating, doing, moving, creating – and our cultural conventions continue to advocate more of the same.

"But all this non-stop activity generates heat: flying unseasonal produce around the world creates heat in the atmosphere, flying ourselves around the world in search of sun has a huge climate impact, consumer lifestyles create heat in the manufacturing and production chains, and all this heat is reflected in the wildfires we are seeing all over the world – even in the Arctic – and also in the bubbling tensions in society, which can be likened to a volcano about to blow its top. As above, so below. As within, so without.

"Humans have forgotten how to live within the ebb and flow of the seasons, where winter brings with it a stillness, a cooling-off, a slowing down, and so we have unleashed the destructive powers of fire. We have forgotten that we are meant to flow with the changing energies of the seasons and that this brings balance, renewal and health. In order to step into our wisdom and return to a state of balance – for ourselves and Gaia – we need to reconnect with the Soul of the Seasons."

Kelsey's words really resonated with us. We have forgotten that we are the weather, and what's more, because Summer is only halfway through the Wheel of the Year, humanity is now stuck at the stage of adolescence. To step into our wisdom, we just need to step into Nature.

The good news is that many people are beginning to acknowledge these truths and are rekindling their awareness of our innate interdependence with Nature, knowing 'deep down' when they are not resonating at their highest potential, when they have become separate from the sustaining natural world. Perhaps you are one of them? Perhaps you have had enough of feeling out of kilter or unbalanced, or unfulfilled?

When there is disharmony in your core, this can often be expressed as stress, ill-health, anger, emotional turmoil and anxiety. But, despair not, because these struggles are also the first clues that your soul seeks another way of expressing its true self. You can choose to see the way your 'dis-ease' emerges as a sign-post that is pointing you towards another way of being, rather than something to be fearful of, or to fight and get rid of at all costs. You may not know which way the signpost is pointing, but that is what this book, *The Soulistic Journey*, is designed to do: to illuminate your path, the one your soul yearns to tread, enabling you to grow in confidence that your evolving self is fulfilling its destiny.

This is where it's worth mentioning your 'sacred point of view', a phrase coined by Seneca teacher Jamie Sams[4]. We write this book from our sacred point of view, rooted in the foundations of our culture, our experiences and our cosmologies as white American/English women. Granted, we are both blessed to be well-travelled in the human and other-than-human realms, yet we do not position ourselves as 'teachers' in the traditional sense of this archetype. In fact, we both have somewhat of an allergic reaction to the way this archetype has been misused in the Western world, because it infers that teachers are somehow superior or know better. No one knows your soul better than you. Instead, we offer our stories, adventures and questions as rich soil for you to till and plant your own seeds of wisdom within.

This book is written and offered from our personal and collective narrative lenses which are beautiful facets of the gems of truth held in Indra's Net of Universal wisdom. Your sacred point of view – of which the purpose of this book and journey is to remember and reconnect with its power – is your source of personal truth. If we share a concept or use a word that doesn't resonate with your personal truth, we ask you to pass it by and instead become curious about what your truth in this regard might be. Your Soulistic Journey cannot be lived by anyone else but you. This is the gift you uniquely bring to the Earth and the story of life in the Universe. We invite you to link hands, hearts and souls with us so that we may all weave a beautiful Soulistic tapestry of truth as we journey together.

THE TRANSFORMATIONAL POWER OF CHOICE

CHOOSING FROM THE HEART

As you begin walking the path of your Soulistic Journey, you may feel quite conflicted at times because the process asks questions of you that, at first, you may not know the answer to. What is beautiful about this journey though, is that you will begin to use this sense of uncertainty as a barometer of development: when you sense confusion or conflict, you will recognise them as important signs that you have entered into new territory where you don't have ready explanations – but the good news is that as you continue your journey of discovery, the answers will unfold.

That being said, you may find yourself getting irritated because you feel there is *no choice* for you but to continue with certain ways of life, even though you know it is not what you *want* to do. You may feel that you have no choice but to continue paying the mortgage; no choice but to stay in a job you dislike;

no choice but to remain with your partner for the sake of the children. Actually, there is always choice, and this journey is about enabling you to see the choices that may not yet have become clear to you – or perhaps it is more the case that you might not have allowed yourself to feel that sense of freedom yet?

Those who believe they have no choice and cannot make changes in their lives are really saying that they are not prepared to move outside their comfort zones. Without realising it, people who feel they have no choices in life have become rigid in their thinking and cynical about life's opportunities. This can become a self-fulfilling prophecy, as cynical thinking 'freezes' the molecular flow of intention so that momentum and energy are dimmed and connection with potentiality is lost or overlooked[5]. We become blind to life's attempts to romance us into new experiences and use the story of 'no choice' as an excuse to stay stuck and wedded to our pain.

COURAGE LIBERATES; CHOICE MOTIVATES

We all have choices, even those who are in the most terrible of circumstances where sometimes the only choice is between life or death. What a choice – but still there is choice: there is the choice not to fear death, but to embrace it and surrender to it; or there is the choice to fight on, to summon your energy and try again. Holocaust survivor, Viktor Frankl sums this up: "*Everything can be taken from a man but one thing: the last of the human freedoms — to choose one's attitude in any given set of circumstances, to choose one's own way.*"

There is a beautiful saying that goes something like this:

In the midst of war there is peace
In the midst of sorrow there is joy
In the midst of hatred there is love

This simple truism is at the heart of choice: even as war is raging around you, you have the choice not to participate and to go peaceably about your day. Even as your heart is filled with grief, you have the choice to embrace it and find the liberation that lies on the other side of sorrow. Even if you feel hatred towards someone, the choice of forgiveness and compassion lies within your heart. But choice does require you to be courageous, a word from Old French that literally means 'feeling from the heart'. Courage liberates; choice motivates.

Choice is an interesting word. As a noun, it infers options, alternatives, selectivity, decisions, preferences. As an adjective, it infers the best, excellence, the finest, the most valuable. In its most powerful active form, as a verb 'choosing' becomes a dynamic process of freedom enacted in every aspect of your life. So, in terms of the Soulistic Journey, choice is about selecting the best way forward in order for you to be in alignment with your Soul Purpose; it is about weighing-up your options and deciding what course of action will be the most valuable to your evolution. It is about stepping into your birthright as a conscious human being on the planet and claiming back your power of choice made in integrity with your heart and your soul. It is about becoming a living, breathing being of conscious liberation.

Returning to paying the mortgage, or the job you dislike, or the partner you no longer love, perhaps it is time to look a little more deeply into the options you have? In the midst of paying your mortgage, can you take a three-month repayment holiday to enable you to attend that art course you've always wanted to do? In the midst of doing a job you hate can you start looking at other options that would allow you to retrain or remove yourself from the unhealthy situation over time? In the midst of the relationship that is breaking down, can you find common ground that could lead to a breakthrough?

But choice isn't always about compromise or changing your attitude towards an existing situation. Sometimes, choice is about having the courage to take action and create change; to cease to do something that no longer serves your greater good; to forge ahead even if others do not accept your choice. As long as whatever you choose to do does not hurt or implicate anyone else, then the choice is yours and you can own this sovereignty regardless of what other people may think, say or do. Remember, when you own your power of choice utterly, it is the most threatening and frightening thing in the world to others who are refusing to do the same. They may try and fight you or persuade you to change your mind, but you will overcome any naysayers or saboteurs if you listen deeply to the choice that your heart wants to make. Listen and take inspired action.

Occasionally, you will be confronted with 'the choiceless choice', wherein you feel in your bones that your soul made a choice for you a long time ago and all you can do is follow the compulsion to act upon the opportunity being presented to you. These kinds of choiceless choices are often indicated by a series of synchronicities that point in a particular direction, or by a situation being unexpectedly resolved or changed without you having to take direct action. The choiceless choice indicates that you are following your Soul Purpose, and changes or resolutions occur naturally, allowing you to experience that which you need to, in order to grow. The choiceless choice is a gift, although sometimes it is hard to see it that way. It is the tough choice that leads you to future bliss and fulfilment, yet you are asked to be brave and forge ahead not knowing where the journey will take you. This is the nature of all soul initiations.

SOMETIMES STASIS OCCURS SO THAT YOU HAVE THE STILL SPACE TO CONTEMPLATE THE CHOICES THAT ARE PRESENTING THEMSELVES

Choosing your course wisely and soulfully is about slowing down and learning to listen to your inner heart wisdom. This is hard because most of us feel we don't have any inner wisdom! But actually, we do. Inner wisdom is that feeling of knowing; knowing that really, you can't do this job anymore and you just have to find a way towards right livelihood; inner wisdom is that small, quiet voice inside that is saying, 'I like this, this is good,' or indeed, 'No – I'm not happy with this'. The practices in this book are chosen to help you slow down and listen deeply to that voice – then the choice to take action inspired by your inner wisdom is yours and yours alone.

There is one final point we would like to make and that is, if your path or choice-making is not clear to you then take no action. Taking no action is a choice in itself. Sometimes stasis occurs so that you have the still space to con-template the choices that are presenting themselves to you before you forge ahead. To pause and sense into 'right action' is a choice made from wisdom.

THE ILLUSION OF SEPARATENESS

WHATEVER THE REASON FOR THE MINDSET OF
DOMINION, THE TIME HAS COME TO RESTORY IT

There is a malaise at the heart of twenty-first century life that is imperilling us all, and that is the misconception that humanity is somehow more evolved, superior to or separate from the natural world. It is a concept that many philosophers have debated over the centuries – why it is that we see ourselves as rulers of Nature – a belief that has given rise to devastation of ecosystems to such a degree that we are now compromising our own future.

Theologically, it seems that permission was granted for human supremacy over the natural world in the Old Testament, specifically in Genesis 1:26, "And God said, Let us make man in our image, after our likeness: and let them have dominion over the fish of the sea, and over the fowl of the air, and over the cattle, and over all the earth, and over every creeping thing that creepeth upon the earth." (*King James Bible*) However, if you go to the Aramaic translations which are much more multifaceted and inclusive, you will find that this passage originally meant that humans were created as, "the living reflection (*betzalmenu*) of the One Being, holding within us the awareness of all the beings that have gone before us in the caravan of life," – not as superior beings over the caravan of life![6]

In the intervening aeons, the interpretation of these words has been under constant scrutiny, with many theologians and thinkers propounding that such an anthropocentric representation of god diminishes our understanding of the Cosmos and the Universal laws to which we are all interconnected.

However, as time goes by, there can be no doubt that, whatever the reason for this mindset of dominion – whether religious, cultural, or scientific – the time has come to restory it. It is now obvious to us that we live in closed-loop systems within the body of Gaia, and that if we poison or abuse those systems, ultimately, we poison and abuse ourselves and all other beings we share this beautiful planet with. We cannot continue to live in the illusion of separateness now we know this truth.

Just so there can be no doubt about how truly connected we are with the ecosystems that surround us, consider this discourse from Silvio Gesell[7], who in 1906 suggested that plants are part of our digestive system:

> *"We cannot conceive man without the Earth any more than without a head or a stomach: the Earth is just as much a part, an organ, of man as his head. Where do the digestive organs of man begin and end? They have no beginning and no end but form a closed system. The substances which man requires to maintain life are indigestible in their raw state and must go through a preparatory digestive process. And this preparatory work is not done by the mouth, but by the plant. It is the plant which collects and transmutes the substances so that they may become nutriments in their further progress through the digestive canal. Plants and the space they occupy are just as much a part of man as his mouth, his teeth or his stomach."*

Isn't that incredible! Over 100 years ago, there was an awareness that we are inextricably linked to the natural world, and yet we still chose a path of separateness. The Soulistic Journey reconnects you to the natural world in ways that reveal the underlying miraculous nature of the matrix of life in which we are but a magnificently intelligent single cell. We are an ecosystem within an ecosystem, within the Universal ecosystem.

Once we truly comprehend that truth, we begin to see the sparkle of creation in everything, as Genevieve describes below in a recent blissful moment of interbeing:

"Today I sat under the shade of a young oak tree. He has been in our garden since we moved here eight-years ago, and we have grown up together. In recent years, due to all the travel with my work, I rarely found time to come and hang out with this incredible being. Since Covid-19 and lockdown, everything has changed — in this case for the better.

As I relaxed in the morning sun and ate my cereal, I gazed up through his branches and noticed the lichens growing up his trunk, the vast array of insects and bees flying through his leaves (I wondered if they tickle him like they tickle me) and the dainty peck marks of the greater spotted woodpecker who I had seen clinging to a branch just a day earlier.

I finished my breakfast and lay back in the grass, luxuriating in the free time between Zoom calls, able to be outside and enjoy a break with my friend. Or perhaps friend(s) is more appropriate. As I lay at the base of this oak being, ants started to crawl across my skin. I resisted the urge to blow them away. A huge bumble bee careened towards my head and only just managed to avoid getting stuck in my hair as she buzzed cumbersomely past. Laughing, I next noticed the daisies caressing my knee, and a money spider adventuring his way across my calf.

Both my oak friend and I are living ecosystems. We are both playing host to a multitude of life in this one eternal moment, even more so when you include the colonies of bacteria, fungi and cellular existences that live their days inside and upon our physical bodies. Oak and I share the same air. And we are both rooted in the soil of our beautiful planet which is, itself, an even richer and vaster ecosystem of life-giving beings. Importantly, we love each other deeply and love all the beings that share our space too.

In quiet moments such as these, each of us can get a sense that our human stories of separateness and isolation are quite ridiculous when set against the wide-ranging narrative of biological, soulful life on Earth. We simply cannot ever be alone, even if we wished to be! We are each a vast and complex ecosystem of physical, mental, emotional and spiritual life. Each thought, feeling and action we make carries a consciousness of its own, yet each is intimately linked to the wider consciousness of 'me', 'we' and all life in our Universe.

My molecules are connected to the molecules of the spider, the ant, the daisies and my dear friend the oak tree. Happily so, for I would miss any one of them should they be absent from my ecosystem awareness for any length of time.

And the same is true for this human ecosystem in which we exist. Our human 'biome' is equally as important and often equally easy to feel separate and distanced from – especially when we are angry or hurt by one of the characters in our 'field'.

Yet our molecules are all equally connected. We breathe the same air and touch the same Earth. We love each other and support each other and need to be reminded of this.

So why not take some time every day to sit, to appreciate, to BE the ecosystem of love and support that you inherently are?

What's in your ecosystem?

When was the last time you stopped to pay attention to it?

How often do you demonstrate your love for it?

When you do, your world, in fact, the whole world, will change.

CORE PRACTICES

Before you embark on your Soulistic Journey of transformation, there are a few Core Practices that will really help you to sink-in to the experience more deeply. It is worth taking the time to embrace these and make them part of your everyday life, in ways that work for you, whenever possible.

FREEFORM WRITING/JOURNALING

JOURNALING REVEALS YOUR TRUTH AT THE MOMENT OF WRITING

This is an absolute jewel of a practice that you will never regret undertaking. You may possibly have attempted it before, but when you allow it to develop into a regular part of your life, journaling becomes essential to your wellbeing; a routine that you will want to continue for the rest of your life – and that is because it reveals your truth at the moment of writing, which can be wonderfully revealing and healing.

Firstly, we suggest that you invest in one or two beautiful notebooks or journals that entice you with their smooth, empty pages just waiting to be filled, and a good pen that is neither scratchy nor blotchy. The tools of this practice are actually very important because the process needs to be enjoyable. It is worth noting that journaling on your laptop or tablet is not the same as writing in a journal. This is because when using your fingers to hold a pen, as a sculptor holds a chisel or a painter holds a brush, you are connecting your hands and heart and bypassing the brain. Your brain is such a 'bossy muscle' – it always wants to be in the equation; but your heart (and your gut for that matter) have their own intelligence that is seldom heard in the noisiness of the brain's dominance. Use a pen and connect directly to your heart.

This is the key to freeform writing[8] or journaling: to 'get your mind out of the way'. This may seem a bit odd at first, as we assume that the mind is necessary to write, but in fact the mind, with all its logic and analysis, often blocks your intuition. In this practice, you are trying to get to the heart of the matter, so it is necessary to still the mind. One way we have found that really helps this process is to imagine yourself removing your conscious mind, as you would remove a hat from your head and putting it to one side. In that hat resides your brain. Put your metaphorical hat away and focus on your heart centre. Then pick up your pen and begin to write and don't stop until you have no more to say or your pen stops moving.

You may need to kick-start the process with some 'easing-in' exercises: what did you dream about last night? How do you feel? What is meaningful to you at this moment in time? You may focus on an object such as a moss-covered stone and really 'feel' its energy with your eyes; how it communicates with you. Then just go with the flow... It doesn't matter if you write jibberish, half-sentences or ideas without clarity – the point is not to write a grammatically correct essay, it is to access how you are really feeling. Even if you don't find it easy at first, keep going. Just write. Eventually the words will start to flow, and what is wonderful is that once you are in the flow, you begin to write your truth in that moment. When you read what you have written, you will easily recognise the point at which you are in the flow, as your writing will be meaningful to you. You may even get 'truth shivers'.

Here is an example of freeform writing taken from my journal, written at the beginning of my Soulistic Journey (Lorna):

THE KEY TO FREEFORM WRITING OR JOURNALING IS TO GET YOUR MIND OUT O THE WAY

Feeling grumpy today – not sure why. Maybe it's the full moon or the incessant wind and rain! Everything irritates me – was cross with the dog on our walk just because he wanted to stop and sniff everything. Poor old Jack – he doesn't mind the rain. Won £10 on the Postcode Lottery! Ten pounds! Wish it was ten thousand. How ungrateful. I quite often feel like things are 'not enough'. What's that all about then? Ten pounds is better than a poke in the eye with a sharp stick, as my Dad would've said. Where does all that 'not enough' stuff come from anyway because actually, I've always had enough. I've never been hungry, or been unable to pay the bills, so where does this 'not enough' feeling come from? Is it a kind of self-sabotage that keeps me from recognising how blessed I am really? Let's face it, I'm rich in lots of ways (loving family, great friends, live in fabulous part of the country, generally happy despite today's grumpiness...) Would I attract abundance into my life if I trusted 'enough' rather than only seeing 'not enough'? There's a thought... Can I manifest enough? (What do I mean by that...) What does abundance mean to me? I must ponder all this and see where it leads

ENJOY YOUR JOURNALING AND READ IT OFTEN. IT NEVER FAILS TO BE REVEALING

So, there we have it – a recognition of a 'shadow' (or mystery) element to my nature: a feeling of lack. What was incumbent upon me after writing this was to explore this feeling and also, the other side of the coin; its 'gift' (or wisdom) element, which is abundance. And whether within this duality there could arise a feeling of sufficiency, a fulcrum where balance and harmony reside. Allowing myself the time to practice journaling on a daily basis gave me this insight and potential resolution to a long-held shadow.

Your freeform writing may not always sparkle with insights and epiphanies; but you may read your journal in weeks and months to come and see how fundamentally you have changed or be reminded of a moment when you understood yourself from a different perspective. You may also write things that only make sense much later on in your journey. As you gain these insights and revelations, writing them down means that they will not be lost, and then when you re-read your journal their meaning becomes clearer. These insights create the golden thread of your journey, a lineage from who you were to who you are. That golden thread can help to keep you on your path and will always be there for you to hold on to.

We recommend, if you can, that you journal or freeform write first thing in the morning. You may only have time for ten minutes or so of writing, but it will set the tone of your day, or it may be that recalling your dreams in your journal helps to resolve a conundrum. Alternatively, it is also great to journal last thing at night, before you go to sleep, so that you drift off in an enlightened state that aids your overall wellbeing. Mostly, enjoy your journaling and read it often. It never fails to be revealing.

IMAGINATION IS ONE OF THE MOST TRANS- FORMATIVE AND POWERFUL TOOLS AT YOUR DISPOSAL

THE ROLE OF IMAGINATION

IMAGINATION GIVES BIRTH TO EVOLUTION

Your imagination is one of the most transformative and powerful tools at your disposal as you walk the Soulistic Journey – in fact, without engaging the imagination, it is likely that you will only skim the surface of the experiences that are just waiting to unfold for you. Read any writings from the mystics and they all place the imagination as primary in the adventure towards the discovery of personal and Universal truth.

Einstein said of the imagination that it is more important than knowledge, for, "knowledge is limited, but imagination embraces the entire world, stimulating progress, giving birth to evolution." Think about that: *imagination gives birth to evolution*. Knowledge is gathered from outer sources whereas imagination seeks and finds your own inner wisdom which is the proverbial 'alchemical gold' of this journey.

If you look around you as you read this book, almost everything you see started off in someone's imagination, perhaps even yours: who painted that picture you treasure? Who designed the bookcase you love? Who wrote that poem you find so moving, or invented your favourite app? Someone who used their imagination; someone who thought outside the box and was willing to create something based on no-thing. That is, until it became a thing that you now treasure.

The word 'imagination' has a bit of a bad rap: many people think of it in terms of fantasy or science fiction, something that's not real and a bit 'airy-fairy' – but actually the imagination is a highly-attuned sixth-sense that we can use to help us formulate that which is beyond words or human concepts. It is our doorway to hidden worlds and unseen realms. Through the imagination we can 'channel' or 'download' thoughts, images, songs, poems, ideas, events, concepts, philosophies – anything that can be formulated. The imagination facilitates *in-formation*; it sources from the metaphysical realm in the present moment, offering a way to sense what is happening on an evolutionary level, just as Einstein intuited.

So, if you have the fleeting thought of, "Oh, that's just my crazy imagination!" go back and contemplate what your crazy imagination is saying to you, because it is absolutely possible that this might be the golden thread of your life's work waiting to be noticed. If, in a state of contemplation you imagine a symbol that looks like The Eye of Horus (for example) then don't dismiss it, follow the thread. What is it? What does it mean to you at this moment in time? Where do its teachings point? To fully utilise your imaginative capabilities, you need to balance discernment with trust, and this can only be learned with practice.

On my first Soulistic Journey, I (Lorna) had an insight that helped me see beyond a self-sabotaging story I was telling myself about having no imagination. During one of the regular Soulistic Circle gatherings, we were discussing the role of our Mentors. I plucked up the courage and confessed that I didn't meet my Mentor at the Soulistic Wheel North Meditation, and that I was really disappointed. A wonderful conversation ensued where we discussed the role of imagination in connecting with your Mentor: how if, during the meditation you imagine (or see in your mind's eye) a wolf, for example, then let that wolf be your Mentor. Dive into the qualities of 'wolf' and 'make like a wolf'. Or, if a word or image passes through your consciousness during a meditation, like 'archway' or 'rocket' – follow those symbols and see where they lead. They are your imagination at play.

I found this to be a real gateway into my journey, because I had in fact heard the name 'Sophia' but gave it no credence, saying that, "it came from nowhere". When I realised that 'nowhere' is the realm of creative imagination, it was like an epiphany for me. Acknowledging that Sophia Goddess of Wisdom could be my Mentor, I went on to connect with the qualities of the great symbolic teacher she is and found much that had meaning for me.

IMAGINATION PRESENTS ITSELF IN MYRIAD FORMS – YOU JUST HAVE TO NOTICE YOUR PARTICULAR FLAVOUR OF IT

Imagination presents itself in myriad forms – you just have to notice your particular flavour of it and then start to develop this like a muscle. We invite you to play with your imaginative abilities, to trust them and follow their lead. Your imagination is a boundless source of potentiality and wisdom which will delight and surprise you in equal measure. To quote the great mystic and scientist Einstein once more, "Imagination is the preview of life's coming attractions." Make sure you pay attention.

THE WAY OF SOULISTIC ALCHEMY

THE ART OF TRANSFORMING THE LEAD OF DISTRACTION INTO THE GOLD OF AWARENESS

The real challenge to humanity at this time – and always – is that of distraction. Most of us are living within a story of 'survival' our entire lives. Our ancestors were also locked into the same story but often with a different context. And now, we find the whole global community facing a collective story of survival, from the triple-whammy impact of climate-change, global recession and Covid-19.

How do you respond to the multifaceted challenges of change? Do you feel a sense of relief that things are transforming or a sense of panic that they are out of control? Are you easily swayed into anxiety by those who preach fear and apocalypse, or can you rise above the fear and hold on to the light of potential opportunity? It is important to be aware of your responses because these emotions are the messengers of alchemical transformation.

To many people, the word 'alchemy' instantly evokes a scene from Merlin's Cave where a cauldron bubbles with foul-smelling contents as it is stirred by the fixated sage; or it is a word they don't really understand that has something to do with turning base metal into gold in a mediaeval alchemist's laboratory. However you understand it, the word alchemy is usually veiled in mythology and layers of meaning, but on your Soulistic Journey we ask you to let go of any preconceptions you may have so that you can demystify your understanding of alchemy.

Soulistic alchemy is the ancient art of transforming lower forms of consciousness to higher forms. You could say that alchemy is a staged process of 'story metamorphosis'. A process that transforms the underpinning narratives by which we live and upgrades them to higher levels of personal and collective meaning. Fear and panic are 'lower' emotions that keep us trapped in inaction, inappropriate action or distraction. Acceptance, curiosity and creativity are 'higher' emotions that unlock hidden resources and connect us back into the web of potential around us. Peace, love and harmony are higher still, and initiate us into a sense of unity with all of life. From this place, the human world stops attracting our attention. We find ourselves lifted to a new plane of existence: being in the world, but not of it.

The process of any alchemical transformation starts with the *prima materia* – the core essence of life. This is the part of you that exists beyond survival consciousness. It is found in the space you arrive at when you allow the noise of the human world to fall away. It is the state you were born into as a baby and will die into when you transition out of this human form. It is the ending and the beginning of all stories.

ALCHEMY IS A STAGED PROCESS OF 'STORY META-MORPHOSIS'

Sometime later, you enter into a stage of *separation* where you experience yourself as isolated and individual. You may feel alone, abandoned and victimised by the external world. Whenever you find yourself blaming or judging, you will be working with the alchemical force of separation. It could be argued that collective human consciousness has been in this stage for some time now. There is only one path out, and that is first to become aware of your thoughts and your habits. Then, in order to move on from this stage you must recognise and let go of anything that doesn't serve your growth. Everything that keeps you small and subject to the social forces at play on the planet must be shed. This path is hard, but the energy that awareness brings can be so powerful, so liberating. Allow it to pass through your stories and cleanse them, letting go of anything that stops you from reconnecting to your own inner wisdom and evolution.

WHAT PERSONAL FOUNDATIONS ARE YOU LAYING RIGHT NOW?

Once you have been able to release your old habitual responses, you move into a process known to alchemists as *conjunction*. The elements of your true story start to join together in a deeper pattern, pointing the way towards your real purpose and destiny.

Fermentation is the next stage of the process. It is often compared to the metamorphosis of a caterpillar into a butterfly, where the imaginal cells fire into action to create a whole new 'you'. This stage of alchemy, that follows conjunction, allows you to embed and solidify your future visions – so it is really important to be careful what you wish for.

What personal foundations are you laying right now? Everything you think, speak, eat and do contributes towards your imaginal cells of the future, even as you read this. What future story are you choosing? Are you getting sucked into the classic human victim narrative of '*Everything bad is happening TO me from outside forces I can't control*'? If the answer is 'Yep', then stop right there. No one else can control your inner beliefs and choices[9]. You alone choose, and you create.

This metamorphosis and liberation of your choice and free will leads to the *distillation* stage of alchemy where you home-in on what truly inspires and ignites you. You enter into a field of clarity, rising phoenix-like from the ashes of your old stories and flying high above the world to see the whole landscape of possibilities open out before your heart and mind. You live from this place, free and unbounded by previous restrictions.

The final stage of the alchemical process is *coagulation*. It is mystical, magical and very difficult to describe in words. It is a time of transcendence, trans-figuration and transmutation, when the purified essence of your life expands in unity and interconnection with everything else and you fully realise that everything in your external life stems from your internal levels of conscious-ness. Indeed, the nature of true unity dictates that there is nothing outside of yourself. 'Me' merges completely with 'we' and you start to reach the stages of non-dual awareness where the story of interconnection comes alive in the cells of your being.

We go into more detail about the practice of Daily Alchemy in August, as you walk the Western Quadrant of the Soulistic Wheel, but it is a process that is central to the evolution of all living beings in the Universe. Are you ready to become the alchemist of your life?

INTUITION AND SYNCHRONICITY

INTRODUCING TWO STEADFAST AND UNIVERSAL GUIDES

The pathways of transformation are many and varied. There is no one guar-anteed way to evolve into your highest potential, and the plethora of books – like this one – that are written to guide you, attest to that. Some books evoke ancient gods and goddesses and indigenous traditions, some follow the Buddhic path of meditation and mindfulness, some use pagan or arcane ritual – there is no one way.

That being said, there are two steadfast Universal 'guides' that never fail to shine a light on your journey – and these guides are Intuition and Synchronicity. Look out for them and honour them, as they travel with you. Be mindful of when they appear in your life and contemplate their gifts. Tuning-in to their presence is a practice that will greatly benefit you as they are guides that come directly from the interface of your inner wisdom and your soul. Get to know how they manifest for you.

Intuition is an enigma – what is it, really? Have you ever felt a profound sense of 'knowing' something? You just *know* this thing so absolutely that there is no questioning it. That is intuition. Have you ever been with a person who is bubbly and friendly, but you have felt deep down that they are desperate and in pain? That is intuition. Have you ever felt really strongly that you should not walk a certain way to work one day? That is intuition and it may have saved you from an accident waiting to happen.

INTUITION
WORKS ON
A DEEPER
LEVEL THAN
INTELLECT
AND HAS
MORE
SUBTLETY AND
FINESSE THAN
INSTINCT

Your intuition works on a much deeper level than your intellect and it has more subtlety and finesse than instinct. It is like a radar that extends beyond your body and connects with the dynamic webs of vibrational energy that interweave all life on Earth, and indeed, the Cosmos. When any part of this web vibrates for any reason, your intuition picks up on it. Most of the time, these energetic waves are 'gated' by your senses because otherwise you would be overwhelmed with multidimensional information, but on occasion your intuition recognises information that will benefit you in some way. So, tune-in to your inner radar and see what it is picking up. It really can help you to avoid pitfalls and gain footholds as you journey.

Synchronicity can sometimes be mistaken for intuition, because they work closely together as part of your spiritual support system. However, synchronicity can be likened to the nodes on the vibrational webs of energy; a connection point that unveils the direction of your path. So, for example, if you were talking to a friend one day about your love of gardening, and then as you walk home, you see a job advert in a shop window for a part-time gardener, then that is a synchronous event that is saying, "Here is an opportunity, if you want it." The key is firstly to notice the synchronicity, as many of us would walk past with our eyes blinkered and our thoughts on whether we remembered to put the washing on the line or not; but if we do notice the synchronicity, we still need to have the courage to walk through the doors of opportunity. We can talk ourselves out of potentiality so easily.

But synchronicity does not judge or give up on us; it works on a much more dynamic level than that. What we think is what we create. This is a fact of quantum physics: molecules are attracted to, or entrained[10] to us, through our conscious and unconscious intentions and beliefs, (which includes the subtle frequencies of our soul journey, too). When we are open to it, this vibration manifests itself as synchronicity and these seemingly magical occurrences are one of the surest signs that you are 'connected' or 'on your path'.

Here's a wonderful example of synchronicity that happened to me (Lorna) recently: In early May, as part of the Soulistic Journey, we had a Beltane Retreat and one of the sessions was about the use of Tarot to illuminate your path. Julie, one of the Wisdom Weavers, who was hosting the session, asked us all to bring our favourite Tarot deck with us. When the time came, I had to confess I didn't have a Tarot deck, and a lively conversation ensued about the decks other participants were using and their various merits. Kelsey (also a Wisdom Weaver) told me about her Wildwood Tarot[11] deck and how much she loved the illustrations. Genevieve also has the same pack – but other recommendations interested me too, and I wasn't sure which deck to choose.

Time passed, and I still hadn't made a decision, when on Saturday morning a week later, I heard the familiar sound of my brother's motorbike coming up the lane. What a treat it was to see him and his partner! After a while, he rummaged around in his backpack and produced a parcel. "This is for you, Lou," he said. Surprised (as it wasn't my birthday), I thanked him and opened the parcel. It was a brand-new Wildwood Tarot deck! I couldn't believe it – not only had I never mentioned Tarot to my brother, but I also didn't know that he had used this deck for several years. "I love it," he said, "and I just thought you would too."

The synchronistic timing of this utterly amazed me, but it also answered the question as to which deck to choose! I mentioned it to Kelsey, who wisely responded, "Well Lorna, you asked the Universe, and the Universe answered!" Since then, the Tarot has become my friend, a gentle voice of wisdom to help unravel some of life's conundrums. If you haven't tried the Tarot, we can heartily recommend the Wildwood deck, or perhaps wait for synchronicity to bring you your own!

SEEING WITH MYTHIC EYES OR SYMBOLIC SIGHT

BELIEVING IS SEEING

'Believing what you see' is at the heart of our next Core Practice, and that is, 'seeing with mythic eyes', or the use of 'symbolic sight'. We use the verb 'to see' in relation to our physical eyes, but we also see with our mind's eye – and, for that matter, with our heart and intuition. Seeing with mythic eyes is all about looking metaphysically at what is being presented to you from deeper and higher levels, beyond those of daily consciousness. It is a way of seeing the events of our lives as a 'living myth' in action and enhances our awareness that we are an actor in and writer of our life story. We can use our mythic eyes to understand our own stories more clearly, and those of our friends and family.

Here's an example. Recently a friend's father had to have a triple-heart bypass. It was a major operation and ultimately, he passed away, unable to recover from the trauma of the surgery. A year or so prior to the surgery, this man's wife had died unexpectedly. I (Lorna) had a strong intuition that my friend's father had died from a broken heart, but I kept this to myself as, obviously, my friend was grieving and needed time to come to terms with what had happened. However, to me, it seemed entirely possible that his father's heart had broken after his wife of many years unexpectedly died, and that the operation to save him was not part of his soul's plan, but provided him with a way to transition out of a life story he no longer wanted to live. There may come a time when I can discuss this with my friend, but that time is not now. However, this is an example of seeing with mythic eyes: looking for the metaphysical perspective and metaphorical clues underlying any given situation.

Seeing with symbolic sight is much the same thing, although what is in question may be more objectified or image based. For example, if you can see that a river delta, the branches of a tree and the structure of the lungs are all reflections of each other, then you can see with symbolic sight: you know that to breathe we need the trees and rivers, and that we are interdependent with them. Or, you may be walking the coast path and see a boat out at sea battling the storm on its way into port, and you may see that as symbolic of the struggle you are having with a colleague at work, and take some comfort in the fact that you too will find safe harbour where you can recuperate. Life is constantly presenting us with a mirror into our unfolding Soul Story. You just need to have the eyes to see it (and the ears to hear it!)

Taking a different perspective on life in this way can often diffuse a potentially difficult situation; it can allow you to manoeuvre around an obstacle without bumping into it head-on. It can offer a new way of seeing things that opens the doors of perception at a more profound level. But it is not easy, and it takes time to see beneath the surface of daily life with your mythic eyes. Just keep practicing. Whenever a situation arises, ask yourself if there is another way of perceiving it. Ask yourself if there is a deeper meaning at work? Before too long, seeing symbolically will come naturally to you and it will greatly enhance your Soulistic Journey.

WHENEVER A SITUATION ARISES, ASK YOURSELF IF THERE IS ANOTHER WAY OF PERCEIVING IT

GUIDES AND MENTORS

TUNING-IN TO YOUR SUPPORT SYSTEM

As with any journey, life is much easier if you have a guide or mentor to whom you can turn for support, advice and inspiration. In this journey, your guides or mentors can be in the metaphysical or imaginal realm or the physical human realm. For example, you may have a friend or family member who you can speak openly with about what you are experiencing as you travel on your journey. You may already have a guide: for example, many people speak of having a connection with their 'guardian angel' or perhaps an ancestor who has passed over, with whom they still feel a connection. For others, guides and mentors may come and go with the seasons, or as their journey progresses.

During my first Soulistic Journey, I (Lorna) took part in a wonderful Soulistic Wheel Mentor Meditation[12], where in my mind's eye, I saw a beautiful white horse with wings, who was absolutely enormous. His forelegs were huge, like the pillars of a temple, but his presence was entirely benign. At that point, the reason why Pegasus came to me through my imagination was not clear at all, but thereafter, I saw him everywhere: depicted in adverts, on the television, even in books I picked up after the meditation – which gave me a profound feeling of synchronicity.

One day, several weeks after this powerful meditation, I met a ceramicist friend in an art gallery who I'd not seen for a few years. We got talking and before I knew it, I'd signed up for her Creativity is Play[13] ceramics course. This was not on my agenda, but I decided to go with the flow. On the first day of the course, as my friend spoke about the creative impulse, she said, "I call this, 'releasing your horse'." And there it was! I knew in that instant that Pegasus came to me as the guardian of my creativity. The course was wonderful and once I'd learned how to release my horse and access creativity through my fingertips rather than my mind, I made a rather odd but powerful 'henge-like' piece, which after it was glazed and fired, I realised was my altarpiece!

We have conveyed this story to demonstrate how your guides and mentors can come to you in the most unexpected ways, through meditation, contemplation or synchronicity; but you can also choose them. If you would like to be accompanied on your journey by any being, be they fictional, mythical, legendary or familial, just ask them to walk with you. Throughout this book, you will see that we refer to these guides and mentors as 'other-than-human', by which we mean the myriad beings whose presence is not human, but in a non-anthropocentric way, can offer incredible insights and support.

Once you have asked for help from your mentors, you will begin to feel their presence; or perhaps in the first instance, you will need to imagine their presence. Imagination is an 'organ of perception' as the German poet and scientist Johann Goethe[14] once wrote. He propounded that other-than-human intelligence in the Universe communicates to us via the organ of perception, the imagination – yet sadly, the imagination is one of the most neglected of all our senses as we discussed earlier in this chapter.

One of the Wisdom Weavers (those who have walked the Soulistic Journey) feels a great kinship with owls and has one as her guide: she enjoys seeing with mythic eyes from the bird's-eye-view of an owl's perspective; similarly, many people feel kinship with lions or elephants, symbolically embracing and embodying their powerful energetic qualities. In some cultures, these creatures are called your spirit animals, familials or totems. They can be your friends and allies, but you must treat them with sacred honour. If you consign your mentors to the realm of make-believe they will often bring you some interesting and challenging tests until you earn their respect.

Be open to your guides and mentors; be respectful of their presence and listen deeply to their wisdom. In the Soulistic Journey Quarterly Meditations you will be guided to greet your mentors and learn how to dance with them.

IMAGINATION IS AN 'ORGAN OF PERCEPTION'

ALTAR AND RITUAL

BRINGING YOUR BODY, HEART AND MIND INTO COHERENCE

Altar and Ritual are words that may have religious connotations for you, so if you prefer, you can use the words 'Shrine and Ceremony' or any others you feel most comfortable with, nonetheless, there is a sanctity in this Core Practice that asks for a degree of devotion as you bring your body, heart and mind into focus, ready for your Soulistic Journey.

We have found that creating an altar (in any shape or form), can be a very affirmative action, because it symbolically connects you to what is currently meaningful in your life and enables a degree of focus. Your altar may need to be small and portable if you don't have space in your home to create one in a permanent place – but this need not be limiting: you can choose a beautiful box, and place in it a few items that you treasure. When you are ready to centre yourself for the next step on your journey, you can just open it and place the items before you for contemplation.

However, you may have a shelf or a table in a corner, or a summerhouse or meditation room where you can create a permanent altar. On it you can place a beautiful cloth, a candle (as fire is always central to this work), and a photo of one or two of your loved ones, mentors or ancestors; on it you can place some incense that you like to burn, or herbs and flowers from the garden that you love; you may include a jewel or stone or crystal that you have a connection with, or perhaps a set of oracle cards[15] that you like to use. In this way, you begin to build a sacred space that is yours and that you can return to again and again as your journey deepens. For example, you may choose to place a large brass key on your altar as a symbol that you have decided to unlock your potential; or you may have a memento from a grandparent who was a guiding influence for you. Whatever you place on your altar is entirely up to you, and how you arrange it and add to it will change over time. The most important thing is to develop a connection with your altar so that you are imbued with the resonance of the sacred objects you have chosen.

When you develop a practice of coming back to your altar space on a regular basis to meditate and honour those energies that are most potent for you, they respond and enhance your experiences of them. It is here that your practice becomes your purpose from the inside out.

To connect with your altar meaningfully, it can be useful to create a ritual that you undertake each time you open to this work. This can be as simple as coming to your altar with a sense of reverence, burning a stick of incense to pervade the air with a sensuous fragrance that brings your body, heart and mind into coherence; or you may like to make a new offering, such as a flower from the garden or a feather, or read aloud a passage from your journal that is important to you; alternatively, you may say a few centring words such as, "In this space, I am open to new insights and experiences," or a mantra such as, "Om mani padme hum," which means you will practice the path of union and wisdom.

Whatever ritual you enter into, it should be simple, meaningful and repeated each time you come to your altar. In that way, the molecules in your body, heart and mind will recognise that you are about to enter a contemplative state and will relax and open up to new experiences.

YOUR DREAMBOARD IS A VISUAL SNAPSHOT OF WHAT IS CURRENTLY MEANINGFUL TO YOU

DREAMBOARDS

A DYNAMIC TIME CAPSULE OF YOUR INTENTIONS

Dreamboards are a visual aspect of your journal – they illustrate your passions, desires, inspirations and learning curves and create a 'snapshot' of what is currently meaningful to you – which is easy to carry wherever you are in the form of a photo on your smartphone or tablet.

Your dreamboard can be a large cork board that forms the backdrop to your altar, or it can be items stuck to the side of your fridge with magnets. It can be a scrapbook, or a beautifully curated collage. However, you make your dreamboard, it is a dynamic, ever-changing artwork of things that inspire you. To start off with, just begin to collect images and words that you love – perhaps of a campervan that you've set your heart on, or a beach that you'd love to revisit; a doodle of the word 'Limitless' that you once had as a henna tattoo, or a photo of your dream house – and pin them to your board. Then, if you have an insight from your journal, write a poem about it or pick the key phrase and pin it to your dreamboard. If you love the lyrics from a particular song, or took a photograph that delights you, pin it to the board.

Over time, you'll develop a beautiful and insightful collection of motifs that inspire you – and perhaps other people who see your dreamboard. It may become a conversation piece within your family, or you may choose to keep it private and mysterious, for your eyes only. However you relate to your dreamboard, the key is to see it as a dynamic time capsule of your motivations and intentions. All that you relate to and all that you're passionate about is in some way encapsulated in what you pin to your dreamboard.

Just as action follows thought, so intention brings manifestation. Your dreamboard is a mechanism that will aid the manifestation of many of these dreams into reality. Often, I (Genevieve), have found old dreamboards in my attic and stopped to reflect on how many of the things I had once populated this vision with, had now come into my life in some way. Your dreamboard is a magical tool of manifestation and vision. Admire it often and remember that dreams are boundless – as long as you take inspired action to give them life.

YOUR GIFTING BAG

THE PRACTICE OF RECIPROCITY

As you journey, you will naturally begin to collect things that have meaning to you which you may keep on your altar – but at certain times, you may wish to take some of these items with you on your travels; some talismans for protection, for cleansing, for gifting. These may include a found feather, a crystal or stone that energises you, a brush of sage and some matches, a pouch of tobacco for offering, a stick of *palo santo*, a pinch of cacao, a driftwood twig, a pinecone, an icon…

Your gifting bag is sacred; keep in it what you will and take it with you wherever you go. It should be small enough to stuff in a pocket, but robust enough to conceal your treasures. When you are in ceremony, whether with others or spontaneously at the foot of a beautiful tree or in a garden or sanctuary, you may wish to honour the moment with an offering from your gifting bag. The energy of exchange is present in every aspect of a healthy ecosystem, so if you wish to come back into an ancient natural balance, gifting is one way to do so. Gift your items back to the natural world and receive any items from her that present themselves to you. In this way the gifting and receiving becomes generous and meaningful.

THE ENERGY OF EXCHANGE IS PRESENT IN EVERY ASPECT OF A HEALTHY ECOSYSTEM

STORYHACKING

A MASTER KEY IN THE GAME OF LIFE

You will see that we have included monthly 'Storyhacks' in the Practice section of this book. Here, we explain how storyhacking is a master key in the game of life on Earth and opens the door for a completely new way of being human. The wonderful truth is, that it is not only possible to hack into your old, self-sabotaging thought patterns and stories regarding issues such as self-esteem, trust and your true purpose in life, but it is equally possible to transform yourself from being the victim to becoming the creator of your life.

Stop for a moment and think:

TRANSFORM YOURSELF FROM BEING THE VICTIM TO BECOMING THE CREATOR OF YOUR LIFE

❀   What is your number one complaint (you know, the one you hear yourself saying repeatedly)?

❀   What frustrates you the most in your life (that is often the source of the complaining)?

❀   What in your life saps your energy and takes away your vitality?

Your honest answers to these questions will give you an insight into where your 'human stories' need hacking. Most people can get to the point of allowing themselves to answer these questions, but very few, have the tenacity, courage and instinct to look themselves in the mirror and move beyond their associated excuse stories and into real change. How about you?

The very fact that you are reading this book is proof that you are open to transforming your life, but real change depends on how comfortable your 'discomfort zone' has become. Sometimes it is possible to be so secure in your state of discomfort that any suggestion of resolving some of the issues you complain about will send you into freefall! For this reason, many people choose to stay in the realm of mediocrity and suppression of their real desires – because change can be scary. But storyhacking offers the key to transforming your energy, vision and vitality in the simplest and most effective way possible – it helps you see yourself from a new perspective. So, here are the three 'core quests' that form the basis of the storyhacker's journey.

REMEMBER – THE CHALLENGE OF ILLUMINATION

Most human problems stem from a deep forgetting of who we really are. All of us wear the masks that society expects – businessperson, parent, entrepreneur – like actors in a play that we have forgotten we are the authors of. The first challenge of any storyhacker is to discern personal truth from lies, authenticity from insecurity and to remember the unique spark of soul genius that you were born with. As you start to remember your true desires and dreams you become self-illumined and self-motivated. You no longer need to seek approval in the outer world because you have remembered your own truth. The superpowers of awareness and choice bloom, as you undertake this quest into your truth.

RECONNECT – THE CHALLENGE OF INTIMACY

We are living in times of advanced isolation. Millions (if not billions) of people across the planet feel lonely and misunderstood. But when you remember who you really are, you are able to lower your social defences, to stop holding back and to show up authentically in the world. Like a moth to a flame, you will find that many people are attracted to your light. So, the second challenge of a storyhacker is one of true connection. How do you show up authentic and real whilst maintaining healthy boundaries from those who would otherwise drain you? How do you become intimate with the human and other-than-human world and tap into the ever-present, eternal well of energy and inspiration that the planet gives freely to each of us? This is the mission of reconnection, where you unlock the superpower of compassion and start to move from separation to interconnection.

This is easier said than done, but if you hold in your heart that you are truly connected to every being – human and other-than-human – and that what you do to them, you do to yourself, then you start to live in a state of connectedness. For example, whenever you notice yourself judging another person, you have placed yourself in a state of 'separateness'; what you are really doing is judging yourself. Notice what you are saying about that person who you have disconnected from and see if you could apply those same judgements to yourself. If you change judgement to compassion, then you become reconnected with yourself and others.

RESTORY – THE CHALLENGE OF IMAGINATION

This is perhaps the biggest challenge of all; one that asks you to leave behind any vestige of separation. You are asked to fully remember, fully reconnect and then fully slay your inner victim – forever. This is the quest of ultimate self-responsibility that leads you to the epiphany that you are the author of your own life. Here you must release any traces of blame, denial or complaint because the final superpower of a storyhacker is hard won and requires a deep and sustained commitment to humility and truth. Here you must continually move beyond any human stories that keep you separate from your own inner power and the inherent power of life in the Universe.

The mission of restorying, brings with it the superpower of creation. You rediscover your ability to think and feel your world into form and allow the biggest story of evolution to be written through your life. It is a grand adventure indeed.

Are you ready?

THE SOULISTIC ARCHETYPES

UNIVERSAL PATTERNS OF CONSCIOUSNESS

Working on the 'archetypal level' is fascinating. Archetypes were first mooted by Carl Gustav Jung[16], who saw that within the collective unconscious, there are patterns of thought that serve to organise and direct human behaviour consciously and subconsciously. This concept was then enhanced over the years by various practitioners of psychotherapy, mysticism and personal development. Now, archetypes are commonly understood to be universal patterns of energy and frequency that influence us to adopt certain identities, make certain decisions and create stories that align to archetypal patterns – whether we are aware of them or not.

Stephen Harrod Buhner, in his book, *Plant Intelligence and the Imaginal Realm*, has this to say about archetypes: "…They are the primary or first things from which all phenomena come. They are the potentials that reside in the quantum multiverse (the imaginal realm). … (Archetypes) prefigure or foreshadow the forms they become in our world. Every form we see in this world is a modified expression of the archetype that underlies it[17]."

Caroline Myss[18] has developed a concept of archetypes, proposing that we all have four archetypes in common, these being The Victim, The Saboteur, The Prostitute and The Child – all expressing certain light and shadow qualities in

> ARCHETYPES ARE THE PRIMARY OR FIRST THINGS FROM WHICH ALL PHENOMENA COME

human nature. Their patterns of behaviour play out in our everyday lives and we're sure you can recognise some of them in your story, as we have done in ours.

Here are examples of the shadow and light or yin and yang qualities of the four universal archetypes:

- ❊ THE VICTIM: It's all my fault (shadow) – I am not responsible for other people's actions (light)

- ❊ THE SABOTEUR: I'm not good enough for this job (shadow) – I will not allow my lack of confidence to spoil this (light)

- ❊ THE PROSTITUTE: I am selling myself short (shadow) – I value myself and my life (light)

- ❊ THE CHILD: I'm afraid of being abandoned (shadow) – Look at the beauty and adventure in the world! (light)

Together with these four archetypes, there are a host of others that influence us: the Femme Fatale, the Fool, the Detective, the Knight, the Thief, the Hermit, the Queen, the Dreamer, the Lover, the Beggar, the Teacher, the Guide and many others. It is possible to select the archetypes that you most recognise or resonate with and in studying their qualities, determine whether any particular archetype has an overbearing or underutilised quality in your life.

Richard Olivier[19], who has also done a significant amount of work in the field of evolutionary archetypes, describes your major archetypal influences as 'actors' who are either on or off the stage of your life story. Sometimes it is helpful to bring a 'weaker' character on stage in order to access new and hidden qualities that exist within you. It also may be equally as beneficial to take a strong archetypal character in your life and 'retire' them for a while so you can expand your capabilities and learn new skills that are outside your comfort zone.

It can be very helpful to look at your life-long patterns of thought – the stories you tell yourself about who you are and what you are capable of – because once you are aware of them you can relate them to certain archetypal influences and then ascertain whether you need them to be more present in your life, or indeed, to step back a little to allow other qualities to flourish.

A really good way to do this is to plot your 'StoryWave' a graph-like visualisation of the highs and lows in your life[20] (See also the April Storyhack on page 183). Once you've plotted your life's high points and low points you can then add to your graph the feelings and circumstances that surrounded these events. It may well be that some archetypal patterns of behaviour emerge from this practice that can help you to determine your strongest archetypes.

Here, Lorna recounts her response to determining her archetypal energies:

"For some time, I had been admonishing myself for being anti-social; not really wanting to spend time with others or go out to parties and gatherings. But when I looked more deeply at the archetypal energies that make up who I am, I realised that actually, I'm not antisocial, but I do have a strong Hermit archetype: it's not that I don't like people or don't want to be with them, it's more that, unless I spend time in my own company, reflecting on what makes me tick, and why I respond in the ways I do, I don't know myself, and I get uncomfortable and begin to make bad decisions. Once I realised this and stopped sabotaging myself about my natural propensity to want to be alone, I began to carve out time for that purpose, but also made a point of reconnecting with those friends who nurture my spiritual journey and who feed my soul. This was a revelation to me!"

Why not take a look at your own archetypes? In the Soulistic Library, we have detailed the work of Jung, Olivier and Myss in this respect, and that will be a good lead-in for your discoveries, however there are lots of other resources available online to help you determine the energetic qualities that have been part of your life to date (just google 'books and cards on archetypes' and see what comes up). It is worth taking your time to understand the basic principles that underlie the archetypal realms – it will be time well spent.

SOLAR AND LUNAR ARCHETYPES

A NEW WORLD CALLS FOR NEW EVOLUTIONARY ARCHETYPES

JOURNEY BEYOND TRADITIONAL ANTHROPO-CENTRIC ARCHETYPES INTO THE REALM OF UNIVERSAL ARCHETYPES

For the Soulistic Journey however, we want to go beyond the human stories we tell ourselves about who we are and why we do what we do; we journey beyond traditional anthropocentric archetypes into the realm of Universal archetypes – energies that flow through us and around us at all times, but of which we are mostly unaware. These energies communicate on subtle and not so subtle levels depending on how open we are to them; they inform the entire web of creation and are the threads that unite humans with 'other-than-human' beings. In the context of this journey they are the Soulistic Solar and Lunar Archetypes.

The Soulistic Solar and Lunar Archetypes as we have presented them, are unique to this journey and this time on Earth. They were 'given' to us – Gen and Lorna – during a profound Vision Quest we undertook as we were planning this book. We had no idea that they would come to us in this way, and no previous association with their symbols or articulation. Through deep contemplation of what we wanted to offer in this book, and after connecting with our human and other-than-human mentors who are supporting our writing journey, we were called into meditation in the symbolic realm. We had not anticipated this at all, but it felt right.

On a big sheet of paper, we drew a line down the middle. One side represented the Solar energies and on the other, the Lunar energies. We closed our eyes and tuned-in, putting our pens to paper and allowing our hands to move without the guidance of our minds or even eyes! As we drew, we swapped sides and continued the process, not speaking but just trusting what was happening. (It was a bit like the old game of Twister, and we were getting tangled up as we kept swapping sides with each other!) We swapped again and again until we had completed all 24 symbols and then sat back in awe of what had been created through our combined energies.

As a next step, we were guided to connect to a name for each of the symbols. As we did so, we found that their names wrote themselves. We can honestly say that the words came to us from somewhere beyond the logical mind, some-where we have come to know as the imaginal realm. Once we had named the pairs of archetypes, their power deepened further and as we began to work with the energies of each one, realising that they were akin to male and female parents who begat a child. Thus, the Unification element of the pairings was 'born'; and so, a final set of 12 symbols emerged.

As this process came to completion, we were taken aback at the power of what had been revealed to us and through us, and when we started working with these archetypes in everyday life, we realised how much wisdom they held individually and in triads. And of course, we now see these archetypes everywhere, because we are aware of them. By their very nature, as archetypes, they are omnipresent, but by presenting them as we have done, we can dance with them as they show up in our lives.

We invite you to enter into the mystery of these energies with us and get to know them as we have. Ask them to infuse your life and show up through syn-chronicity, intuition and mirrored wisdom: to embrace their energies as your own because they are you – in archetypal form.

The Solar and Lunar Archetypes work in conjunction with the Soulistic Wheel of the year. They form the Solar (masculine), Lunar, (feminine) and Unification, (inner synthesis) aspects of our journey through each month and phase of the Earth year. They create harmonic fields of possibility and interconnect in fluid webs of frequency, underpinning life as we perceive it, and as we create it. Their pairings allow us to see how the balance of the Divine Masculine through the solar archetypes and the Divine Feminine through the lunar archetypes combine to create an overarching quality which can be likened to the 'child' or 'offspring' of these energies: Unity.

Within each archetype itself there are energising 'yin/yang' qualities, which we call the 'Mystery' and 'Wisdom' aspects. These are neither good nor bad, simply opportunities to dive more deeply into the insights they hold. An easy way to understand these is to look at the archetype of 'Flow' as an example (see page 113). The Mystery aspect of Flow can emanate in feelings of being stuck or wading through mud; Mystery asks you to contemplate why you may be feeling this way and what is causing the feeling of constriction. What lurks in the shadows? What is veiled so that you cannot see? The Wisdom aspect of Flow asks you to recognise when you are floating in the river of life, and how, when you surrender to this energy, everything falls into place and the direction you are flowing in comes with ease and grace. Wisdom asks you to ponder what it is that creates this sense of ease? What is the gift of this archetype? What abundance is being offered to you?

Each month we ask that you sink into and contemplate the qualities of these patterns and energies. But don't worry – it's not as complex as it seems at first glance and we will guide you through the process so that before too long, recognising the prevailing archetypal energies that you are experiencing becomes second nature. So, as you embark upon your Soulistic Journey, look at the archetype keys for each month and become aware of how they manifest in your life. Are any of these energies dominant or dormant in your life? If you would like to activate these energies, speak your desire aloud: "As I walk with the Phoenix Moon in May, I resolve to respect and unlock my innate creativity and choose to make time to bring my dreams to life."

Remember, it really is, 'the intention that counts', because your intentions create thoughts and your thoughts create your reality. But more than that, contemplate how might the activation of and reconnection to these energies create a sense of beneficence and sovereignty as you walk your Soulistic Journey? How might they change your experience of life?

In 'The Library' section of this book, you will see a list of the Soulistic Archetypes for each month of the year. You can refer to these at any time to give you guidance and support on your journey. In 'The Practice' section of this book, we will delve into each archetype more deeply and explain how these energies may manifest for you as you move throughout the wheel of the year. The important thing is not to be overwhelmed by this concept, especially if it is new to you, but just relax and see if the archetypes resonate with you.

THE PRACTICE

THE SOULISTIC WHEEL OF LIFE

YOUR SOULISTIC ADVENTURE BEGINS!

Now you are ready to take the first steps on your Soulistic Wheel, a cycle which has a timeframe of a year and a day, an ancient shamanic practice that takes you from beginning to end and beginning again, symbolised by the ouroboros, where the snake eats its own tail – because in reality, there is no end to this journey; once you set foot upon it, you will walk the eternal spiral, remembering, reliving and restorying these experiences to relate to your spiritual path at any given time.

We (Genevieve and Lorna), like to step into our annual journey in the North of the wheel around November, because this time of the yearly cycle on Earth allows us to withdraw our energy from the outer world and start to focus within on remembrance of our soul path – but your journey begins wherever you are. There is no reason why you cannot step onto the Soulistic Wheel at any time of year and connect with the energies that are present. It is all part of the flow of life on this planet and in our Universe – and as you continue your journey you will start to enjoy this ebb and flow of energy as your relationship with Gaia deepens and you recognise her gifts.

Each month we invite you to undertake a couple of specific practices which are designed to immerse you in the timeless field beyond your current stories, where anything is possible. The practices have both a physical and metaphysical potency and are open to many levels of interpretation, depending on how deeply you dive into the experience. The more you give, the more you will receive. This is a Universal law and applies here as in the rest of life.

Enjoy your journey of discovery: engage your imagination in the process, go where you are led, respect and act on your intuition, notice the magic of synchronicity – and with this potent brew, allow the deep alchemical process of personal transformation to evolve. Step into your soul's journey through life.

F

REJUVE

M

NORTH QUARTER MEDITATION

REMEMBERING

Make yourself comfortable and breathe deeply for a minute or two until you feel still and settled. As you breathe, envisage your breath taking you deeply down into your Heart Centre, the hub of your personal Soulistic wheel, where the four directions meet with the energy of above and below. Imagine this sacred circle as a room – it is the room of your heart, a place you will come to as you undertake your Quarterly Meditations. What does it look like in this place? Is it dark, comfortable and cosy – or open, clear and light? Does it have windows, and if so, what is the view out of them?

Once you can envision the room of your heart and feel comfortable within it, find the central point and sit or stand there. Take a deep breath and look around you; first to the East, where the element of fire resides. Feel the warmth coming from the East; the energy of the rising sun, with its potential to burn up old stories and release you from self-limiting habits. Then turn to the South, where Water is in its element. Feel the generous ease and flow that water embodies, how it can resolve any feelings of restriction, how it can wash away your fears. Then slowly turn to the West, the element of Earth. Feel how the Earth holds you and nourishes you; feel how abundant and energised Earth is. Know that just by standing on the Earth in your bare feet, you can reconnect with her sacred spirit. Then turn to the North, and the element of Air; feel that freshness and clarity that can instantly give you a new perspective, feel the lightness of Air and know that you can mirror that lightness in your decisions and choices.

In this Quarter, you are facing the North of Winter, the element of Air. This is the aspect of the divine human mind where you are encouraged to welcome the truth of your remembering and the liberation of relinquishing.

These four directions and their elements are your touchstones. Know that at any time, you can envision being in your Heart Centre and you can reconnect with it for sustenance. Within the directions, over and above all elements and residing in your Heart Centre is the fifth element of ether; the essence and the mystery. The all-encompassing one-ness. Ether is of this world and not of this world. It is the essential element that enables transcendence into the cosmological realm. Your Heart Centre is filled with this bridging element of ether; feel how it moves you beyond this realm.

Continue to breathe deeply and imagine yourself now leaving your Heart Centre and travelling upwards into the firmament of our Universe, deep into the Cosmic realms. How liberating it is to swim among the stars, looking down on the jewel of blue that is Planet Earth. Allow yourself to travel beyond the Milky Way to the edge of the Universe, where you find a doorway, a portal between our Universe and the Multiverse – the Cosmos. You are invited to slip through that doorway into the timeless, eternal realm where angels and archetypes reside. As you move into this new realm, you will see before you a Cosmic medicine wheel; a mirror of the one in your Heart Centre. An archangel stands guardian at each of the four sacred directions – creating a blessed and safe space for you, a place where only the energies and guides that reflect your highest good can enter.

Come to rest in the middle of this beautiful Cosmic Temple. Notice how you feel resting here as your 'Universal/Univer-soul Self'; relax in the harmonious energies that flow from all directions and anchor you gently in the centre of the wheel. Then turn to face the North and notice the doorway that is placed there. Watch as the door slowly opens, and prepare to welcome whoever or whatever comes through – an archetype sent by your higher self. Their form may be from the deep ancestral realms, a king or queen, god or goddess, or a human archetype like a jester or a wizard, a mythological creature such as a unicorn or phoenix, an animal like a bear, wolf or owl, or indeed a form that is not immediately recognisable to you. You may wish to take their hands or touch their being in an act of sacred connection and communion noticing any words, images, symbols, feelings or colours that come to you as you interface in this way. Remember to trust your imagination and don't over-analyse what comes to your mind. You know you are safe and protected here by the guardian angels and your higher soul self.

This being is offering to walk with you as a teacher and guide of Divine Law for the dark quarter of Winter. Your Mentor will support you in myriad ways; in your remembering, in your questioning, in your weaving – and you can always ask them for help or guidance. Their wisdom may be hard to discern at first, but just walk with your Mentor and be open to whatever teaching comes your way.

Now your Mentor leads you back towards the Universal portal where you entered the archetypal realm. You follow, safe in the knowledge that this immortal being is always here in spirit for you. You begin to slowly and gently traverse the Cosmic realms, back down towards your Heart Centre, and come to rest there. Your Mentor has accompanied you and stands behind you, with their hands on your shoulders.

Come back into your body now and rest in the blessings of your journey.

See page 364, Endnote 12 for links to the recorded version of this Meditation if you prefer to listen to it rather than read it.

REMEMBERING

In the darkness of winter
Deep memory stirs
The dreamworld and the dayworld fuse
Ancient stories are revealed
All that is asked is for you to stop, sit and wait
To open your heart, mind and soul
To timeless, ancestral wisdom, innate
Will you find the courage to remember
Knowing that you will be forever changed?
Will you answer the call of your Soul Adventure
Knowing that once begun, your whole life will be rearranged?

This is now a time of increasing darkness, when the Earth and the Cosmos draw into themselves, whilst drawing into you. Wrapped in a blanket of reflection, we retreat and rest by the fires of our soul's calling. It is a time of integration and transmutation; a space of alchemy and magic. Deep magic. Memories from past existences flicker into our dreams and visions, prompting us to go fully into the narrative weft and weave of our lives. This is the quarter of shadow and light, shapeshifting ancestors and reclamation.

Many of us hope that it may be possible to time travel at some point in the future. We have visions of a kind of technology that can transport us back to the past or forward to the future, like the teleportation machine in Star Trek. But in fact, we time travel constantly through our ability to remember the past and imagine the future, and in our dreams, we travel the astral planes too. We are time travellers already!

The North Quarter of the Soulistic Wheel is a time for remembering; a time for the gentle recollection of all that we have been, all that has brought us to this point in time, and all that we have learned. There is a sacred quality to this kind of remembrance because it comes not from a place of judgement or blame, but from a deep honouring of our life's journey, acknowledging the suffering and the hardship, the joy and the beauty.

As we travel back with our memories and ponder our lives from the perspective of the 'here and now', we can see how everything happens for a reason, although at the time, that kind of clarity of vision is not always possible. As the saying goes, we all have 20:20 vision with hindsight! When we allow ourselves to truly remember, we can see our path more clearly, like a golden thread that links the past to the present and the future; we can see how it unfolded according to the choices we made and sometimes even without us having to make choices – as if through fate or divine providence.

For me (Lorna), one of the most profound golden threads that I can recollect runs like this: my sister had a son, and her son went to school with Merlin. We got to know Merlin and his parents and went to many parties at their house. Merlin's older sister, Star got married to a man called Giles. Giles wrote a book and was talking about it with his father in law, Brian. Brian mentioned that he knew someone who published books (Lorna). Giles contacted Lorna (me) and we worked together. Giles was pleased with how we produced his book and recommended us to his friend, Genevieve. Genevieve and I became friends and we wrote this book together. So, you could say that if it were not for my sister having a baby, this book may not exist!

Remembering kindles a profound faith in the future, because we can see how our past fits together like the pieces in a jigsaw puzzle, and so we can be reassured that this process will continue, and that if we choose wisely, it can continue in a direction that fulfils our Soul Purpose. What golden threads can

REMEMBERING
KINDLES A
PROFOUND
FAITH IN THE
FUTURE

you see weaving through your own life? Take a moment to reflect and recall all that has brought you to this point in time.

Remembering is also about looking for the clues that may help to light your soul's journey – all of those things that gave you the greatest pleasure, or a sense of satisfaction or fulfilment, are like little candles that illuminate a pathway. Can you see yours? Sometimes it is possible to remember the decisions that your parents and grandparents made that may still be impacting your life now. If these ancestral choices no longer serve your greater good, then it is time to re-story them. This book will show you how.

The wonderful thing about remembering is that, as a form of contemplation, there is not much you need do other than observe your thoughts as they arise and write them in your journal. Memories also surface in the dreamworld (as does imagination – your connection to the future), so be curious about your dreams too. Just write down anything that seems significant, no matter how slight and see if you can join the dots. Open your heart and mind to this process, without judgement. What arises may astound you.

NOVEMBER

A LIMINAL STATE OF 'BEING AND NOT BEING'
WHERE RESILIENCE ACCOMPANIES MYSTERY

NOVEMBER EARTH SIGNS

November sees the return of the darkness as the lengthening, colder nights signal to plants and animals that it is time to rest; time to return to a state of dormancy where energy is conserved and transformed. The Autumn leaves that have fallen, slowly break down into a nutrient-rich mulch that will in turn nourish trees and shrubs in the Spring; perennial plants that have set seed will wither and withdraw their energy into their root system, bulb or tuber – they may look dead, but they are very much alive, in a liminal state of 'being and not being' where reunion with the seed core of the whole is taking place so that the plant can put forth new shoots in the Spring.

Animals, too, withdraw at this time of year: badgers, hedgehogs, bears and many others go into a state of hibernation where they lower their bodily activity to the minimum necessary to sustain life, allowing them to survive the harsh realities of winter when food is scarce. But transformation is afoot in this time of the Weavers' Moon. Many of the hibernating animals are also gestating, creating new life within, as they rest. Gestation is a lovely word, deriving from the Latin *gestare*, which means to carry, so the process encompasses both carrying the mystery of new life, and patience whilst Nature runs its course. It cannot be rushed or hurried along. It takes as long as it takes.

At this time of year, there is deep natural mystery afoot: despite incredible developments in science, we still don't fully understand how a caterpillar pupates and overwinters, all the time transforming into a butterfly. We still marvel at how geese migrate many hundreds of miles and know where to find the exact same winter feeding-grounds each year. We don't really know how kingfishers survive the weeks of muddied floodwaters when fishing is impossible, or where the nuthatch sleeps at night to shelter from the rainstorms. Mystery is alive and pulsating in the dark months of the year, and resilience accompanies magic in this eternal dance, where despite the odds, life returns with the light.

We invite you to marvel at the mysteries of November: at the immensity of dark skies and the enigmatic twinkle of the stars that call us into our imagination; of the enlivening vibration of winter's entangling winds, of the perfect formation and purity of ice crystals, the steadfast resilience of the birds, and the innate wisdom of the animals... Which of these qualities can you embrace as you walk through November? Are you ready to welcome the quieting of the year?

NOVEMBER COSMOLOGICAL SIGNS

SCORPIO TO SAGITTARIUS

I CIRCULATE

As you move from the hidden darkness of Scorpio into the vast realms of potential represented by Sagittarius, feel into how willing you are to 'let go and let in' the constant stream of deep insights and intentions you are presented with. Your ability to 'circulate' energy, love, resources, connections and ideas creates your reality in the month of November, as you move deeper into remembering who you are as a cosmic being living an earthly existence.

You are asked to acknowledge all that may have been hidden from sight over lifetimes and eons until now, whilst setting new intentions for your future. No easy combination! It is far too tempting to get sucked into the seductive patterns of the past and become distracted with times, places and identities that are no longer relevant to your current path of soul development.

The real task in this month is to surrender all your stories to the fires of transformation, accepting both your darkness and your light in equal measure, whilst allowing your narratives (past, present and future) to circulate through you and out into the world.

WEAVERS' MOON

– traditionally a time of weaving warm clothes for the winter, we invite you to weave the old stories of how things were with the new threads of your intentions for transformation and growth in the coming cycle.

NOVEMBER SOULISTIC ARCHETYPES

SOLAR ARCHETYPE: PURITY

You are walking the North Quarter of the Soulistic Wheel at a time when energies turn inward towards reunification (involution). All you have experienced during the course of the year is coalescing into a pure essence of awareness. By tuning-in to this essence with your mythic eyes, you can begin to ascertain a clearer picture of all you have encountered. It is time to look more deeply at some of your stories in this pure light: what are the deeper mysteries at work here? Do the stories you tell yourself about your work and dreams still hold true for you, or are they more like habits that you are afraid to let go of? Are your stories embedded in self-sabotage and victimhood, or do they ring with a purity of vision and purpose? What is the wisdom held within your stories? What is essential for your evolution and what are you prepared to let go of?

Above, around and pulsing through you, is the energetic quality of purity, which clarifies everything to its purest essence. Feel into it – sometimes communication is beyond words, so your emotions and feelings are an integral part of this process. When you begin to embody purity of thought, action and purpose, you become lighter, less serious and more playful. Radiate your purest inner light and you will attract to yourself that which your soul desires.

In a state of contemplation, as you sit in front of your altar, or in Nature, take a few moments to recollect your experiences of the last few months; reflect on all that has happened and make a note in your journal of anything that sticks in your mind as having been 'pivotal': whether or not it was a painful or joyful experience. Can you see a deeper meaning in what happened? What is the essence of this event? What mystery is at its core? What wisdom does it reveal? If you express yourself through drawing, painting or song, see if any of these insights inspires your creativity. Drill down to the core word or image and add it to your dreamboard.

PURITY
CLARIFIES
EVERYTHING
TO ITS
ESSENCE

YOUR
DREAMS ARE
THE GATEWAY
TO OTHER
WORLDS

LUNAR ARCHETYPE: VIBRATION

You are dreaming in the North Quarter of the Soulistic Wheel and your dreams are the gateway to other worlds. Below the frenetic vibrational layers of the intellect lays the vastness of your subconscious, wherein deep wisdom flows. When you are in the quantum realm of your dreams, you can tune-in to the subtle vibrations of these mythic realities which can often reveal insights that are hidden in the day world.

The mystery of dreams is obscure and subtle, and often it is difficult to even remember your dreams – but, can you recall how you *feel* when you emerge from your dreams? Feelings often reveal more than the details of dreams. How do you feel when you awaken from sleep? If you experience emotions such as foreboding, anxiety or disquiet, tune in to that vibration (by which we mean, just sit and observe your feelings without judgement). Are you able to trace the source of your sensitivity? What does that reveal? Do you choose to create noise and chaos (another form of vibration) in your life to cover up a deeper mystery that you don't want to look at? And if so, fear not, for within the vibrational frequency of destruction and chaos there is always creativity and potential. Wisdom is asking you to uncover the layers of meaning in your dreams and tune-in to their highest vibration.

Keep a Dream Diary by your bed. When you awaken, make a note of your dreams, even if it's just a snippet, and include your feelings and emotions as you recall these dreams. Or, doodle your dreams… doodles offer fascinating insights into your subconscious. Doodles are an abstract language of line and emotion[21] that can be revealing and profound. As time goes by, you may notice some patterns emerging: times when you have 'anxiety dreams' may link with your own periodic cycles or the moon's cycles of waxing and waning; recurring dreams may be triggered by a certain person or event. Contemplate your dreams with interest and read your Dream Diary often.

UNIFICATION: TRANSCENDENCE

The pathways of Above (solar) and Below (lunar) merge within your Heart Centre, that place of stillness, silence and transcendence. Transcendence is a choice you make when you are ready to embody the wisdom that radiates from your Heart Centre. Transcendence has intentional energy that guides you on your journey beyond the boundaries of everything you thought and believed was possible in your life. It is a magical journey for it subtly changes everything, leading you into the mystic, metaphysical realms of symbolism and alchemy.

If you wish it, you can pupate from your 'caterpillar' state into your soulful butterfly. This takes time and patience and the transcendence is attenuated – it happens by degrees. At first, you may look the same on the outside, but feel differently on the inside. Continue on the path of Transcendence, allowing your old stories and identities to melt and eventually, undoubtedly, you will transform beyond the person you thought you were here to be. It is a path less travelled, but it is open to you should you choose to surrender to your soul journey.

Contemplate your Heart Centre for it is your touchstone and portal. It is the node that connects you to the web of life in our Universe; and your unique vibrational frequency radiates from it outwards, connecting you with all beings. From your Heart Centre you shall be known. See it as a temple, a shrine, a homecoming.

YOU CAN PUPATE FROM YOUR 'CATERPILLAR' STATE INTO YOUR SOULFUL BUTTERFLY

NOVEMBER PRACTICES

WISDOM WEAVING

GET OUT OF YOUR MIND AND INTO YOUR HEART

November is the time of the Weaver's Moon, when in a bygone era, wool from the summer shearing had been spun into yarn and warmer clothes were woven on the looms during the dark days of Winter. In recent years, the arts of knitting and crocheting have had something of a renaissance, perhaps because of a yearning for that meditative state that weaving induces, a state that the busyness of modernity often precludes.

When I was a young girl (Lorna), I used to love sitting next to my grandmothers as they were knitting or crocheting. I remember feeling absolutely peaceful and happy – it was my favourite thing. I was hypnotised by their fingers which seemed to know just the right time to make the complex movements that turned the yarn into beautifully patterned fabric, and as they did so, my grandmothers would quieten and begin to tell stories about their lives. Those precious moments were imbued with a sense of tranquillity that I have found can be rare in adult life – that is, unless I'm sitting next to one of several friends, who are also keen knitters, when without fail, that sense of pure peacefulness overwhelms me.

Children sitting at the feet of their grandparents is a tradition we should cherish and encourage. Our elders – our parents and grandparents and those in our communities who still have a remembrance of how to live harmoniously with the natural and other-than-human worlds – have great wisdom to impart. In Indigenous cultures, the elders are revered as those who embody a depth of understanding that engenders discernment, foresight and good decision-making on behalf of the community. They know how to weave ancestral stories into tapestries of meaning and communal wellbeing.

THERE IS REALLY ONLY ONE PROBLEM IN THE WORLD: THE MIND IS TELLING THE HEART WHAT TO DO

According to Unangan Elder, Ilarion Kuuyux Merculieff, founder of Wisdom Weavers of the World[22], there is really only one problem from which all crises arise – from climate change to species extinction, economic injustice to war – and it is that, "the mind is telling the heart what to do." Ilarion Merculieff is a 'Messenger' – that is what 'Kuuyux' means, and his message to humanity is a simple one. We need to, "Get out of our minds and into our hearts and live in the present moment." From there, we find a deeper, more intuitive perspective that can help to balance our thinking. Kuuyux says, "When you drop into your heart, you remember who you are." When you do this and act from the heart, you come face to face with your true self, and in doing so, you can begin to weave your new story.

This is the basis of Wisdom Weaving: as often as you can, practice 'Getting out of your mind and into your heart' – because when you stop thinking, you start to feel; you start to taste and discern and allow your other senses and perceptive abilities to come into play, and from that place, you can begin to weave. One of the greetings the Unangan people use is, "This morning tastes good." How often do you stop to 'feel' the morning; how it smells, how it tastes? In general, we humans tend only to think about what day it is or what time it is, what work we have to do, or what is being told to us in the news media or by our colleagues, therefore allowing our thinking mind to dominate our feeling heart. So, as part of your Wisdom Weaving practice, begin to feel the morning, begin to taste the day. Then ask yourself, "What is my heart saying to me this day? What is my heart asking me to do?"

It really does take courage to sink into the wisdom of the heart, but the beautiful thing is that the etymology of the word *courage* derives from Old French *'corage'* and literally means, *from the heart.* So, the courage you need to work from your heart resides in your heart – this is a wonderful reflection of sacred geometry, of the holographic nature of the Universe.

Wisdom Weaving is about pouring your energy into that which you want to create, that which you dream about, and then setting your intention – without thought, but from your heart at a cellular level within your body. Set your intention with deep faith and trust that in weaving this new tapestry it will unfold in front of your eyes. In fact, this cannot fail to happen for dreams are born of the imagination and imagination resides in the fertile womb of the Great Mother in the heart of the Cosmos; the pure potentiality of the Divine Feminine, the space between thoughts.

Wisdom Weaving is almost the antithesis of campaigning or activism for in these pursuits the focus is on 'stopping something', but as Kuuyux says, "When we try to stop something we are reacting and pouring all our intention, our mental, physical and spiritual energy into this process, so in fact we give it more energy, we make it bigger." The key is to weave a new story into being, to dream a new picture and imbue that with energy. How often have you made a resolution to stop doing something – to stop drinking alcohol, to stop eating sugar, to stop binging on social media – only to find yourself doing more of those things? It is because your focus is on those things. So rather than trying to stop and perhaps berating yourself for not being able to do so, delve into your heart's desire and bring forth a new story that gives you joy and which you can focus on. In this way, you will free yourself from the dominance of your mind, you will let your heart speak and begin to weave your wisdom.

The wisdom of the heart preoccupied another beloved sage, the Sufi poet and mystic Jalāl ad-Dīn Muhammad Rūmī, who lived in the 13th century in Persia (now Iran). Rūmī wrote, "Everyone has been made for some particular work, and the desire for that work has been put in every heart." He asks, "Why are you knocking at every other door? Go knock on the door of your own heart." His words are as pertinent to us now as they were over 700 years ago. You will find what you seek if you allow the wisdom of your heart to weave its magic through you and to do this, all you need to do is relinquish the dominance of your mind. Of course, this is much easier said than done!

So, how do you begin to weave this new picture of you? It involves feeling into and then unravelling any stories you may be holding onto about yourself that you sense are no longer relevant or no longer serve you. With compassion in your heart, let these stories blow to the four winds. There is no right or wrong about what you are choosing to let go of, for it has brought you to this place of discernment, but now it is time to listen to your heart and find out what new story wants to be woven. It is also worth noting that we are not advocating heart wisdom at the expense of your thinking mind but to find your own state of balance between the two, giving space for your intuitive heart wisdom rather than always prioritising the mind and its logical analysis. The whole Soulistic Journey is about finding balance so that nuance rather than duality is the outcome.

The best way to hear the wisdom of your heart is to allow yourself to be still, and to feel into the silence between thoughts. Breathing slowly and deeply is one of the best ways to let go of your mind-chatter, but it is not easy and it takes time to learn how to drop into this space. In our 'Unfurling Yoga' section on page 145, we detail some techniques that may help you drop into your heart space. Don't berate yourself if you find it hard because Wisdom Weaving is a lifetime occupation – it doesn't ever stop; you just keep adding to the Great Loom that holds your picture; you just create a new motif here and a new colour theme there. Embrace the pattern and beautiful design of your tapestry and behold with excitement what emerges. See it all as part of your coat of many colours. As your weaving reveals the shadow and contour of your story, try to accept what arises without judgement or blame – be openhearted towards yourself and the choices you have made and continue to make. We are all on a journey and at the heart of wisdom is compassion towards self and others.

Wisdom weaving is best done slowly and with the intention of creating balance in your life. When it's done in anger or impatiently, it just creates more knots and is usually a sign that your mind has taken control of the weave again! Have a go at weaving some new stories about yourself and your future; not focusing on what you 'ought to stop' but on what you dream of.

THE HEART OF WISDOM IS COMPASSION TOWARDS SELF AND OTHERS

ALL
CREATIVITY
BEGINS IN
THE DARK

HONOURING THE DARKNESS

DARKNESS IS THE PROVINCE OF INITIATION

Do you fear the dark? Most humans do in some form or another, so it is natural as the days draw-in and the darkness comes back to reclaim the land in an enveloping embrace, that we resist the coming of the darker months of the year. We resist the dark because we associate it with the abyss, the tunnel wherein there is no light, the locked closet from which we cannot escape, the cloaked and sinister being – all shadowy archetypes that embody fear – and so most of us prefer the daylight hours and the summer warmth; the translucency, the dynamism of growth and abundance, when we can see that which is before us. Yet the darkness is incredibly fertile and potent in ways that we can only begin to imagine, and those shadows contain within them pearls of wisdom if we fully embrace them and learn how to see with our inner eye of symbolic sight.

My grandfather was famous for saying, "All creativity begins in the dark," and I love this saying. For me (Genevieve), it certainly is true: when I travel into the black abyss of night time, dreaming and visioning beyond my conscious mind's reach, or in my early morning meditations when it is often still pitch dark outside, or in the darkness of uncertainty and confusion when the way is not clear until I tune-in and go into that tumult, these journeys into darkness are always full of epiphany and insight, once I open up and receive the wisdom that lays within. It is at this point, to paraphrase T. S. Eliot, that the darkness becomes light.

It is also true that the darkness of our mother's womb is our first reality and yet our time of greatest safety; and it is true that the deep dark of the Universal Mother's cosmic void, beyond all time and space, is a place embedded in potentiality, a place of fertility of the highest order. All of these shades of dark and shadow offer the Soulistic Journeyer a plethora of wisdom and teachings, when we see and hear with our inner sense of imagination.

One way to become comfortable with darkness and honour its velveteen embrace is when you are brave enough to venture beyond the confines of your home, at night. You may ask why it is necessary to do this if you are able to commune in the darkness of your dreams, but remember what we said about how your pathway often becomes clear when you move out of your comfort zone? This is very much the case with darkness. Darkness is the province of initiation and in facing your fear of it you are able to access many hidden gifts and insights. But, if the thought of wandering around the landscape at night fills you with dread then perhaps ease yourself into this practice by heading out for your adventure at dusk, the time when the 'veils' between this realm and other realms are thinned, a time when many a quester finds themselves drawn into new territory and initiations.

I 'danced with the darkness' quite recently and it was indeed an initiatory experience. Here's my story:

"After a long day in front of the computer, I found myself needing to get out of the house, just after dinner. Living in Avebury for part of the year, there are plenty of places that I could have wandered, but on this particular evening as the sun was setting low over the hills in tones of orange and peach, I found my feet taking me towards the Adam and Eve Stones. They are not terribly far from my home and I was filled with ease as I wandered down the path towards these two impressive stone guardians, also known as the Long Stones. As I approached the meadow in which they stand sentinel, a voice in my heart said, "Now you must walk the eight-fold infinity loop between them."

I baulked for a moment, realising the scope of the task being presented to me. I was being asked to honour the stones and energies there by entering into communion with them – but walking eight large figure-of-eight loops between these two stones is no quick task, and the night was drawing-in fast. As always, when a challenge is gifted to us, we can either back out and go home (no shame there,) or embrace the new territory with courage. So, I started walking.

I knew where the centre point of the stones was and orientated myself through feeling the Earth under my feet and noting the edges of the field as the light disappeared and the shadows became my friends. With each infinity loop I walked, I faced down yet another inane fear that reared its head. Unknown shapes and movements of energy wove their way around the stones, through the long grasses and then encircled me, and each time I had to remind myself that I was alone here (at least in the human world) and that I was infinitely protected by the stone guardians themselves and my own guardian angel (in the other-than-human worlds).

As I walked, gradually allowing my eyes to adjust to the light that is in the darkness, I noticed how I began to relax and feel safe wrapped in this blanket of shadow. Cloaked in the mystery of this magnificent place, I embraced the darkness and serenely walked all eight loops. Any fearful thoughts were vanquished, an almost trance-like state settling upon me – until I was finished and able to stop, bend down and kiss the grass under my feet in gratitude for my experience. And a ripple of awareness arose; that, 'Courage begins in the darkness too'.

And that was my lesson. That I am courageous, and I can face my fears; that in welcoming the initiations that life offers me, I deepen into who I really am and relax in the knowledge that each small step of awakening opens another vista on my journey."

As I was talking with Lorna about this experience, she told me that it reminded her of a beautiful conversation she'd had with her friend Natalie. Natalie dances with the dark regularly; she says sometimes she finds it quite scary, but it always brings her a revelation. One time, she had decided to go for a high tide midnight swim at The Quay – a local swimming spot. Although it was summer, nobody else was there, and being in the dark phase of the moon, there was no celestial light other than starlight. Natalie had always wanted to night-swim, but still felt a shiver of fear at the thought of it. Nonetheless, she plucked-up her courage, stripped off and dove into the inky waters. And as she did so, the most marvellous thing happened: phosphorescence sparkled from her fingertips and toes, rippling out a shimmering echo of starlight in the waters and delighting Natalie to the core. If she hadn't stepped out of her comfort zone, she would never have known such beauty exists in the darkest depths.

This practice of Honouring the Darkness can be done in a variety of ways and certainly isn't limited to the winter months, but as darkness is thrust upon us in winter, it gives us an opportunity to be more creative in how we work with it. Some of the other practices in this book such as An Invitation to Hibernation and Death Practices also weave a dance with darkness.

So why not embark on your own shadow adventure? It needn't be grand. Just a walk down the street or in the local park or woods, in the dark, will do to begin with and you can see where that leads. How does it make you feel? What emotions and mind-chatter comes up for you? What revelations does the darkness offer you? Remember to journal your experiences so that you can read and ponder this journey over the course of time, because always, revelation takes its own sweet time to unveil itself.

Whatever your approach, begin to embrace and honour the darkness. For she is your friend and in her fertile expanse you may find a way to unravel and reweave some of your own challenges.

BEAUTY EXISTS
EVEN IN THE
DARKEST
DEPTHS

AS WITHIN,
SO WITHOUT

NOVEMBER STORYHACK

GENEVIEVE GUIDES YOU IN THE GENTLE ART OF
RESTORYING YOUR LIFE...

THE TRUTH EXISTS WITHIN YOU AND WITHOUT YOU

You are in the North Quarter of the Soulistic Wheel and at this time, like me, you may find yourself looking back over the year that is coming to pass. Of late, I have been remembering. I have been reconnecting to ancient ancestral memories and in doing so, that has helped me to restory who I thought I was and the lessons I thought I was learning. You see, this is a never-ending journey: just when you think you have come to a place of understanding, you realise there is always more to learn and remember!

I have been rethinking what it means to love and to forgive. I have been letting go and letting in. But, the biggest revelation of all has been somewhat stereotypical and even clichéd. I have heard it thousands of times before and yet never really believed it... until now, of course. The thing that has made this year of challenge and metamorphosis massively unique has been the realisation that every insight has come from one source: ME.

Each time I have asked a question, the answer came from within. Each time I stumbled upon an emotionally challenging memory it came because I called it forth from the depths of my unconscious. Each time I healed, it came because I invited it and said 'yes' to the resolution. All my answers came from within. All my healing came from the inside out. Just like the teachers, mystics and angels have always said it would.

My truth existed all along within the rich soil of my experiences, stories and memories. My transformation came from within. I realised that the mirror of the world and the Universe only exists to remind me of my own choice to dive fully into the depths of my life and weave new realities from the truths that exists there.

The adventure of life really is one of remembering. Remembering who you are and why you are really here. Remembering the story that you came into human form to love/live. Remembering that you have choice and that all truth comes from within. As within, so without.

Hermes Trismegistus said that a very long time ago. Or perhaps you know him as Thoth, the Egyptian God of Writing, Magic and Wisdom, Master of Alchemy, who knew the secret I am discovering – that you can discover. That we are all a mirror of life. The whole Universe exists within the microcosm of us.

As my friend, the writer and physicist, Jude Currivan says, "We live within a vast cosmic hologram where the Universe is in-form-ation". Our truth is constructed from the stories we choose to live within... and without. Our truth is mirrored back to us from every aspect of life. It lives through us and all around us. It could even be said that the ultimate revelation is that we ARE truth in human form."

ME = WE = ALL

Someone very wise and loving once said, "I AM the truth, the way and the life." And so are you.

DECEMBER

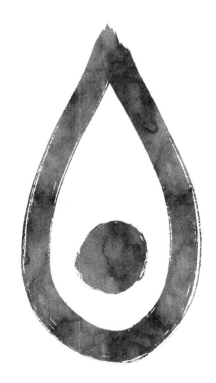

WHEN THE SUN CATCHES BEAUTY
AT A RARE ANGLE
AND A SUSURRATION OF SLOWNESS
INVITES US TO REST

DECEMBER EARTH SIGNS

December, the darkest of months, sees the living world fall asleep. Not much stirs in the bare branches of the oak, and the birds have ceased singing except for the friendly robin who churrs quietly in the hedge as you pass. In December, humans retreat from the cold and the wet, yet the natural world endures it with fortitude. After days of drenching rain, the blackbird appears on the lawn, handsome in his resplendent black plumage and yellow beak, his head cocked looking for grubs and worms. Survival is encoded in his memory.

December rarely gets much light: it can be grey from dawn till dusk, but when the low sun does shine it catches beauty at a rare angle: a swathe of sunlight in the dense woodland embellishes the intense purple of the newly-forming alder buds and the fiery orange of the willow tips like at no other time of year. There is colour in December, but it is fleeting, a reminder of things to come.

The dearth of light in December emboldens sleep; sleep wraps her tendrils around the apple tree and the rose, as they slumber in the cool winter winds. Sleep hushes the bees on all but the warmest of days and lulls the bats and moths into rest. Sleep whispers to us on the wind too, a susurration of slowness, an invitation to stop, to pause, to reflect.

December also brings us the Winter Solstice around the 21st-22nd, the exact date being determined by the moment when the sun passes through 270 degrees of geocentric longitude. This is an ancient and powerful celebration of the shortest day in the Northern Hemisphere and therefore by its very nature, the gradual return of the light as we move towards the Spring. Many cultures and traditions celebrate the Winter Solstice as a 'power day' when the veils between worlds are thin and many other-than-human beings come in to communicate with us. However you choose to celebrate the Solstice on your Soulistic Journey, remember that light can be found in the deepest of dark.

At the turning of the Gregorian year, where endings are beginnings, we invite you into stillness, to enjoy the peacefulness of the season.

DECEMBER COSMOLOGICAL SIGNS

SAGITTARIUS TO CAPRICORN

I EXPLORE

The winter months bring you to a space of inner quietude where your journey becomes deeper and introspective. Sagittarius invites you to remember your dreams and visions, which are often left by the wayside as you speed along the roads and pathways of life's lessons. As you now slow into Winter, you can embrace more of your soul essence; your purpose returns as a pulse that you can align to and structure your life around, so that you can move forward through this North Quarter with ease and joy.

You are invited to explore a new yet ancient story as you continue to remember your sense of self, heritage, ancestry and artistry. You are invited to muster up the courage to walk new paths through the mists of time and space, connecting to something beyond your logical mind – the imaginal realm, which is longing to be explored by you!

Your goals and aspirations will then become soul-infused as you deepen into a form of action that magnetises you forward into a new adventure – one that you courted and yet was not foreseen.

THE IMAGINAL REALM IS LONGING TO BE EXPLORED BY YOU

Full Circle Moon

– a time of beginnings and endings, when the darkness is full and fecund. The Pole Star glittering True North reminds you that now is the time to reset your spiritual compass for the year to come. Rejoice in the mystery that the darkness brings and dance in the blessed illumination of the Full Circle Moon.

DECEMBER SOULISTIC ARCHETYPES

SOLAR ARCHETYPE: UNITY

You are at the zenith of the North Quarter of the Soulistic Wheel where reunion brings you into wholeness – all paths become one and lead to the Winter Solstice. It is a time of reacquaintance with your ancestors by telling their stories around the mid-winter fires, acknowledging with love in your heart that truly, you are kin to all life on this Earth. Mystery asks you to feel compassion for the travails of all human and other-than-human ancestors, even if their actions have hurt you. Wisdom asks you to love yourself unconditionally, too.

Unity is omnipotent and omnipresent throughout the Universe – stop for a moment and contemplate that statement… It is not a spiritual cliché – you really are unified with every being – and understanding this ignites epiphany. Consider your relationship to the wolves of Yellowstone Park. Studies have shown[23] that the wolves keep the ecosystem in a state of perfect balance by preying on deer and other herbivores which would otherwise devour tree saplings and trigger loss of forest cover, in turn affecting the climate in that area and by consequence impacting the global climate. This phenomenon is known as a 'trophic cascade'. So, you really do have a unifying interconnection with wolves because wolves affect the global climate which in turn impacts you.

Similarly, consider the magnificently beautiful great whales of the ocean. Like wolves, they too are guardians of the climate through the trophic cascades they create in their own ecological niche in the oceans, helping to sustain the health of the entire oceanic realm, on which you are also interdependent[24]. So you are intimately interconnected with whales and wolves. In fact, you (I/We) are one with the entire Cosmos and once this fundamental truth is accepted you *become* Unity, the Divine Lover – because anything less abnegates the perfection of creation. Unity is all form, all manifestation.

Wisdom asks you to contemplate and embrace your homecoming into unity and to honour the holographic reality of the Universe. As above, so below. As

CONTEMPLATE AND EMBRACE YOUR HOME-COMING INTO UNITY

within, so without. The microcosm is the macrocosm. Can you see the truth of this through your new-found mythic eyes?

What 'other-than-human' being do you truly love? (And if there is not an 'other-than-human' being that you love, consider why that might be.) Take a photograph of, or paint/draw this being. Add it to your dreamboard.

LUNAR ARCHETYPE: ALCHEMY (THE DIVINE FLAME)

You are experiencing the fecund climax of the North Quarter of the Soulistic Wheel, a time when it is 'better to light a candle than to curse the darkness'. All flame derives from the alchemical Divine Flame, the animating principle that allows for unity – without the Alchemy of the Divine Flame, all would remain inert. Mystery asks what it is that could 'light your fire'? What motivates you from lethargy to creativity? What energetic impetus do you need in order to move beyond the stagnation of your comfort zones? Can you remember the things you loved to do as a small child? This may give you a clue to your spark of Soul Purpose, for when we were children, our dreams had not been educated out of us.

The Divine Flame gives birth to all the archetypal energies which are often revealed in dreamtime. Is there an energy that is expressing through your dreams? Do you dream of flying or of drowning? Of being loved or being alone? Do you dream of sailing or of struggling through quicksand? Do you connect with spirit in your dreams or do you descend into fear? What does Alchemy want to birth through you?

Remember, in the mystery is the wisdom; the shadows reveal hidden gifts if you are fearless enough to go in search of them. Shadows are only places where the light has not yet come to pass.

The Divine Flame of Alchemy fans the embers of your heart's longing into a fire of creativity; it will animate you to begin again when you feel like giving up. Dare to hope.

Make a list of all that you feel you have achieved during the course of this year; all the things you are proud of, no matter how insignificant. Call this list 'Candles' and pin it to your dreamboard. When you feel like giving up or giving in, look at your Candles, burning bright in remembrance of what you are capable of.

UNIFICATION: TRUTH

The paths from Above and Below merge within your Heart Centre, that beautiful place of stillness and silence where Truth prevails. Your own unique Truth resides beyond the current stories you are telling yourself and it will eventually call you home to this place after a long and mysterious journey.

You may feel a sense of completion at the close of the year, beholding the truths in your heart and all they have taught you. At this time of the Winter Solstice, if you wish to, you can now 'die' to who you have been in all those old stories, because through contemplating their mysteries and wisdom, they will have served their purpose. If you wish to, you can offer them up as part of your Fire Ceremony so they can ignite and burn away to become unified with the Akashic Library of all our human stories that are held in perpetuity.

You are pure and unified spirit, animated by the Divine Flame and ready for the next spiral of life's mystery – for it is not all over! Truth reveals that the wheel continues to turn, life goes on, and in your ending is your beginning. The great 'Ouroboros of Infinity' spins on. It is time to take another step into the mystic.

What personal truths can you divine from your experience of the year that is passing? Are you living your current Truth? On a small piece of paper, write down a word or phrase that represents your core Truth at this time. Put it in a safe place so that this time next year, you can refer to it and see how your Truth expands as you dance the Soulistic Journey.

DECEMBER PRACTICES

FIRE CEREMONY

DESTRUCTION BRINGS CREATION IN ITS WAKE

At this time of the year, when in the UK at least, it is sometimes so grey that it seems as if the day hardly dawns before night casts her spell once again, what could be better than lighting a fire? Fire gives us light and warms us to the core, imbuing us with a feeling of comfort and wellbeing; its flickering dance mesmerises and transports us to other worlds – how often have you gazed into the flames of a fire and lost all sense of time? Fire is alchemical, it transforms things: wood to ash, liquids to gases, raw ingredients into meals.

Fire is also the great destroyer – it can quickly alter form and matter for ever, and sometimes this can be devastating. But the great theosophist, Alice Bailey, taught us that, 'Only through destruction do we get creation.' In other words, for something to be born, something else has to die, or to put it more accurately, has to transform. The destructive power of fire brings creation in its wake. You only need look at the green shoots of regrowth against the blackened trunks of a forest fire to know that this is true.

This Fire Ceremony is all about creativity. It is about creating space for old feelings or habitual thinking to burn away making space for the birth of new energies and motivations. The best time to have your Fire Ceremony is during the Winter Solstice, 21st-22nd December when it can be a really meaningful ritual by marking the return of the light and the intention to allow creativity into your life.

Here's how to do it.

❋   If you have an outdoor fire-pit or chimnea, then use that for your ceremony. If you don't have this, but do have a wood-burning stove indoors, then use this instead. If you have no access to a place for fire-making, then you can use a candle.

❋   Build your fire in a mindful state, placing each piece of wood on it with reverence, knowing that it will be transformed forever into another state – this act requires humility.

❋   If possible, go for a short walk to find seasonal and symbolic items that you can place in your fire: a sprig of holly; some withered sage; a nub of frankincense from your Gifting Bag if you have some; a pine cone… anything that feels significant to you at this moment in time.

❋   Whilst you are building your fire, set aside several sticks or twigs that you can use later. Light your fire and keep feeding it so that it grows more intense in heat and colour. Whilst you do this, quieten your mind so you are nearing a state of meditation. The best way to do this is just to watch the flickering flames. Watch the dance of energy before you and how the wood relinquishes its form. Watch as the flames lick and curl and caress; surrender to their power and transformative beauty.

✳ As you settle into the vibrational energy of fire, ask yourself if there is anything in your life that you would like to transform. Then pick up one of your twigs and say aloud whatever it is that you would like to change: 'I would like to transform my habitual judgement of others into unconditional love.' Then throw the stick on the fire and watch it literally transform in front of your eyes. The next time you catch yourself in judgement of others, remember that you have already transformed that habit into Love and change your perspective. Perhaps you would like to relinquish the anxiety that you hold regarding your current job? Pick up a twig, throw it in the fire and say aloud, "I choose to let go of any feelings of anxiety about my work and trust that the best outcomes for me will unfold." Then watch your anxieties burn in the fire, making space for something more creative.

✳ If you are using a candle for this practice, you can wave a stick of palo santo incense through the flame and watch wood turn to fragrant smoke, a transformative process akin to that you are seeking.

You can hold a Fire Ceremony at any time of the year and for any transformational purpose, where you wish to change one perspective into another. But as with all these practices, choose wisely and ask for only those things that bring harmony into your life. The old adage, 'Be careful what you wish for' is always one to bear in mind, because in this practice as with all of them, your words become your actions. Here are the words of Mahatma Gandhi to remind us of this truth:

> "Your beliefs become your thoughts,
> Your thoughts become your words,
> Your words become your actions,
> Your actions become your habits,
> Your habits become your values,
> Your values become your destiny."

INVITATION TO HIBERNATE

NESTLE, RUMMAGE AND SQUIRM...

A key aspect of the Soulistic Journey is a deep reconnection with the natural world, taking our cues from Mother Nature and slowing down to her pace. What reveals itself when we do this is wonderfully transformative, but it takes faith and patience to walk this path and in these days of technological instant gratification, patience is fast becoming a lost art.

In the cold, silent days of Winter, it is hard to imagine the abundance of Summer, where all is fruitful and burgeoning – all we see are the grey-brown hues of a seemingly barren landscape and this can make us feel quite desolate. Winter is often a time when melancholy and depression arise for many. But what if we 'hack' that perspective? What if, instead of seeing the land as barren, we see it as fallow. Those who tend the land know that leaving it fallow is an essential aspect of fertility. The land needs time to rest and recuperate after the activities of Spring and Summer and it does so during the Mystery Time of Winter.

In fact, prior to the industrial revolution, it was common that once every seven years, a field would be left fallow for the whole year so that it could truly rest and recuperate. In the Jewish culture, this tradition was reflected in the practice of 'Sabbatical' - where once every seven years, land-workers were able to take a year off, because it was recognised that for them to be as healthy as the land they tilled, they also needed to lie fallow. Nowadays, when do we ever give ourselves time to properly rest, beyond the snatched fortnight of a holiday – let alone a Sabbatical?

In December, it is time to lay fallow, to slow down into hibernation mode. Okay – so most of us have to work and we have families to support and houses to clean – but this invitation is not about being absent for a year, or even a week, it is about carving out a niche of time on a regular basis throughout the month and beyond where you 'hibernate'. This is how you do it.

IT IS TIME TO LAY FALLOW, TO SLOW DOWN INTO HIBERNATION MODE

❋ Announce to your family and friends, or commit to the process in writing via your journal, that every Thursday evening (or whatever evening, or timeframe that works best for you) for the next month (or however long you can realistically commit to this), you will be hibernating. Ideally, your hibernation practice should take place at a time when you don't usually allow yourself to rest.

❋ Enjoy the raised eyebrows and disbelief. Insist that during this time, you should not be disturbed – barring an emergency.

❋ Make like a grizzly-bear and create your den. If you share a bedroom with another human being, is there an alternative space where you can hibernate? If not, then be ready to pack down your den after each session. If you have a shed, summerhouse or a spare room, then mark out your territory! Your den should be small and cosy, dark and sumptuous: collect drapes to hang, and soft furry blankets to snuggle in; have plenty of cushions to curl into and hot water bottles at the ready if it is cold. You may like to hang golden fairy lights above your head to remind you of the stars. As with our animal cousins, even though your den is likely to be inside, it should feel connected to the outside, so you might like to play the sound of a river, the ocean or the wind in the trees on your smartphone – there are many Nature Sounds apps to choose from – or you may prefer silence. Light some incense and a candle, for nothing is quite as soporific as flickering candlelight. Bring into your den anything that helps you to truly relax.

❋ Admire the beautiful space you have created just for you.

❋ At the appointed time, wear only loose-fitting comfortable clothes and no shoes. Crawl into your den space and ensure you have at least an hour - preferably two or three – when you will not be disturbed. Set a gentle alarm on your smartphone to rouse you out of your hibernation at the time you choose.

❋   Nestle, rummage, squirm. Get comfy. Then begin to slow…

❋   Focus on your breathing: breathe in through your nose, two-three
hold… Out through your mouth, two-three hold… Slower: in through
your nose, two-three hold… Out through your mouth, two-three hold…
Slower still: in, two-three hold… out, two-three hold… in, two-three
hold… out, two-three hold…

❋   Relax and tune-in to the silence or the Nature sounds. Keep breathing slowly.

❋   You may fall asleep or you may just breathe – but do absolutely
nothing else.

Sounds easy, doesn't it! But, it's surprising how long it takes our chattering
minds to become still. If you're adept at meditation, you may easily be able
to slip into a meditative state where you become still within, but if, like many
of us it is difficult to 'let go' of the busyness of the day, then hibernation may
take a bit of practice. Do stick with this practice, because how often do you
truly allow yourself to do nothing? Watching TV, reading, darning the kids'
socks, writing the shopping list, having friends around for dinner – this is not
doing nothing. Gift yourself a few hours each week during the Mystery Time
of Winter to just do nothing. Remember, doing nothing takes dedication and
practice but it will pay off in the long run!

Hibernation takes you beyond meditation into surrender. And what are you
surrendering to? Your own natural rhythm and tempo that exists in every cell of
your being. You were born with this instinct but have learned to cover it over
with the busyness and noise of modern life.

If any insights come to you whilst hibernating, then write them down after the
session so that you may ponder upon them, but hibernation is all about true
relaxation at a fundamental level. Really, it asks nothing of you except commitment to surrender.

HIBERNATION
TAKES YOU
BEYOND
MEDITATION
INTO
SURRENDER

DECEMBER STORYHACK

GENEVIEVE GUIDES YOU IN THE GENTLE ART OF RESTORYING YOUR LIFE...

BECOMING AN OBSERVER

JOY IS THE ULTIMATE STORYHACK TO A BUSY, STRESSED-OUT MIND

Have you ever heard the phrase, 'Being in the world but not of it'? This has been rolling through my head increasingly of late, as I have travelled from one seemingly tumultuous political environment to another. Whether the politics being played out are personal, organisational or national doesn't really matter. It's all made of the same messy human narratives that have the potential to suck us into their vortex of fear of the unknown. The process of breaking down in order to eventually break through is one that few of us are good at. Indeed, I would challenge whether anyone living through these times of intense chaos and transformation becomes good at this process when they are in the middle of it!

My solution to the turbulence of my internal and external world has been to retain a secret part of my consciousness who sits quietly in the background and *observes* the scenes unfolding around her. She has patiently listened, watching for the seen and unseen dynamics; noticing what has been said and left unsaid. She has sensed in her body the pain of unexpressed fear, the untapped exhilaration of hidden vision and the embarrassment of words spoken in hasty anger.

Most of all, she took me by the hand more than once and led me out beyond the human world into the wider ecosystems of our planet. We found a quiet spot underneath a large 'Tree of Heaven' (yes, that really is its name) and sat for 30 minutes each day. As I (we) sat there, she repeatedly 'shushed' my over-active brain that wanted to label the plants and animals that came into our world. She reminded me to breathe really deeply and relax my tense muscles that were clenched with the winter cold. Then in the relative silence, she would put her arms around me and communicate one overarching emotion above all else.

Joy
Quiet joy
Instant joy
Ever-present joy

The joy that comes from knowing that we are alive, that we have been blessed with another day of adventure, that we have so much to be grateful for. Joy is the ultimate storyhack to a busy, stressed-out mind. Joy is the fastest way to dispel our sense of self-judgment for not being (good) enough. Joy is the turbo-charger for attracting new opportunities your way.

Since I have allowed her – my observer – to lead me out of my busy mind, I have had more exciting epiphanies and new opportunities than in the previous 12 months.

She works fast, my inner observer. All I had to do was allow her to do her thing.

JOY IS THE FASTEST WAY TO DISPEL OUR SENSE OF SELF-JUDGMENT

JANUARY

WHEN THE SOFTEST THING IN THE UNIVERSE
CAN OVERCOME THE HARDEST THING
IN THE UNIVERSE

JANUARY EARTH SIGNS

Having passed the longest night of the year, January brings a gradual, almost imperceptible return of the light, yet this blessing can be overshadowed by bitterly cold storms and relentless rain and often, snow. But wrap-up warmly and step outside and you will find that somehow, poking through the frigid snow-encrusted Earth, a green shoot has appeared. It looks so tender, so fragile, but it can resist ice. It is the first stirrings of the snowdrop, that most longed-for of flowers in the northern hemisphere.

Look more closely and you'll find that, miraculously, the sunshine yellow of a winter aconite has unfurled beneath the birch tree; that the periwinkle is starring the hedgerows with blue; the celandine is forming buds. What resilience and fortitude! What vision to keep pushing up through the cold, hard soil to emerge into the perilous world above ground. Yet, emerge they do. How is it that beings seemly so soft and delicate can survive the harshest month? As it says in *The Tao*, 'The softest thing in the Universe can overcome the hardest thing in the Universe.' What a metaphor to live our lives by.

January also brings us the spectacle of starling murmurations where thousands of birds fly as one, creating the most incredible shapes and patterns in the sky as they slowly descend to their overnight perches. The phenomenon of murmuration is facilitated by 'swarm intelligence', where there is no one leader, but where there is an emergence of energy which individual birds respond to. So, if one bird flies higher than the others or in a different direction, then the rest will naturally move to surround it, thereby creating the pulsing and fluctuating patterns that so often resemble that of a bird. It is the microcosm and the macrocosm in a scintillating dance, one of Nature's wonders.

In January we invite you to feel into the emerging energy of Spring and to respond creatively to its ebbs and flows.

FEEL INTO THE EMERGING ENERGY OF SPRING AND RESPOND CREATIVELY TO ITS EBBS AND FLOWS

JANUARY COSMOLOGICAL SIGNS

CAPRICORN TO AQUARIUS

I ACHIEVE

As the Gregorian calendar leads you through the turning of another annual cycle, you are invited to follow the energy of Capricorn into the new year with vigour. At this time, you may find yourself accelerating into commitments and goals, looking to achieve something new – but keep an eye out for the 'trickster energy' of false hope and pipe dreams.

In the cold light of day, January is a time to assess the goals you wish to keep and pursue from the previous year and those you wish to redesign into something that feels more authentic and aligned to your emerging Soulistic identity. Now is a time to sense into what 'achievement' really delivers when you accomplish it and whether this still feels relevant to your emerging story.

You are invited to move beyond resolutions and into resolve, as a sense of determination breaks through your resistance and fuels you with the energy needed to move into the next stage of your journey.

White Owl Moon

– in the light of the January full moon, we catch the essence of White Owl, she who moves silently across the Earth, her all-seeing eyes attuned to what moves, her hearing acute and sensitive. Be like White Owl, sensing what is presenting itself to you.

JANUARY SOULISTIC ARCHETYPES

SOLAR ARCHETYPE: FLOW

You are walking in the final weeks of the North Quarter of the Soulistic Wheel, yet you may feel stuck and unmotivated, or lacking in energy, as if you are wading through thick mud. This is because you have yet to fully emerge from the 'cave' of your winter hibernation and like most of us in the northern hemisphere at this time, you are still only taking tentative steps into the light and then retreating back to the warmth and security of home. This is natural and understandable, but a remembrance of Spring is vibrating in your cells, nonetheless.

Do not push yourself at this time – honour your own energy levels – but notice how the sun's flow of energy emerges by degrees and emulate that with a slow, graceful unfurling of your creativity after the winter sleep of reunion. As you feel a corresponding rise in your own energies with that of our great solar benefactor, which bathes us and our planet with its enlivening properties, it is time to begin remembering what it is that truly enlivens your soul; what it is that is calling you forth into its Flow, this coming year.

Venture out of your winter home and allow the molecules of sunlight to flow around you and caress your skin; recognise the energetic invitation to open to the potential of new opportunities and ways of being. Let the flowing energy of light take you by the hand and lead you into the forest of your life story. Mystery asks you to be courageous, to look at your story and see if there is a new path you would like to take. Wisdom knows that this is an invitation into the heart of your adventure for a new year.

Will you accept this challenge and take your first few steps into the new? Will you bathe in the light of the lengthening days and allow any feelings of restriction to melt into motivation? Know that if and when you do, the qualities of Flow will lift you, guiding the way with the magic of synchronicity. Flow is powerful and creative; it is possible to divert the Flow of energy through fear and cynicism, but courage says wade into the Flow and see where it leads!

Who is your archetypal mentor at this time? Who did you meet at the North Quarter meditation? What was their gift to you? (Perhaps reciprocate their gift to you with something from your gifting bag?) Ask them through dialogue on the imaginal realm any question that may be in the forefront of your mind. Allow the answer to Flow to you on the wind.

LUNAR ARECHETYPE: COMPLEMENTARITY

You are emerging from below into the light, as the final weeks of Winter and your own journey through the North Quarter of the Soulistic Wheel draw to a close. Open your eyes and look around you; see how, despite the cold, there is enough warmth and daylight for life to reappear in all its glorious diversity. There is Complementarity between the light and the dark that is divinely whole. There is Complementarity between Winter and Spring that allows for growth. Without one, there could not be the other. Mystery may fill your heart with hopes and fears, but Complementarity distils them into choice. What choices are showing up for you right now? Can you see their new shoots arising?

Complementarity often shows her face in opposites and contradictions, but what may seem paradoxical is actually at the heart of wisdom. What is Wisdom whispering to you as your energy begins to flow in this turning of the year? Paradox may also show you a mirror image of yourself; you may find yourself judging a friend for their actions and then realise that you do the same thing yourself. Always, when we judge others, we are judging ourselves. The gift of paradox is clarity, though it takes a degree of playful enquiry to see through oppositional energies. In truth, we are all mirrors of each other and are therefore able to remind each other when we have strayed off the path of our true destiny.

Sit at your altar for a while and come into a state of contemplation. Consider the things that you would love to do in the coming year – be they momentous or relatively insignificant. Make a list of

them and pin the list to your dreamboard. You have now created some intentions. How are you going to act on your intentions?

UNIFICATION: CLARITY

The paths from Above and Below merge within your Heart Centre, that place of stillness and silence where Clarity resides. The potential of Clarity is immense because Clarity illuminates the path you knew you came here to walk and have been seeking ever since you were born. Clarity shows you the way through synchronicity and intuition.

That can be a scary thought – fulfilling your potential – it may ask more of you than you are ready to give, but trust in the flow of your life. All aspects of your life experience have led you here, to read this. You *are* ready.

Clarity calls to you to own your aspirations – can you see them clearly now? When things become crystal clear to you that were previously murky and unresolved, that is when your path appears. Look at the list you made in the Lunar Archetype of Complementarity – are any of these aspirations at the centre of your soul journey, the core of your story? Do any of them have a degree of Clarity that makes them stand out from the others? Will you follow Clarity, leaving behind outworn beliefs and stories of who you thought you were? Of course you will! If not now, when?

Sit comfortably beside your altar, or in Nature if you prefer, and take some time to be by yourself, undisturbed. As you did in the North Quarter Mentor Meditation, envisage that you are sitting within your Heart Centre, in the middle of your unique inner Wheel. You are comfortable at rest here in this place of great beauty. Let go of all thoughts and allow your mind to settle. As your mind settles, like the reflective surface of a scrying pool, Clarity will emerge. What is Clarity's gift to you?

JANUARY PRACTICES

GRATITUDE MEMO

GRATITUDE EMPOWERS YOU WITH POSITIVITY

Have you ever felt an overwhelming sense of thankfulness? Have you ever thought, "I'm so lucky…" or "I feel so blessed…"? That emotion is gratitude. Gratitude is unconditional in that it doesn't depend on you giving or receiving anything; it arises of its own volition – often quite unexpectedly – from your heart centre and pervades your whole being. It feels like being saturated by a blissful, golden energy. You might even find tears of joy and grace coming. Let them come, bathe in them, for tears of gratitude are so healing.

The experience of gratitude can be fleeting and intense, but it does infuse you with a sense of wellbeing. Gratitude is good for your mental, emotional and physical health and it empowers you with positivity.

Studies have shown that people who count their blessings tend to be happier and suffer less from depression and anxiety because they focus on what is good in their lives, rather than what is not going to plan. Expressing gratitude also has the ability to liberate you from holding on to toxic emotions by shifting your attention away from resentment, envy or anger, towards those things that bring you happiness.

Twenty-first century life is frenetic, complex and demanding. It leaves little time to 'stand and stare' at the beauty of a cherry tree coming into blossom, or the glory of a sunset. Yet giving yourself permission to slow down often brings with it a sense of gratitude. Try this, next time you are dashing from A to B. Just stop and breathe and notice something that gives you pleasure.

GRATITUDE ARISES OF ITS OWN VOLITION FROM YOUR HEART CENTRE

In your Soulistic Journey, you are awakening to all sorts of energies and experiences that you may have previously been unaware of. Gratitude is one of them: it's often there, but usually overlooked – batted away in an effort to 'get on' with life. The good news is that your experience of gratitude can be enhanced with practice so that eventually, your default-setting is gratitude. One way to do this is through Gratitude Memos.

- Once a week on a certain time and date of your choosing, get into the habit of writing a Gratitude Memo. This can be done in your Journal, because it's wonderful to read these memos a few months later and recall all the good things that have happened to you.

- Start off by writing a few lines about what you have enjoyed in the last few days: 'On Saturday, I went to the market and bought the ripest, juiciest mango I have ever tasted. It was delicious.' Or, 'I rang my old housemate from Uni yesterday, and we had a wonderful catch-up. I won't leave it so long next time.' Then write about the people who make you happy; what you love about them and why you are glad that they are in your life; write about what you enjoy doing and what that feeling is like; write about the little things: the smell of a rose in the garden; the wag of your dog's tail when you return from work…

- Take time to think of all the things in your life, big and small, that you are grateful for; the people you would like to give thanks to and the things that bring you joy. You may like to make an offering on your altar from your gifting bag – a pebble, a feather, a crystal, some incense – to remind you whenever you pass, of your feelings of gratitude.

- In your daily life, if you notice that your inner voice is grumbling about something, try and alchemise that thought by focusing on something good that has happened to you recently.

This is not about seeing the world through rose-tinted spectacles; it's about *choosing* to focus on that which brings you happiness rather than that which

THIS IS ABOUT CHOOSING TO FOCUS ON THAT WHICH BRINGS YOU HAPPINESS brings you down. The phrase, 'bring you down' is accurate, as that is what actually occurs: fear, anger, envy, anxiety, stress… all these negative emotions lower your vibrational rate and can often cascade into a vortex of depression. So, counting your blessings really is good for your wellbeing. Gratitude Memos will help to get you into the habit of thankfulness.

ENTERING THE DREAMWORLD

DREAMS WILL BE YOUR TEACHERS IF YOU ALLOW THEM

AS YOU SLEEP YOUR SOUL ROAMS FREE WITHIN YOUR DREAMS

Is this life a dream? Are we walking through an imaginal realm, full of characters that we designed and created to dance with, before we were born? My experience (Genevieve) would tell me so. But this is something that each of us must discover and interpret in our own time and from walking our own path.

The dreamworld is one of untapped potential, archetypal beings, symbols and alternative realities waiting to be explored. As you sleep, your conscious habits of distraction and avoidance retreat into the background and are momentarily silenced as your soul roams free within your dreams, learning valuable lessons about what is happening in the day world.

The 'dreamweave' (as Jamie Sams, Seneca Medicine Woman, would call it), welcomes you into its metaphors and mysteries, showing you mirrors of your true inner beliefs, emotions, thoughtforms and desires. It is here that you are able to perceive the vast and complex inner workings of your psyche. This is one of the reasons that master mythologist and psychologist Carl Jung advocated dreamworking so passionately: because it is in this realm that you have the ability to embrace and transform the raw materials of your soul journey and bring them back into your day world, thereby enhancing and transforming your life in myriad ways.

Sounds implausible? Perhaps that's because as children, we were all fed a diet of cultural misinformation that told us, 'dreams are just the fantasy workings of your mind and are nothing to pay attention to.' Or perhaps on a more personal level, you may experience a kind of resistance about exploring your dreamweave because you don't really want to know the real substance of your soul's longings and passions?

But eventually, these inner callings surface in one form or another. In my experience, it is better to address what is being revealed by consciously working with your dreams, than to try and avoid or deny your deepest inner urges. Or perhaps you are entirely the opposite and cannot wait to romance and court your inner visions in the dreamweave? "Tapping the dreamweave allows us to understand the unseen circles of energy that influence and define our waking experiences, showing us how to come full circle and how to dance the next level of our personal growth cycles." - Jamie Sams, *Dancing the Dream*

Dreamworking has been a core practice of mine for decades as it provides both a training ground for life's lessons and challenges as well as a rich tapestry of mythic stories to fuel our inspiration and awareness in the day world. Often, if I have a question I am working with or a dilemma that I just can't seem to 'mental' my way through, I will cease thinking and dream on it. This can take many forms and I find it most powerful when I follow these 3 simple steps.

❋   I set aside any expectations I may have for the experience I will have in the dreamweave (i.e. that I will remember it, that I will have a lucid dream, that I will travel etc). I will have no judgement about what arises.

❋   I create a container of ceremony around the dreamspace itself. Often, on a conscious dreamworking night, I will light a candle and say a prayer before I sleep. I will also call in my guides from the archetypal realm to assist me in my journey. On waking (as well as recording anything I remember in my journal) I will light the candle again and express gratitude for my adventures in whatever form they took.

✻ As soon as possible after waking, I repeat the dream out loud (at least as much as I can remember) in the first person, present tense. For example: "*I am* walking down the street, I **see** my friend walking towards me. She **has** green eyes…" This ensures that you relive the dream in as much detail as possible and you will often find that other details spring back into life and you remember much more about the context.

✻ Then I simply allow the dream to 'work me' for the following few days. It can be powerful to share your dream with others but please try to stay away from dream interpretation, either by yourself or anyone you share it with. The dreamweave speaks in riddles and metaphors; it rarely allows for a simple or universal translation. The idea is to dance with your dream and see what emerges as you contemplate it over a series of days, weeks or even years. I regularly remember some of my vivid dreams, years if not decades after I had them. Dreams will be your teachers if you allow them.

Many ancient or indigenous cultures use dreaming as one of the primary forms of collective decision making. Often in Native American practices, groups of women (and men) will enter into a collective dream intention to 'dream on behalf of the people'. Each person is presented with one piece of the puzzle and this is shared in council so the tribe can make sense of the question from many angles.

Just like in the day world, the dreamweave is complex and takes years (and lifetimes) of practice to learn to navigate its waters. You could start your own practice in the darker months of the year when sleep and hibernation are key. Or try intentional dreaming, on full or new moons, when the veils between the worlds are thin and the dreamweave is easier to enter.

There is no right or wrong way. Just dream.

JANUARY STORYHACK

GENEVIEVE GUIDES YOU IN THE GENTLE ART OF RESTORYING YOUR LIFE...

LESSONS FROM BEING LOST

CONSCIOUSLY KNOWING THAT YOU DON'T KNOW

On a bright and chilly January day, I went out into the forest near my house in Wiltshire to deliberately get lost; to wander paths that I have never walked before and listen to what the quiet, wise voice of Nature had to teach me about myself. My key lesson revolved around my fear and joy of getting lost. Here are some of the lessons that came to me as I wandered through the sunlit forest, with an open heart, listening, learning and remembering.

Sometimes on the paths of life, there aren't signs where you expect them to be – and sometimes there are, it's just that you're not looking for them!

When you travel consciously through your challenges and lessons, it is easy to feel afraid of getting lost in the jungle of life, and so you start to look for signs that can lead the way. Whether you want to be pointed towards 'the right decision' or the 'easiest path', it is human nature to want to be told where to go and what is the best thing to do. Sometimes however, there are no signs. Sometimes, you are asked to continue onwards in faith and trust, believing in yourself as you put one foot in front of the other. Sometimes life's signposts need to be lacking so that you can be still and hear your own deep intuition.

On the other hand, humans also have a habit of becoming too narrow-focussed, looking and seeing only what we want to see and filtering out the majority

SOMETIMES
LIFE'S
SIGNPOSTS
NEED TO BE
LACKING
SO THAT
YOU CAN BE
STILL AND
HEAR YOUR
OWN DEEP
INTUITION

FEEL YOUR
FEAR AND
CONTINUE
REGARDLESS

of the world in favour of the elements that we understand. Sometimes, there are signs there for you to be guided by, but you may not see them. To do so, you need to develop the 'mythic' eyes to see them. These signs don't always appear in the form that you expect, but if you remember to stop and look for them, they are there, nonetheless.

When you gather your courage and forge ahead on an unfamiliar path, you find that the great unknown is not as scary as you thought it would be.

The unknown is naturally scary. It is uncertain and is more often than not uncontrollable. To fear this is perfectly understandable. To continue anyway is courageous. It is a common trick of the ego to make you rigid with fear so you are paralysed and stay within the safe boundaries of your comfort zones – however, when you break free and move forward anyway, often you find that the 'unknown' is not only safe and exciting but actually a new flavour of the 'known'. You remember the feelings of excitement and ultimate freedom that come with feeling your fear and continuing regardless. This is true human spirit and the only road home to your soul.

Sometimes when you are lost, there is nothing else to do but keep walking until you find what you are looking for.

Action speaks louder than words. Movement creates momentum and new outcomes. When you walk in trust, you are able to feel safe, no matter where you are. When you consciously 'know that you don't know', sometimes the best policy is just to keep putting one foot in front of the other until you find the path or the lesson you are looking for.

A journey is not about how far you go, whether you make it to your destination or if you receive some grand vision that inspires you. It's actually just about exploring, playing, adventuring – wondering at the beauty of life and seeing the connections between all things and knowing, truly, you are never alone. If you can do this much every day then you have fulfilled your ultimate purpose.

So often your ego tricks you into thinking that it's all about the destination. That it is 'how fast', 'how rich', 'how much' you can get. This is the cause of much pain and suffering in the world and the human psyche. How often are you told that life is about the journey not the goal or ultimate destination? Hardly ever. But in reality, life is about how well you travel your path not what you get at the end of it. When you remember this in every cell of your being, every step you take is full of joy and wonder. You can look around and feel life pulsing under each footstep. You are complete and enough right now, as you are, no matter where you are going and where you have come from.

Sometimes you think that you are forging new roads and finding new ways and yet you recognise things are strangely familiar. You realise that you have come right back around in a circle again and know exactly where you are.

Life is tricky and old habits die hard. Sometimes your ego tricks you into thinking that you are making new choices and creating new circumstances in your life, only for you to find out that you are actually operating from the same old beliefs and patterns of thinking and behaving as before! Whether these cycles refer to your relationships, your career, your hobbies or ways of interacting with the world, it is up to you to recognise when you are at a point when you can break the cycle and choose something new. As Einstein said, 'Insanity is believing that we will get different results by repeating the same patterns of thinking over and over again'. To get new results, you need new thinking. The key is to recognise when you have come full circle and then, knowing this, you can make the choice to change.

Sometimes at the beginning of a journey or a challenge, you think to yourself, 'There is no way I am ever going to complete this. There is no way I will ever find the energy, motivation or the strength of will to come through.' Yet by taking one step at a time, suddenly you find yourself having completed everything you set out to do and it not having been nearly as hard as you thought.

LIFE IS ABOUT
HOW WELL
YOU TRAVEL
YOUR PATH
NOT WHAT
YOU GET AT
THE END OF IT

WHEN YOU
FORGET TO
TRUST LIFE,
YOU FALL
INTO FEAR

Like all of us, you are bound to make up stories based in fear of the unknown, along the lines of: 'Why start when I don't even know if I will finish?' or 'Why bother even trying when everything seems stacked against me?' These stories keep you locked in your comfort zones – if you let them. They keep you in the stasis of the ego, trapped in fear of failure. True freedom is knowing that whether you finish or not, real success is trying anyway. Often when you focus on just taking one step at a time, you find that you actually tackled the challenge with an ease and grace that you never expected. Often your success surprises you and you see that your stories were just that... Stories.

In those moments when you think that you haven't got the strength or the courage to carry on and that you will just retreat back to the safe paths that you 'know' will get you home, you decide to just climb the next hill to see what is in the distance. Trust your instincts here, and when you do, you will see that you were on the right path the whole time. That moving forward it not only safe but exactly where you want to be going. Trust in yourself and in the spirit of life moving through you. When you are 'in trust', you are completely You. You are one with the world. You are always on the right path.

Trust is the superhero power that we all crave. It is the foundation for all success and from it springs all of life. Would animals in the harshest of conditions reproduce and search for food if they didn't trust that life would provide for them? Would humans overcome seemingly insurmountable obstacles if we didn't ultimately believe and trust that life 'has our back' and everything will ultimately be okay?

Trust comes from your own deep inner knowing that you are connected to all around you and when you remember this, you always know what to do and where to go. When you forget to trust life, you fall into fear. You allow your ego to create stories based on 'what might happen if' and if you listen to these fears then you are trapped in illusion once again. Moving forward in faith requires courage. It requires that you trust that the Universe will take care of you and lead you. It requires that you remember the truth at the core of life which is, that you are already safe, already home, already on the right path no matter where you choose to wander.

Do you accept your own unique adventure? And if you accept it, are you willing to enjoy every single step through the forest of life? Because if not, then feel free to go ahead and accept someone else's dream. Accept the dream of society that tells you who you 'should be'; or accept the dream of your parents, your teachers or your friends. But, if you accept someone else's dream, it will never lead you home.

This is life's invitation:

Accept your path
Heed your own call to adventure
Listen to the whisperings of your soul
Trust that you have the courage to follow your path through the forest
Trust that you are never alone
And you will always find your way home.

Before I end this storyhack, I am reminded of a speech made by Nelson Mandela, where he quoted Marianne Williamson's wise words, which bear repeating here:

"Our deepest fear is not that we are weak.
Our deepest fear is that we are powerful beyond measure.
It is our light, not our darkness that most frightens us.
We ask ourselves, who am I to be brilliant, gorgeous, talented, fabulous?
Actually, who are you not to be?
You are a child of God.
Your playing small does not serve the world...
As we are liberated from our own fear, our presence automatically
liberates others."

TRUST IS THE
SUPERHERO
POWER THAT
WE ALL CRAVE

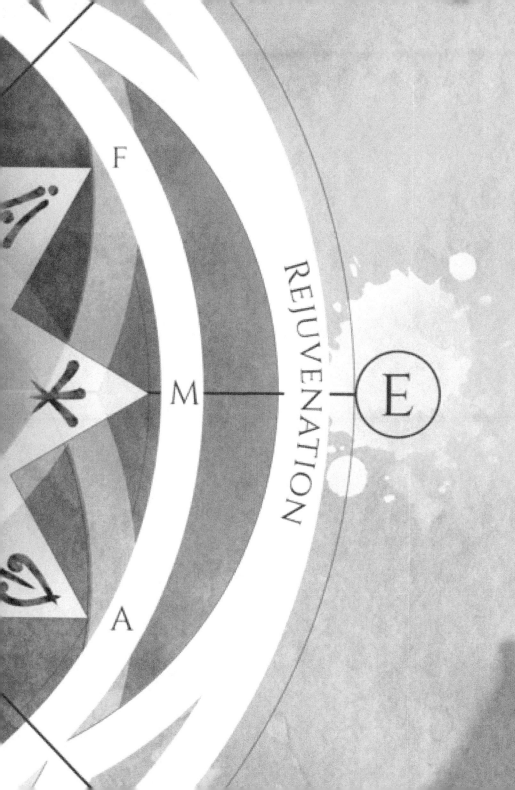

F

M   REJUVENATION   E

A

EAST

EAST QUARTER MEDITATION

REJUVENATION

Make yourself comfortable and breathe deeply for a minute or two until you feel still and settled. With your mind's eye, imagine your Heart Centre as the hub of your personal Soulistic Wheel, where the four directions meet with the energy of above and below. Imagine this sacred circle as a room – it is the room of your heart, the same place you came to in your North Quarter Meditation. Does it look the same or has it changed in any way? Take some time to reconnect with this beautiful space.

Once you can fully imagine the room of your heart, and feel comfortable within it, find the central point and sit or stand there. Take a deep breath and look around you; first to the East, where the element of fire resides. Feel the warmth coming from the East; the energy of the rising sun, with its potential to burn up old stories and release you from self-limiting habits. Then turn to the South, the element of Water. Feel the generous ease and flow that water embodies, how it can resolve any feelings of restriction, how it can wash away your fears. Slowly turn to the West, the element of Earth. Feel how the Earth holds you and nourishes you; feel how abundant and energised Earth is. Know that Earth always offers you her sacred reconnection. Then turn North, to the element of Air; feel that freshness and clarity that gives you a new perspective, feel the lightness of Air and know that you can mirror that lightness in your choices.

In this Quarter, you are facing the East of Springtime, the element of Fire. This is the aspect of the divine spark of soul light before it comes into form. You are asked to welcome the truth of your rejuvenation. Follow the sparks you encounter like a firefly dancing with its kin. What will you discover?

These four directions and their elements are your touchstones. Know that at any time, you can envision being in your Heart Centre and you can find sustenance there. Within the directions, over and above all elements and residing in your Heart Centre is the fifth element of ether; the essence and the mystery. The all-encompassing one-ness. Ether is of this world and not of this world. It is the essential element that enables transcendence into the cosmological realm. Your Heart Centre is filled with this bridging element of ether; feel how it moves you beyond this realm.

Continue to breathe deeply and envision yourself now leaving your Heart Centre and travelling upwards into the firmament of our Universe, deep into the cosmic realms. How liberating it is to swim among the stars, looking down on the jewel of blue that is Planet Earth. Allow yourself to travel beyond the Milky Way to the edge of the Universe, where you find a doorway, a portal between our Universe and the Cosmos. You are invited to slip through that doorway into the timeless, eternal realm where angels and archetypes reside. As you move into this new realm, you will see before you a Cosmic medicine wheel; a mirror of the one in your Heart Centre. As before, archangels stand in guardianship of the four sacred directions – creating a blessed and safe space for you, a place where only the energies and guides that reflect your highest good can enter.

Come to rest in the middle of this beautiful Cosmic wheel. Notice how you feel resting here as your 'Universoul Self'; relax in the harmonious energies that flow from all directions and anchor you gently in the centre of the wheel. Then turn to face the North and bow to the wisdom of your Mentor who resides there, thanking them for all they have taught you in the North Quarter; then face East and notice the doorway that is placed there. Watch as the door slowly opens and welcome whoever or whatever comes through, knowing they are a guide sent from your higher self. You may wish to take their hands or touch their being in an act of sacred connection and communion, noticing any words, images, symbols, feelings or colours that come to you as you interface in this way. Remember to trust your imagination and don't over-analyse what comes to your mind.

This being is offering to walk with you as a teacher of Sacred Law, for the rejuvenating quarter of Spring. They will support you in myriad ways; in your remembering, in your questioning, in your weaving – and you can always ask them for help or guidance. Their wisdom may be hard to discern at first, but just walk with your Mentor and be open to whatever teaching comes your way.

Now your Mentor leads you back towards the Universal portal where you entered the archetypal realm. You follow, safe in the knowledge that this immortal being is always here in spirit for you. You begin to slowly and gently traverse the Cosmic realms, back down towards your Heart Centre, and come to rest there. Your Mentor has accompanied you and stands behind you with their hands on your shoulders. Your Mentor from the North greets your Mentor from the East.

Come back into your body now and rest in the blessings of your journey.

See page 364, Endnote 12 for links to the recorded version of this Meditation if you prefer to listen to it rather than read it.

REJUVENATION

The land and skies awaken
Stirring us into creation
The waters of life arise within us
Encouraging rejuvenation
Earth's spirit and essence begins to bloom
The human family rejoices
And comes out of winter's womb
Embrace the new year and new story
As within, so without
Choose the seeds you sow wisely
Dispel darkness and doubt.

Seed germinates deep underground and starts its epic journey upwards towards the light of Spring. As Earth warms and the sunlight intensifies, life begins to express itself in new and unique ways, reflecting the energy of this moment. Movement returns inside and outside and we notice where we feel stuck and worn from the colder months. Compelled like the seedlings, we heed the call to adventure and find new paths presented to us for roaming. Our cells radiate the energy we choose to feed them with, and we are offered new choices that fuel the health of our ecosystems.

Rejuvenation is the elixir of youth – literally: the etymology of the word means to return to a younger (juvenile) state; which is why the word is used *ad inifinitum* in the beauty industry. The promise of a face cream that can make you look younger, however, is an empty one. If 'younger looking skin' is attainable, it is not through using expensive chemical concoctions; it's through enlightenment on a metaphysical level so that you have more reason to smile than to frown. A smile really is the best face-lift ever invented.

This phase of rejuvenation is all about deepening your connection with who you were as a youngster (and still are now); remembering what your greatest joys and passions were then and reclaiming that youthful zest for life. Who you were as a child, before your imagination was educated out of you by school, culture and custom, is the clue to your Soul Purpose; for that is when you expressed the pure intention of your soul; that is when you were nearer to your true self. Can you remember what gave you great joy as a child? Rejuvenating those passions may ease your journey into one of flow and bliss.

As you rejuvenate the essence of your inner child in this Quarter, you may feel a sense of excitement and energy for the potential on the horizon that you can't yet see unfolding.

When I was a child (Lorna), I didn't have dolls or teddy bears – I didn't really like them, and I didn't see the point of them. They seemed lifeless and dull to me. Whilst my playful sister's bedroom was strewn with toys, mine was tidy to an almost obsessive degree, with a small desk and an Olivetti typewriter in one corner, where I would dash-out story after story in my imaginary worlds. My sister thought I was SO boring.

It took another 50 years and my own Soulistic Journey to give myself permission to write my stories; my saboteur archetype having previously berated me with a million and one reasons why I was not good enough to be a storyteller. But now, after a deep dive into my Soul Purpose and a thorough wipe clean of my self-limiting narrative lenses, I can accept that it was what I was born to do.

I have rejuvenated that passion. I have said 'YES!' to my Soul Purpose. What golden threads link to your past, and what is lying dormant for you, just waiting to be rejuvenated?

WHAT GOLDEN THREADS LINK TO YOUR PAST, JUST WAITING TO BE REJUVENATED?

FEBRUARY

STORM CLOUDS BRING
THE WINDS OF CHANGE

FEBRUARY EARTH SIGNS

February is a most fickle month; the shortest of the year but perhaps the hardest to endure. A traditional rhyme says it all:

'February fills the dyke, be it black or be it white'

meaning that whether it's rain or snow, there's going to be a lot of precipitation! In these days of climate change, in the northern hemisphere snow is becoming a rarity; instead, torrential rain for days on end brings rivers into full spate often flooding the valleys and plains. All seems brown and grey and dreary.

There will be a time, only a few short months away, when we will be thankful for the full dykes and reservoirs as Summer heat dries and cracks the Earth, though in February it is hard to envisage walking barefoot on warm, silken grass. February is a time to remember the gifts that Nature bestows when we can least imagine them; a time to recall the verdant exuberance of Summer when it seems like Winter will never end – and trust that all will come to pass once again.

February bestows promise in the small things: the nodding heads of bright hellebores and the startling hue of violets; in the first resplendence of daffodils and the courage of primroses; it's in the tentative call of the blackbird as he limbers-up for his Spring song; in the swelling of leaf buds on the chestnut and ash.

Hold on to that promise as the storm clouds pass. Remember that sunshine always comes after the rains and keep that as a metaphor for whatever personal storms you may be experiencing at this time. Though it is hard, let us bless the wet and the wilderness.

FEBRUARY IS A TIME TO REMEMBER THE GIFTS THAT NATURE BESTOWS, WHEN WE CAN LEAST REMEMBER THEM

FEBRUARY COSMOLOGICAL SIGNS

AQUARIUS TO PISCES

I ASPIRE

A new energy now comes into your personal and collective world, one that has not yet been seen or experienced in previous cycles. You are inspired to aspire. You don't necessarily know where this energy is leading you, but you follow it anyway, gaining in confidence and momentum with every step forward you take.

Aquarius leads you on a new mission towards personal and collective change. Place your life and your story in service of something greater and aspire to make a positive difference in the world unfolding around you.

You are caught in the momentum of a new way of being and living – one that is soulful, true and full of joy. You become hope in action and take new steps towards a vision that has been waiting for you to claim since before you were born.

ASPIRE TO MAKE A POSITIVE DIFFERENCE IN THE WORLD UNFOLDING AROUND YOU

WINDS OF CHANGE MOON

– February heralds the awakening energies of Spring, brought to us by tumultuous winds and storms. The Winds of Change Moon scours us clean, ready for new beginnings.

FEBRUARY SOULISTIC ARCHETYPES

SOLAR ARCHETYPE: BALANCE

You are commencing your journey into the Eastern Quarter of the Soulistic Wheel as Earth energies begin to rise. This can be a time of confusion because your old stories have burned away in the passing of the year, but your new stories may not yet be clear. As the days lengthen, plants and animals begin to respond to the light, but always they remain in a finely tuned state of Balance, neither pushing forward nor holding back: timing is everything and it is linked to the light. In contrast, humanity can often feel disillusioned, unbalanced and impatient at this time of year, longing for warmer days and sunnier skies.

Mystery asks you to examine where your feelings of uncertainty, disorientation or impulsiveness come from. Perhaps the stories you hold about yourself have been so shaken by the journey you are making that you no longer know which way to turn? When in doubt do nothing. Aim to stay balanced and healthy in your lifestyle choices, and tune-in to your voice of inner wisdom, balancing silence and solitude with community and connection.

The easiest way to retain your equilibrium is to surrender to all that is currently happening; accept unequivocally the road that is being paved for you right now, even if it seems that nothing at all is unfolding. Look to the balanced, exquisite timing of Nature and know that you are part of that web of life. Remember, too, that paths, like rivers, never run in straight lines. Your journey is always a spiral, never linear, and every choice you have made in your life has brought you to this point. Trust that.

The archetype of Balance also helps you to re-story your attitude to life and death, because without death, life would become unsustainably out of Balance. Wisdom asks you to contemplate what you see as 'the end' as also 'the beginning'. As we do throughout this book, we can look to the natural world for a metaphor of this: a jay may predate a tree-creeper's nest, which we feel sad about because of the death of the beautiful tree-creeper chicks, yet the jay's own chicks will cache acorns their entire lives and not eat them all, resulting in natural reforestation that creates essential habitat for the tree-creepers. Nature's 'small deaths' always create life and so, with your mythic eyes, you can learn to see death – of who you thought you were, your dreams, even your own physical death – as integral to life and essential for Balance.

If you can surrender to the mystery that is unfolding, there will be unexpected moments of calm, where you can relax in a state of equilibrium which is a foundational element of epiphany and revelation. You have burned away your old stories and opened your heart to a deeper dive into your Soul Purpose during the North Quarter – these are hugely powerful intentions and transformation takes its own sweet time. Balance is a barometer of change, indicative of forces at play and at rest. The fulcrum is your Heart Centre.

Choose the middle way of Balance in all things and you will find this greatly aids your journey.

Find an artefact for your altar that represents 'Balance' to you. This could be two pebbles balanced one upon the other or a beautiful mandala painting; anything that represents the perfection of Balance. Placing it on your altar will be a daily reminder that balance is an aspiration (I Aspire).

LUNAR ARCHETYPE: PEACE

As you set out on your journey into the Eastern Quarter of the Soulistic Wheel, a certain fleeting and exquisite feeling may envelop you. It is the peacefulness that resides in your core and which is nourished by love. On your Soulistic Journey you are being asked to make choices that honour your Soul Purpose and your happiness – this is a form of love for the self, and from it, Peace arises. Peace indicates that you are integrated in body, mind, heart and soul. It is a sign that you are 'on track'.

Conversely, your choices will inevitably create profound transformations that can be scary: all change brings with it death (of the old) and fear (of the new). And so, your state of peacefulness will wane if you are conflicted, distracted and fearful, because Peace needs equanimity in order to flourish. Mystery asks you to find the root of any 'dis-ease' so that Peace may prevail and embrace you in that glorious feeling of tranquillity and interconnectedness.

Relaxed in a state of peacefulness, you will find greater clarity emerges regarding your eternally spiralling journey through the Universe, because remember, you are an eternal being, playing in form. Take a deep breath and relax into the Peace and perfect tempo of your soul journey. There is no need to rush forwards, only to dream and envision the future you wish to create.

What does Peace feel like to you? What words come closest to describing that feeling? Create a WordCloud[25] of these words and add it to your dreamboard (which must be looking fantastic by now!) Speak aloud the words from this WordCloud, often.

UNIFICATION: BLISS

The paths from Above and Below merge within your Heart Centre, that place of stillness and silence where Bliss resides. That delicious upwelling of joyfulness you may feel when all is peaceful and in balance is Bliss.

Bliss brings with it the gift of inner gnosis (knowing) that all ever has been and always will be perfect in the Universal story of life. This is hard to accept when you see death, suffering and hardship all around. You may ask yourself, 'How can I know that all is perfect in the world, when there is so much pain and suffering?' But, when you see with mythic eyes in deep time, your gnosis is confirmed: everything happens for a reason – to allow for great teaching, wisdom and awareness to arise – and even death can be seen as just, right and wondrous. With this gnosis a sense of elation radiates from your Heart

Centre. It is so powerful it changes the way you look; you cannot help but smile because you know heaven truly is on Earth; people will say you look radiant.

You will experience Bliss when you release any judgment of right or wrong, good or bad, success or failure; in fact, Bliss cannot be experienced at all if you are in a state of duality where all is assessed from a perspective of 'either/or'. Bliss comes from the holistic place of 'and/we'; it is inclusive and accepting. Bliss is the precursor to heightened awareness and divine inter-being.

You know that saying, 'She was really blissed-out'? Go for it! What makes you blissed-out? Perhaps it is dancing barefoot on the warming Earth? Or a long, hot bath with essential oils and a glass of wine? Perhaps it's a day-long forest trek, or a brisk wild swim in the glittering ocean? Whatever it is that gives you Bliss, give yourself permission and get blissed-out.

BLISS CANNOT BE EXPERIENCED IF YOU ARE IN A STATE OF DUALITY

FEBRUARY PRACTICES

DEEP LISTENING

THE ART OF BEING OMNIPRESENT

There is a fundamental difference between hearing and listening: they are not the same thing. We all hear a multitude of sounds throughout the day – as I write this, I can hear a dog bark, a blackbird sing, a tractor in the distance and someone whistling as they walk past our house. I hear all these things, but I am not really listening to them – my sensory system 'gates out' anything that isn't immediately necessary for me to attend to. Listening, on the other hand, requires focus and attention – it is not passive like hearing; it requires active contemplation.

But even when we think we are listening, we're not really, we are mostly formulating our response. Next time you are in a conversation, pay attention to what is really happening: are you truly and respectfully listening to what is being said, or are you waiting impatiently – sometimes interrupting – to have your say? Or, next time you are listening to music, are you really listening, or are you thinking about something else – like what to have for dinner, or why your friend hasn't answered your email?

Deep listening requires an approach that is not centred around your response: it asks for your undivided attention, so that you can hold whatever it is you are hearing in a sacred space, where it can develop its own energy and meaning without your influence. This takes practice, because we're all very often so keen to pitch-in our 'two-pennies worth' that we just jump in, not really listening but wanting only to have our say. Have you ever done that and regretted not holding your tongue? I know I have. It is worth asking yourself, *Why do I find my contribution more interesting or exciting than that which I'm listening to? What am I trying to prove or influence by saying this?* To paraphrase Pythagoras, "Let the words you speak be worthy of the silence they break." Sit with that one for a while and observe the feelings that arise around keeping your counsel.

Interestingly, up to 50% of any given conversation is non-verbal: communication comes in other ways via the eyes, body-language, and breath. Deep listening, therefore, asks you to focus with all your senses so that you can read body language, make eye contact and be fully present – you are *feeling* what is being said as much as listening. You are omnipresent in that moment.

What is transformative about deep listening is the opportunity it gives others to express themselves and be truly heard, sometimes for the very first time. Deep listening is a precious gift to bestow upon someone, because in the silence of listening, a connection can be made with the collective consciousness – the

LET THE WORDS YOU SPEAK BE WORTHY OF THE SILENCE THEY BREAK

omnipresence of knowing – and this silences allows for the creation of a conduit or channel that enables the speaker to 'download' and resolve their own conundrums. Epiphanies readily ensue.

The art of deep listening quietens your own mind, creating a positive feedback loop that then allows you to listen even more deeply. Sometimes, when you are practicing deep listening, what you actually hear is your own heart wisdom: a kind of knowing that is beyond words and beyond sound.

So, the beautiful paradox of deep listening is that it is not about hearing at all, but it is about quietening into silence, wherein resides true knowledge. Try it, and see how beneficial it is to listen deeply, without responding, in an open-hearted, focussed, attentive manner. Try it next time your Mum calls, or your friend pops-in for a cuppa. Listen and create the space for transformation to occur before your eyes. Deep listening is a form of kindness, and a gift to yourself as much as the person you are communicating with.

UNFURLING YOGA

AN INNER JOURNEY WITH OUTER BENEFITS

Yoga[26] in its essence means union. It also means to 'yoke' yourself to a practice until the deeper aspects of its meaning unfurl inside you and help you to expand and evolve. I (Genevieve) have been practicing yoga in various forms for the last 15 years and for me, I still feel like I am a beginner whenever I come to my mat. Yoga is an inner journey with multiple outer benefits that emerge over time. In coming to this practice, you learn about your inner beliefs, thoughts and feelings and how they create the stories that you live when you're off your mat. As my first yoga teacher was fond of saying, "How you do things on your mat is how you do everything in life!"

Every day you come to your mat, the flow of each yoga posture is different because your body, mind and emotions are different hour to hour and minute to minute. This is the beauty of this particular practice. It's an ongoing adventure in awareness and humility. Oh, and YOU are your best teacher. Now, don't get me wrong – if you already have a yoga practice or intend on starting one then having an experienced teacher to help you enter into poses and breathwork correctly is recommended. But, don't confuse the outer form of perfectly performed poses with the inner ritual of your transformation – by which I mean that YOU are the source and the destination of any yoga ceremony, and every time you come to your mat you are entering into a ceremony with your soul. Ana Forrest[27] (one of my yoga teachers) taught me that.

In the colder months of the year, your body needs to move to keep your circulation moving and to fire-up your digestion and metabolism. Your muscles that will often contract in the cold, are begging for you to gently and rhythmically open them so they can continue to feed that lifegiving blood and good vitalising energy throughout your bodily systems. Likewise, your mind and emotions crave a calming, grounding way of focusing within, that complements the overall energies of the season. Thus, you are invited to enter into unfurling yoga.

I use the word 'unfurling' because like the early flowers that begin to show themselves in various parts of the world right now, we also start to attune to the energies of early Springtime and begin to 'unfurl our wings' into a new season. Whatever your level of yoga experience or practice, the main aspects of unfurling that you are invited to explore for yourself are:

EVERY TIME YOU COME TO THE MAT YOU ARE ENTERING INTO A CEREMONY WITH YOUR SOUL

- ❈ **Deep breathing** (pranayama) – that brings you into a state of present moment awareness. Stay with your breath until you feel your mind relax and your emotions start to calm. You are your own barometer here and only you will know what this feels like.

- ❈ **Deep awareness** of your body inside out – what feels tight and contracted and how can you bring gentle movement to those parts of your body to stretch and welcome in new energy and blood flow? Do whatever feels good to your unique body (even if it looks weird) and breathe into the areas of tightness until they start to feel different. Again – only you can know what 'different' feels like for you.

※ **Deep self-love** – okay, so this one is the hardest of all, mostly because we are each our own worst critic and say things to ourselves that we would never think of saying to anyone else because it's so horrible. So, for this core practice (yoga begins as a practice for the mind before you even get to the body), we are asking you to put aside your self-criticism, your self-competition and your self-loathing. Yes... loathing. If you do nothing else but sit on your mat and practice putting these emotions to one side, then you will be one of the most skilled yogis on the planet! Each time one of these self-deprecating thoughts arise, notice it. Notice how it makes you feel in your emotions and in your body. Not good, I would surmise! Once you have noticed such a thought, imagine that you can pick it up out of your mind or body and place it to one side of your mat (sometimes these thoughts appear as black balls of energy or sludgy goop... see how you experience them). If you choose to pick them back up again at the end of your practice, then so be it – but why would you?

Oh, and watch the excuses: the "I don't have time for yoga" excuse, is one of the most common – but even if you come to your mat for 5-10 mins a day and just breathe, that is enough. This is closely followed by the "I'm not flexible enough," or the "I'm too old/tight/out of shape" excuses. As you can see from the practice outlined above, these are all the games your inner critic, who doesn't want you to purge your sense of self-criticism from your systems. Smile and come to your mat to breathe. From here all else becomes easy.

Taking the first step in these life practices is really the hardest part. Once you have started a consistent practice it doesn't matter how it looks or whether you believe that what you are doing is 'real yoga'. Remember, yoga means union. So, it is truly about the practice of coming into union with your true soul self and getting everything that distracts you from this out of the way.

FEBRUARY STORYHACK

GENEVIEVE GUIDES YOU IN THE GENTLE ART OF RESTORYING YOUR LIFE...

FORGIVENESS AS FREEDOM

HARNESSING ONE OF THE UNIVERSE'S HIDDEN SUPERPOWERS

Recently, my grandfather passed from this world into another. He was ready, but his readiness has been a long process of coming to terms with the parts of himself and the fragments of his story that needed to be healed before he could let go. This process brought him pain – because forgiving ourselves and others always does – but it also brought my grandfather release and transcendence.

In honouring my grandfather and his life/death passing, I am also honouring my own ability to embrace, forgive, trust and create freedom in my life. I am allowing forgiveness to move through me and out into the world as a force of love.

Forgiveness comes in the moments that really matter, like those of separation or death, when you are asked to be bigger, wider, more expansive than you have ever been before. Forgiveness opens doors that you have tried to close and lock. Forgiveness breathes you into places you have tried to forget. Forgiveness is a mirror into the parts of your soul that you have rejected. Yet, when you forgive, you create freedom. When you forgive, you are liberated. When you forgive, you love.

Forgiveness is one of the Universe's hidden superpowers, one that we are all asked to harness at some point in our existence. Forgiveness is a doorway

> FORGIVENESS IS A MIRROR INTO THE PARTS OF YOUR SOUL THAT YOU HAVE REJECTED

that, when you are willing to walk through, changes everything from the inside out – because forgiveness starts with you.

Before you can truly know peace, you must forgive all that you have deemed unworthy; you must trust in a power beyond your human narrative to show you a higher, wider, more complete picture, because a lack of forgiveness always comes from a partial story.

When you expand your heart, mind and soul to embrace the bigger picture of things, you allow forgiveness as a sense of Universal perfection to flow into every part of your existence, and then you are shown divine timing, synchronicity and soul lessons in play. You see karma, not just as cause and effect, but as dynamic choice: sovereignty and free will in action. You open up to the Universal story that plays out through your soul over eons, and you know that there is definitely more to the grand game of life than you are able to see in your human form. Through forgiveness, you remember how to trust again. Trust and forgiveness go hand in hand, heart in heart.

So perhaps today is a moment when you can allow yourself to embrace forgiveness and allow yourself to experience freedom?

Maybe today is the day you allow your story to expand?

A LACK OF
FORGIVENESS
ALWAYS
COMES FROM
A PARTIAL
STORY

MARCH

THE GATEWAY TO SPRING
SEES THE DANCE OF LOVE UNFOLD

MARCH EARTH SIGNS

As we transition from Winter into Spring, March heralds that change with hosts of golden daffodils dancing in the breeze and the appearance of frogspawn in ponds. Though it can still be cold with biting winds, transformation is afoot in March. If you pause and listen deeply you will hear a choir of birds announce the turning of the seasons, their songs exquisitely melodic and ethereal. Take some time to stop and stare in March and see what is really going on.

The dance of love begins as the female March hare boxes with the males, fending them off until she is ready to mate. She stands her ground firmly on her hind legs, fearless and feisty – she sets the pace and the males must acquiesce to her; and then we hear the sweet song of the thrush, and watch as she brings soft moss for her nest, a green 'beard' hanging from her beak; the rooks tumble in the air for sheer joy cackling as they plummet, then race off to find yet another sinuous twig to add to their haphazard nests. The first butterflies grace the meadows, orange-tips searching for their favourite flower, lady's smock, from which to sip the nectar; and early purple orchids live up to their name, their spotted leaves giving way to a spike of tiny flowers later in the month.

March is the gateway to Spring. It brings great hope and bursts of joyfulness for we have survived the Mystery Time and come now into a season of growth and rejuvenation. March winds may blow, it may even snow, but the sun climbs inexorably higher in the sky with each passing day and our cold bones are warmed by those blessed rays. Rejoice in March and all that is to come.

MARCH COSMOLOGICAL SIGNS

PISCES TO ARIES

I DREAM

Just as you thought you had found a degree of clarity in the aspirational realms of Aquarius, it slips from your fingers and you dive into the vast cosmic pool of potential. The primal waters of Pisces wash over you and you are lost momentarily in the flood of possibility. What you experience in the realm of Pisces – 'I Dream' – cannot be named, because as soon as you attempt to describe this potentiality, you confine it and therefore limit its eternal expanse.

Your sleeping and waking life becomes the dream. You move through inner and outer landscapes of opportunity and illusion. Your task is to discern one from the other. You come to know yourself as both individual and collective. As Me, We and All.

If you are conscious of it, you can choose to become a 'dreamer', entering lucidly into Indra's Net of consciousness and way-finding your path into a deep cosmological sense of soul and story.

DIVE INTO THE
VAST COSMIC
POOL OF
POTENTIAL

DREAMING MOON

– the March full moon and Spring Equinox mark a magical time of transition from Winter to Spring. Now is the time to dream into being the intentions you have set that create balance between the darkness and light in your stories.

MARCH SOULISTIC ARCHETYPES

SOLAR ARCHETYPE: FREEDOM

As you come to the mid-way point of your journey through the East Quarter of the Soulistic Wheel, the energy of balance comes to its apex at the Spring Equinox. All is in exquisite equilibrium as the days and nights are of equal length and your own energies are primed for the frenetic ecstasy of Spring to come. Can you feel this rejuvenation in your body? It is a reawakening which brings with it the Freedom to fly on high like a bird, unfettered by any chains of conditioning, about what you can and can't achieve. Now is the time to shoot forth your arrow of intention, for the energy that Freedom brings makes all things seem possible.

Freedom is a pioneer, a courageous out-rider, a harbinger, but for many, such feelings of liberty and boundlessness bring with them a sense of anxiety of what may come to pass and in that anxiety, a choice to stay put in your comfort zone may feel like the safest option. But what you are seeking can never be found in your comfort zone. Mystery asks you to examine why you feel trapped or fearful. What is at the heart of your discomfort? Can you follow the thread of that feeling to its roots, so that you are able to reweave it? Wisdom reminds you that your biggest fears point to your greatest breakthroughs.

Imagine that you are flying above this beautiful Earth – what can you see that inspires or motivates you? Where is your 'arrow of desire' pointing? A sense of Freedom will lead you into new beginnings and remind you of your own ability to fly beyond any restrictions you may believe you are trapped by. Freedom is a guide to your future.

> THE ENERGY THAT FREEDOM BRINGS MAKES ALL THINGS SEEM POSSIBLE

What is your favourite symbol of Freedom? Is it a bird flying on high, or a broken chain signifying the time you walked away from something that was holding you back? Is your symbol of freedom an opened bird cage, or the dove of peace with an olive branch in her beak? Is your symbol of freedom a distant mountain peak or

a diving dolphin? Have a tattoo of your Freedom Symbol so that you will never forget that Freedom is yours if you want it – or if you don't want to have a tattoo, make a piece of jewellery or a painting of your symbol so you can see it every day.

LUNAR ARCHETYPE: KNOWING

You are floating in the magical undertow of the River of Dreams to the half-way point of your adventure through the Eastern Quarter of the Soulistic Wheel. Can you hear the persistent inner voice of Knowing whispering to you as you journey, or do you still feel uncertainty about your life goals? She of Knowing has always been there for you, but until now, her voice may have been drowned out by one of many human archetypes that can dominate your awareness. Perhaps you are overwhelmed by the voice of the victim (nobody loves me); or the saboteur (I can't do that because I didn't go to university); the judge (I think it's a terrible idea); or the addict (I want more even though I know it is not good for me)? Perhaps so, yet despite these voices of self-doubt, you still have a sense of Knowing, or at least you are beginning to feel on a deeply soulful level, what is healthful and nourishing for your being.

Knowing has alchemical powers, because it enables the retelling of your personal stories in a new light. You may have felt confused and unhappy in the past, but now you are beginning to know yourself in a new light, because you are unravelling the knots of your stories and reweaving new ones. Knowing is a feeling that comes from the heart – it is not an intellectual construct as many people think; it is a feeling. Mystery asks you to identify the feeling of Knowing when something is right, and to recognise the unfolding patterns that indicate and define your life lessons. Your mentors or guides will be deeply interconnected with your sense of Knowing, for they know too. Dialogue with them.

Knowing presents you with the threefold path of your lifetime – the past, present and future – all are her domains and indeed, she moves simultaneously through them, facilitating your evolution, flowing like a river through your life.

Knowledge is keeper of your life lessons, hard won through your childhood, adulthood and elderhood, reminding you when you are about to repeat the same patterns and offering you the potential to redirect your flow.

Your unique Knowing is ancient and wise. Listen to her as she whispers in the shadows of your dreams.

Is there something you have always known about yourself yet have never allowed into expression? Now is the time to ac–knowledge that. Write about it in your journal and set an intention to act upon this Knowing.

UNIFICATION: FUTURE

As the paths of Above and Below meet in your Heart Centre, the hub of your Soulistic Wheel, you are beginning to sense into your Future. Future teaches you that when you combine self-knowledge and wisdom with inspiration and courage, you create your dreams in reality. You will come to know the wisdom of all things; even that which you may once have perceived as failure is integral for your Future – for without it, what lessons would you have learned?

Future waits excitedly for you at the threshold of new journeys, beckoning you forward. The mysterious alchemy of this moment is that when you choose to follow, Future becomes your Now.

Knowing as you now do that what you think becomes your reality – begin to observe your thoughts on a daily basis. Catch yourself if you are thinking negatively about any person or situation and transmute that judgement, opinion or fear into a smile. That is all that's necessary – a smile allows the light in and defuses the thought. Your Future happiness is based on smiling now.

MARCH PRACTICES

ACCEPTING CHANGE

IT'S HARD TO HOLD ON TO LIFE AS YOU KNOW IT WHEN YOUR COMFORT ZONES NO LONGER FEEL COMFORTABLE

If you started your Soulistic Journey at the Winter Solstice, you will be coming to the end of your first quarter of the Wheel now, and it is likely that – even if you haven't been able to participate in all the practices – you will be noticing changes in your behaviour. You may be feeling fundamentally different in your response to life's challenges; you may also be making choices that affect your relationships and career; or even moving into unchartered territory as you make transitions that have exponential repercussions in all aspects of your life.

Do not panic!! Change is a constant in life; indeed it is one of the few things we can be certain of – but when you embark upon a spiritual journey, such as you are doing by reading this book, change may happen at an unprecedented rate – and this is because you are activating change at a cellular level by the choices you are making. Sometimes it's hard to hold on to life as you know it when your comfort zones no longer feel comfortable and you find yourself sailing on a sea of uncertainty.

There is a wonderful book by Buddhist nun, Pema Chödrön[28], called *Comfortable with Uncertainty* and whilst the book is a highly recommended read, the title says it all: learning to be comfortable with the uncertainty of change is the only place to be; because change happens whether we like it or not. Even as you walk your spiritual path, unexpected and uncalled-for change may happen such as the death of a loved one or the loss of a job. In this practice, we recommend becoming comfortable with uncertainty by surrendering to change.

The word 'surrender' gets a bit of a bad rap these days: it has a negative connotation of failure or loss; but in fact, surrender is a beautiful word that has Anglo-French origins in the terms 'to deliver, hand-over or yield'. If you yield to uncertainty you are no longer in control; yielding becomes an act of faith where you accept that you made certain choices that have set the wheels in motion (change) and that you are comfortable with that process. Faith demonstrates a deep trust in the unfolding of life from higher levels than our human mind is capable of comprehending. Faith allows the Universe to bestow you with miraculous outcomes. This does not mean that you cannot change the outcome (because change is a constant), but it does mean that you can let go of any anxiety by yielding or surrendering in the current moment.

The practice of surrender is delightfully easy and eminently difficult! It's one of life's great paradoxes: how can anything so easy be so hard? The answer is because we cling on with all our might to the 'known' and do not, under any circumstances want to step into the unknown and release the façade of control we believe we have, even when we know we need to! But it is possible to hone your ability to accept change by cultivating a few practices.

The first step is to transform your thought patterns from anxiety to acceptance; so, when you catch yourself using words like, *should, ought, might, must, can't* or *afraid*, try to take a deep breath and rephrase what you are saying. These words are rooted in self-doubt and come from your 'inner critic' or saboteur – but why should you accept that your inner critic knows best? A friend once said to me, "I would never let anyone talk to me the way I talk to myself!" So, why not accept the wisdom in this statement and stop that nagging voice of self-sabotage taking centre stage in your life. Take a deep breath and rephrase whatever it is you are saying so that it transforms from criticism or judgement to acceptance and compassion – most especially for yourself.

Another wonderful method to allay any anxiety you may feel relating to change or uncertainty is mindful breathing. When you feel that tell-tale knot in your stomach, stop whatever it is you are doing and breathe deeply and slowly for several minutes, at the same time recognising that at this moment in time, all

FAITH ALLOWS
THE UNIVERSE
TO BESTOW
YOU WITH
MIRACULOUS
OUTCOMES

is well. Breathe in and hold; breathe out slowly and hold. In those moments between breathing in and out, you are free to let go and let in; let go of anxiety and let in tranquillity; let go of expectation and let in acceptance... Mindful, deep breathing has instant and miraculous healing abilities.

Finally, you can turn the nature of change in on itself by recognising that 'this too shall pass' – an ancient Persian adage that recognises that even change itself will lapse. So, if you are feeling uncertain, uncomfortable or anxious, it won't last forever; things will change. For change to happen, change has to happen! Take some solace in that fact.

ENERGETIC MOVEMENT

YOUR EVOLVING PERSONAL PRACTICE

The practice of energetic movement is an ancient one and there exists a vast array of traditional forms from almost every land and culture – such as yoga, qigong, tai chi, breathwork, meditation... (the list is endless) – that testify to its efficacy. The variants of these systems are as diverse as any ecosystem on Earth.

I (Genevieve) have practiced a wide range of such 'energy medicines' over my lifetime (and perhaps many lifetimes), but I have found the most powerful to be those that are self-crafted. What I mean by this is that traditional teachers and knowledge systems are simply the doorways through which true 'practice' emerges and evolves.

As a child, when big waves of energy would hit me, I'd stand in a corner of the room and shake my hands and arms violently until the surge had passed and I felt able to stand still again. At other times, I'd have an emotional meltdown and my poor family would have to pick up the pieces. In my late 20s I still felt energy deeply within my body, particularly in my endocrine and nervous systems. To say, I was 'sensitive' was an understatement and very quickly I found (much like when I was a small child), that if I was unable to shift energy through and around my system, then I would become overwhelmed.

Do you recognise this scenario? You probably do, because it's common to almost every animate being on Earth. Have you ever heard the phrase 'fight or flight'? Add to this the words 'freeze and shake' and we have the whole instinctive response pattern that every animal lifeform on this planet uses to cope with perceived 'threat'.

The thing is, what happens when you suddenly feel overwhelmed or upset and you can't see a cause for this – there's no threat to speak of? Often this is symptomatic of energy surges in your immediate environment – be they solar, lunar, electromagnetic in origin from technology, from your own pervading thought patterns, or even part of the zeitgeist of collective consciousness. Knowing how to recognise these symptoms and then clear them is an essential practice, especially in the Spring when the Earth's own energies arise and so there are multiple variants of energy coursing around your bodily system at any one time!

THE ALCHEMY OF BREATH

One of the classic and most effective ways I have learned to shift big energy, is to breathe. Yes, I know it sounds clichéd, but sighing is a super-effective mechanism for releasing pent up frustration, energetic blocks or anxiety caused by 'energy locks'. (An energy lock is when you feel tightness in a specific part of your body, and you can't understand where it is coming from or why it's there).

THE ALCHEMY OF MOVEMENT

The next practice in shifting energy comes from the physical movement of your body. In our modern world, we spend way too much time sitting down. Sometimes we will be hunched over desks and computers for hours without moving; something that was unknown to our ancestors. If you feel blocked,

locked or constricted, get up and move, dance, do yoga, stretch or walk (preferably outside). Then your tension will begin to ease and you will be able to breathe again, having moved your stuck energy.

THE ALCHEMY OF NATURE

Then of course, there is the vital ingredient in our general health and wellbeing: the Earth all around us. Nature is medicine. Walking barefoot has been proven to earth the electrical currents that run through our nervous systems; walking in a forest (known as forest bathing) shows an instant reduction in stress-causing hormones such as adrenaline and cortisol; sitting with your back against a tree will transform the quality of your thoughts and allow any stuck energy to move through your skin, into the nervous system of the tree and down into the Earth.

These ancient energetic movement systems all aid the shift of energy, but as with all things in life, what you create for yourself reflects your needs in a more relevant way than a 'generic' solution. So, I suggest that you experiment with your movement practices, adding a few yoga stretches, a couple of tai chi stances, a dance on the lawn, a jog with the dog… and make your practice your own. After all – you ARE Nature and you know yourself better than anyone does. So, find what's most natural to you and practice it… again and again.

MARCH STORYHACK

GENEVIEVE GUIDES YOU IN THE GENTLE ART OF
RESTORYING YOUR LIFE...

LOVING REMINISCENCE

YOUR MEMORIES ARE FERTILE GROUND FOR THE CREATION OF YOUR FUTURE

To recall past events and learn lessons from them is one of the oldest mythic traditions in the human lineage. Since ancient times, people have gathered to recall legends, retell tribal stories and teach young ones through remembering the adventures of those who came before them. Therefore, it comes as no surprise that it is the inner landscape of our memories that holds the most fertile ground for the creation of our future.

In my view, too many teachers train people to forget the past. For experiences of trauma and abuse, this is (perhaps) understandable on one level. And yet, I believe, it's the tough times in our lives that hold the most transformative 'gold'. The trick, then, is to be able to remember the lesson without the emotional drama of the experience itself. It is no easy task but there is one super-hack that facilitates the process. Love.

Love is the lens that turns fear into courage.

Love is the lens that transforms isolation into connection.

Love is the force that transmutes anger and replaces it with compassion.

TO LOOK AT
THE STORIES
OF OUR PAST
THROUGH THE
LENS OF LOVE
REQUIRES
THAT WE
LET GO OF
COMPARISON,
COMPETITION
AND
CRITICISM

To look at the stories of our past through the lens of love requires that we let go of comparison, competition and criticism. We must reminisce not resist, nor judge.

Let me give some examples –

※ Instead of remembering your history through a lens that emphasises what is lacking now in comparison to 'then', hack your view. Choose to see how your past created the very conditions that have allowed you to be who you are NOW, whoever that is.

※ Rather than comparing former experiences to current ones and finding either lacking in some way, try to see your growth through time as a dynamic story of evolution that interconnects with the people and places in your narrative. Without difficult experiences to hone your sense of self, you would never learn who you are. It may just be that now is a difficult experience, period. Great! Your opportunity to learn is at its highest!

※ Finally, rather than critiquing your life (past, present or future) in any way, try seeing it through the lens of love. What is it that you cherish, value and gain in energy from? It is rare to encounter a person who is totally unable to find anything of value in their existence. Everyone is able to mine their life experiences and find numerous examples of power, bravery and joy. What are yours?

True narrative reminiscing is a process where you can indulge yourself, mining your past memories for gold that you can use in your future creations, if you choose to. Of course, you could choose to mine for lead too! I know plenty of people who prefer this narrative of victimhood to one of golden empowerment.

So, next time you find yourself sharing old stories with friends, stop and choose to seek gold. See through the lens of everything you have loved and use this empowering framework of 'personal proof' to create a future story that turbo-charges your sense of purpose and faith in the magic of life.

Gift yourself love not comparison.

Gift yourself joy not lack.

Gift yourself and others insight into the human adventure, not a negative critique of it.

Enter into the practice of loving reminiscence and see how fast your future narrative changes for the better. I do it every day.

APRIL

WHERE NATURE GIVES GENEROUSLY
AND UNCONDITIONALLY

APRIL EARTH SIGNS

Blessed April! Warmer winds and lengthening days bathe the whole of Gaia with an energy that is palpable. The hawthorn and beech leaves unfurl with the most luminous green imaginable, and the contrast of this lustrous green with the iridescence of bluebells is heavenly. On a warm late April day, there is nothing better than finding a spot under a beech tree in a bluebell wood and bathe in the perfume and splendour of these other-than-human beings. If you allow yourself to really sense the energy – *feeling* it with all your senses, including your imagination – it is possible to connect with the metaphysical foreground of all that surrounds you. It may be a fleeting glimpse, but it is a reminder that you are inextricably connected to all life on Earth. All beings in the woods are your family.

The swallows and house martins return in April, and so does the cuckoo, a welcome and rare visitor, loved by many. She knows that now is the time of nest-building, when the birds create a place of safety for their young. They busily flit and flirt, knowing that time is of the essence, and now is the time. Their lives are focused and have meaning. They know exactly what it is they must do.

April is also the time of seed-sowing, where you can choose that which nourishes you in the coming months. If you choose wisely, you can enjoy the fruits of your sowing throughout the year.

Nature's abundance is humbling; she gives generously of herself, unconditionally. Each Spring, she offers the potential for growth, transformation and harvest. Her template is one that you can learn from as you walk the Soulistic Wheel. What can you give abundantly whilst asking for nothing in return? What do you want to transform at this time of emergence and growth?

WHAT DO
YOU WANT TO
TRANSFORM
AT THIS
TIME OF
EMERGENCE
AND
GROWTH?

APRIL COSMOLOGICAL SIGNS

ARIES TO TAURUS

I AM

Having emerged from the watery depths of the unknown, a new sense of identity and persona takes root. The Aries energy of 'I AM' claims your breath and facilitates your re-emergence into a new archetypal pattern.

You come to know yourself in new ways, having journeyed through the depths and the heights. All of this takes root in your body and expresses itself, sometimes violently, as opinion, polarity and restriction.

The only way to expand is to first contract, and 'I AM' in Aries brings you back to the 'small self' so the larger soul can recapitulate into a new form later in the wheel of the year. Your task is to remember your soulful, cosmic enormity so that your human identity can let go at the appropriate moment in your journey.

GREEN MOON

– all is emerging with quickening energy. Shimmering
green is the colour of Spring, reflected in this month's
full moon. The Green Moon is a perfect time to sow
the seeds of your intentions for the year ahead.

APRIL SOULISTIC ARCHETYPES

SOLAR ARCHETYPE: ABUNDANCE

Spring is in the air as you walk the final stage of the Eastern Quarter of the Soulistic Wheel. You feel rejuvenated by the practices you are undertaking and the new insights that you are bringing into actualisation. These gifts and others are at the heart of true Abundance which is not about money or 'things' at all; Abundance is about choosing that which makes you joyful and healthful. When these life choices become your norm, Abundance is everlasting and fills your cup to overflowing.

Many people spend their lives in a state of anxiety about lack of Abundance because they cannot see what true Abundance is. We cannot reiterate enough that Abundance is not about money. Abundance will shape-shift to present you with what is needed in your life, and always with perfect timing – but it takes the development of your intuition and your symbolic sight to see Abundance for what it really is.

A timely example of this is the Coronavirus lockdown situation in 2020. For many people who were fortunate enough not to contract the illness, lockdown presented an Abundance of time. Those who made the choice to use this Abundance to fulfil long-held dreams of painting or writing, gardening or resting have felt incredibly nourished by the experience. Those who fell into the realm of 'fear and lack', generated by the media and our societal anxiety around change, spent the time feeling worried, stressed and angry. When lockdown eased, those who spent time in Abundance and those who spent time in fear still faced the same reality. How did you spend your time?

Abundance is firmly rooted in unconditional love. If you look at the natural world, you will see Abundance at the heart of everything. The humble apple tree flowers in March and April, its open-centred pinkish-white flowers are a perfect landing-pad for bees, who pollinate the blossoms in return for nectar; there is a reciprocal gift here. Throughout the Summer, the apples grow firm and plump, thanks to the beneficence of the rain and the fertility of the soil. When the apples are ripe, they fall from the tree or are harvested by humans, and nourish many beings, the seeds within being distributed by birds or via compost, to create new plants. There is a reciprocal gift here too: eat me and regenerate me. The apple tree does not discriminate which beings can and cannot partake of its gifts. The lesson here is that Abundance does not derive from controlling or hoarding; Abundance derives from gifting and sharing, unconditionally with love. It is a wonderful paradox: that to receive, you must give.

Abundance reminds you that you are the creator of your reality and that your thoughts and feelings give birth to your experiences. Open your heart and receive the wisdom of Abundance with gratitude.

Can you identify what it is that gives you the greatest feeling of Abundance? Contemplate what Abundance really means to you? Spend the next few days gifting random acts of kindness[29] (an offer to babysit for a friend, feeding the birds, collecting a prescription for your neighbour, a celebratory meal for your family...) by way of thanks for the Abundance in your life.

LUNAR ARCHETYPE: HARMONY

You are dreaming into the last days of the Eastern Quarter of your Soulistic Wheel. Your sense of vitality and exhilaration permeates your sleeping and waking life as Harmony sings you into wellbeing. Harmony is a state you feel when you are making choices that are aligned with your Soul Purpose. As you do this, your energetic resonance accords with the tonality of the Universe, enabling you to weave your unique song with hers, creating a state of grace.

This state of grace expresses itself not only in feelings of at-one-ness, but also in the experience of everything falling into place. It is as if you don't have to make any decisions or do anything, because life blossoms before you in ways that you have longed for – it is all harmonious and perfect in its unfolding. All this is because of the intentions you have set as part of your Soulistic Journey to date.

If, however, you are still feeling rather lacklustre, fatigued and out of balance, this could indicate that you are still working through certain levels of 'illusion' that have built up in your life. For example, you may be holding on to the 'security' of a job you dislike because of the financial implications you fear if you let it go. This is totally understandable. Developing your sense of trust in life and in your soul destiny takes time and commitment. Don't denigrate yourself or your decisions – just be mindful of where you are right now, wisely accepting that your journey takes as long as it takes and will twist and turn as new paths unfold. There is no judgement, just potential.

Harmony feels joyful because she operates on the soul level. She is the great stabiliser, bringing exactly the right energy, at exactly the right time to create new levels of evolution, if you invite her into your life. If you do, then you can expect both destruction (of old stories that no longer serve you) and creation of new, more empowering narratives of healing. Harmony reminds you that life involves a constant cycle of rebirth and surrender. When you surrender to your true purpose, even if it means relinquishing things you once felt were integral to your wellbeing, there will always be a rebirth: of adventure, of journeying, of mystery, of wisdom – of Harmony.

> *How are you feeling right now? Do you feel a sense of Harmony, or do you feel a sense of discord? What choices have you made that you feel have elicited a degree of Harmony in your life? What choices can you make to alleviate any feelings of discord? Be sure to contemplate the archetype of Harmony and the mystery and wisdom inherent in the choices you have made. If you feel moved to do so, create a piece of art (a poem, a painting, a sculpture, a song…) that exemplifies how you are feeling right now, as the Soulistic Wheel turns towards the South.*

HARMONY IS A STATE YOU FEEL WHEN YOU ARE MAKING CHOICES THAT ARE ALIGNED WITH YOUR SOUL PURPOSE

UNIFICATION: EVOLUTION

The paths from Above and Below merge in your Heart Centre and co-create the child called Evolution. You are now becoming the architect of your personal Evolution, intentionally moving towards the soul expression you choose. What an achievement! How courageous you are. Take a moment to reflect on the changes that are manifesting as you evolve into this new, wise being.

The potentiality of Evolution lives within you – within your very genes – ready to move you forward in the direction of your dreams and your destiny. Scientists have invested much time and effort decoding our genetic make-up, and some of us feel unfairly predisposed towards health issues that are not of our making – because of our genetic inheritance – but the good news is, to paraphrase the inspirational epigeneticist, Bruce Lipton[30], you are not a victim of your genes.

The science of epigenetics proves that factors over and above (*epi*) your genes can influence your life outcomes, your Evolution. These factors include environmental impacts, nutritional factors and the nature of your thoughts. Bruce tells us, "The moment you change your perception is the moment you rewrite the chemistry in your body. […] We are conscious co-creators in the Evolution of life. We have free will and we have choices, which are in turn totally dependent on our awareness."

What is wonderful is that it is never too late – whenever you come to this realisation that you co-create your own Evolutionary path, it will be the perfect moment – for above all things, Evolution has exquisite timing. Evolution is patient and indulges your foibles, never retracting any benefaction or gifts, because Evolution is ever-unfolding, dancing in the cells of every being, compelling us all to keep moving towards new life, new stories and new adventures.

What is triggering a negative emotional reaction in you? Is it an argument you had with your best friend? Is it a job offer you turned down? Is it a health issue that makes you feel anxious? Look deeply into the mystery that lies within this situation and using your mythic eyes, hack into the stories you are telling yourself about it. Can you change your perception? Can you tell your friend that you love and respect them even if your opinions differ? Can you truly forgive yourself for turning down the job offer and expect that in future, you will have the courage to walk through the doors of opportunity? Can you focus on the things in your life that give you joy despite the pain of your ill health? Or can you intuit a link or connection to any habit or thought pattern that is exacerbating your illness? Just by thinking differently about these situations you are healing yourself, step by step. Don't let your thoughts make you sick.

YOU ARE THE ARCHITECT OF YOUR PERSONAL EVOLUTION, MOVING TOWARDS THE SOUL EXPRESSION YOU CHOOSE

APRIL PRACTICES

SOUL GARDENING

NURTURING AND GROWING YOUR INTENTIONS

As the days get longer in April, the soil begins to warm up and the sun's energy potentises the microflora and fauna in the Earth, enabling germination. This seedbed is further tended by the gardener who adds extra nutrients like compost, to nourish the seedlings when they emerge. The gentle Spring rains – so different from the cleansing Winter torrents – replenish the cells in the seeds with life-giving water and before long, new life burgeons. Sowing seeds and seeing them thrust through the ground, transformed from tiny brown husks into verdant green shoots, is witness to a miracle.

At this time of year, you can also sow metaphorical 'seeds of intention'. As you move from the North Quarter of remembrance on the Soulistic Wheel into the Eastern Quarter of rejuvenation, you may feel your own energies catalysing; you may recall ideas and projects that you mulled-over during your Hibernation Practice that now begin to take root in your consciousness, or you may feel intuitively that a new approach to an existing situation is necessary. Notice if you are drawn to anything through your meditations and contemplations. What wants to germinate in you at this time?

Sowing the seeds of intention will direct the path of your Soulistic Journey, so be careful that you don't grasp onto the first idea that comes to you, but sit with it and contemplate whether this is truly the direction you choose. If you are a little impatient and prone to jump on any bandwagon without really thinking about it, then step back and recognise that intention-setting needs to come from a different place: not from the habitual brain-driven, survival-led domain, but from the deeper, intuitive soul level. How do you tell the difference? The answer is to listen to your heart. This sounds a little clichéd, but clichés are truths nonetheless. What does your heart desire at this time?

Once you are aware of the intention(s) you would like to set, then you can begin Soul Gardening.

SOWING THE SEEDS OF INTENTION WILL DIRECT THE PATH OF YOUR SOULISTIC JOURNEY

* As with actual gardening, for the seed of your intention to germinate, you need to prepare a good seedbed. So, if your intention is to paint, then is it possible to find a studio space for yourself; somewhere you can go that will nurture your creativity? Or, if your intention is to walk the Santiago de Compostella pilgrimage trail, can you set a date or book the time off work? The seedbed phase of Soul Gardening is important because it is the first step towards actualisation. Take your time with this and contemplate what is needed for your intentions to take root.

* Once you have begun to prepare the seedbed (and this is an ongoing process, because just as with Earth gardening, you will continue to

nurture it with water and feed, weeding and pinching out) you can now plant your seed. Write your intention(s) on a piece of paper or card and pin it to your dreamboard. Be creative; make it a beautiful thing to behold, because you will see it every day. You may like to draw offshoots around your intention that remind you of the reasons you have made this choice, such as: Personal Wellbeing, Dream Come True, Joyfulness, etc. This image will remind you that you have set this intention and that it is important to you.

❋ Continue to work on your seedbed, watering it with energy, pulling-out any negative thoughts, nipping any problems in the bud by thinking strategically, and hoeing away any distractions.

❋ Journal how you see your intention germinating and coming into being. What does it feel like? What do you need to do next? How is your life changing because of this choice you have made?

Soul Gardening mirrors Earth Gardening. It is a joyful cycle of transformation, growth, stability and change. Your intention will come to fruition and bloom, but then it will change, even disintegrate, or develop into a new form. What is key is to tend the intention, but not control it. If you try to control Nature in the garden, what often happens is that the energy and vigour dissipates; Nature knows how to do things and enjoys our cooperation, but any notion of control is ultimately self-defeating. It is the same with Soul Gardening. Your intuition comes from your heart centre – it is wise and timeless – but your bossy brain always wants to be in control, and this diverts the energy and ultimate fruition of your intention. A successful gardener has knowledge and experience but really does work from a place of intuition, knowing when the time is right to transplant and pinch-out.

It is interesting to note how many phrases that we use in everyday life come from the gardening world: to 'nip it in the bud', to 'branch out', to 'face the sun', to 'harden off'… Notice when these phrases come to mind – how do they relate to your intention? What do you need to 'nip in the bud' before it becomes a problem? Where are you not facing the sun and therefore not allowing for full growth? What needs to be hardened off, so that it can withstand certain forces outside of your control?

Soul Gardening is a metaphor. It is a wonderful way to nurture and grow your intentions. It needs patience, observation, contemplation and flexibility to flourish. Most of all, it requires acceptance that things rarely go to plan, but the results are often better than you imagined!

SPRING PILGRIMAGE

A DEEP COMMUNICATION BEYOND WORDS

How often do you take off your shoes and stand on the warm grass flexing like a tree in the Spring breeze? How often do you allow yourself time to gaze at cherry blossom and marvel at its own rhythmic cycle of coming into flower at the same time every year? If your answer is, 'Not very often,' then you're not alone. These days we rarely notice that the blue-black dart in the sky is a swallow returning to these shores after an epic migration from Africa; and we may miss altogether the prickles of green in the hedgerow that announce the hawthorn is coming into leaf, to be swiftly followed by the chestnut and the beech and all the other trees. These are rhythmic events – they happen every year, around the same time (although climate change is moving Springtime earlier each season) and they are Nature's indication that we are in the time of rejuvenation, when energy begins to flow and all becomes vibrant.

So, for this practice – and to encourage your own energy and vitality to flow – we invite you to dance, in your own way, to Nature's rhythms by taking a Spring Pilgrimage. A pilgrimage is a journey to a place that you consider special, to pay your respects – it doesn't have to be a religious or spiritual place although that's absolutely fine if you are drawn there; but it must be a place that is meaningful to you for one reason or another.

Choose a beautiful Spring day to take your walk. Pack a rucksack with water, snacks, a diary, binoculars perhaps, and anything else you think you'll need – you may be walking for several hours, so think ahead. Make a mental map of your journey, or if it is complex, take a map with you, but do try to carry as little extraneous equipment as possible; you don't want to be weighed down with unnecessary baggage – although do take a garland of spring flowers, or a libation of any kind to leave at your place of pilgrimage, if you wish.

Before you set-off on your Spring Pilgrimage, take a few moments to breathe deeply and loosen yourself from the shackles of your daily thought patterns. Pilgrimages should be approached in a state of quiet mindfulness and devotion to the mystery unfolding before you. Thich Nhat Hanh and his Buddhist community practice walking meditation[31] as a way of stilling the mind – walking is a tried and tested way to unite body and mind; to 'let go and let in' – so just try to focus on putting one foot in front of the other, knowing that eventually you will reach your destination.

In many cultures, pilgrimages are undertaken for quite a duration of time; this is so that the rhythm of walking can permeate one's being to the very core. After many days, the 'destination' becomes only a facet of the experience; the spiritual transformation takes place on the journey itself, not at the journey's end. Some pilgrims choose to make the journey even more challenging by genuflecting the whole way, or by walking backwards, but for our purposes, the point of the exercise is to walk to a meaningful place with a clear mind, open to observing all that befalls you on the journey but not attaching your thoughts to anything.

GIFT YOURSELF
TIME TO GET
OUT INTO
NATURE

Here is a piece I (Lorna) wrote in my journal after undertaking a Spring Pilgrimage:

THE BLACK POOL

I'd been planning to walk to Blackpool beach for weeks – but there'd always been a reason why not to: it was cold/windy/raining or I didn't have time, or a new client had just asked me to do an urgent job… or a million other reasons why not to gift myself the time to get out in Nature. But as the Spring Pilgrimage is one of this month's practices, I knew the time was now!

I set out for the three-mile round trip on the most beautiful Spring afternoon imaginable. The sky was cloudless, and the breeze had shifted from a chilly easterly to a balmy southerly, bathing me in voluptuous caresses of warmth. Yet even as I set out, I felt my saboteur archetype berating me from her perch on my shoulder: 'You should be working' she said to me; 'You ought to finish that article before you go…' But I bade her be quiet and stop being so, 'Shouldy' – I'm getting quite good at putting her in her place these days.

As I put one foot in front of the other, I felt myself settle; I felt a part of me – that bit that gnaws at my innards whenever I do something 'unscheduled' – recede; and I heard myself breathe-in deeply and sigh a couple of times. My mind did try to intercede with mundanity, but for once, I was able to detach from 'work' mode and really feel centred within myself. It was a lovely feeling.

I walked down the steep hill, into the wooded combe flanked by the Abbey River that leads to the sea, and the black pool that gives the beach its name. I could hear a willow warbler – first of the season – so I knew that this tiny migrating bird had made it home, and that the cuckoo was sure to follow. I saw nestled in the roots of a tree the first early purple orchid, and the first flush of bluebells, the scent sending me into a swoon. The beauty of this vista knocked me for six – 'It's all still here, on my doorstep, just doing its thing, without the need for any validation or recognition from me. Nature just IS. Wow.'

I continued walking, the sun on my back, the lull of the ocean in the distance, through the valley and into the woodland that meets the river. As I continued to walk, I felt my whole body relax. I knew where I was headed and there was nothing else to do except walk and observe. At first, my attention was taken by the glorious sights all around but slowly, even that connection became secondary to my sense of listening. I heard Nature rather than just seeing it: the birdsong, so uplifting and ethereal; the soughing of the breeze in the budding branches, the slow drag of the pebbles as each wave threw and then drew them along the shore; but even this receded…

The listening became internal; I listened to my mind chatter, but didn't respond to it, and so my mind continued to quieten. I didn't formulate a response to any thought that came to mind, I just listened. This sense of listening seemed to emanate from me into the valley so that I felt attuned to all the beings around me, and they to me; as if the valley was listening to me, too. It felt like a very deep communication, beyond words.

I FELT ATTUNED TO ALL BEINGS AND THEY TO ME

In this blissful state, time seemed to stretch and expand. I didn't know how long I'd been walking and lingering, and it didn't matter. As I walked through the kissing gate and onto the springy grass of the foreshore, I took off my shoes and felt the ground beneath my feet, knowing that the free radicals in my body were being earthed and neutralised by this connection. I lay on my front amongst the wild thyme at the cliff edge, overlooking Blackpool beach and the eponymous black pool that forms at the culmination of the river's own journey.

The pool has changed its shape totally since I was last here, the winter storms heaving the rocks and pebbles to form a dam wall that the river cannot breach. The pool that forms behind is long and thin like a miniature loch, not round and deep as it was last year. I always enjoy this unexpected element of change in a landscape that feels so ancient.

Then suddenly, I see a friend hopping over the boulders on the beach, having just enjoyed a high tide swim, and instantly, my deep reverie dissipates; my brain kicks-in with cheerful glee at seeing my friend and we have much to discuss, not having seen each other for weeks. But that sense of deep listening – that will stay with me. It was profound and felt very healing; like my body had been washed clean from the inside[32].

This Spring Pilgrimage story shows us that what happens when we walk mindfully, is not always what we expect to happen. If we can approach the journey with humility and open heartedness, who knows what we will find?

APRIL STORYHACK

GENEVIEVE GUIDES YOU IN THE GENTLE ART OF
RESTORYING YOUR LIFE...

STORY RHYTHMS

YOUR STORIES HAVE RHYTHM,
BUT YOU ARE THE CONDUCTOR!

Of late, I have been thinking a lot about the nature of story and its energetic elements; of how the words in ancient myths carry power through the way we voice them; how when we read stories aloud, they carry a different resonance than when we absorb them silently. How narratives transform when they are combined with sacred sound and frequency to create healing journeys that take us deeply into the imaginal realms.

Stories have frequency. In this particular hack, I ask you to feel into the particular lessons (tests) and blessings (gifts) that your life story and experiences have presented you with, thus far. Make a list of these highs and lows in your life, then plot them, much like a graph, along a piece of paper mapping the heights and depths against a yearly timeline and drawing a line to connect them all.

What you end up with is a diagram that looks much like a brainwave or even a heart wave. The line that connects your life experiences shows you the relative frequency of your life at any given point and the resonance of your narrative journey. Isn't that amazing – to see the rhythm of your life?

Of course, it is society's current state of consciousness, belief systems and cultural identities that helps each of us determine whether an experience is a 'high' or a 'low' within the overall rhythm of our lives and what we once thought of as a high might yet be seen as a low in years to come. What's interesting, though, is that repeating this exercise at least annually, allows you to see how your overall perspective flows like a wave as you journey through life. It also shows you what frequency your stories are creating in the world. Do you have a life that is dominated by 'highs' or burdened by 'lows'? Do you have an undulating frequency that gives you a taste of the lessons that come from both ends of this spectrum?

The 'storywave' frequency can be seen somewhat like your heartbeat. Imagine that you are hooked up to a monitor in the hospital and can see your heart beat regularly pulsing in green every time it beats. Similarly, every life experience and the story you create about it forms a pulse. Each day has a rhythm. Each year has a pattern and a tempo, much like a drumbeat. Or a pulse. Or a frequency band on the radio.

YOUR STORIES
ARE THE
MUSIC THAT
YOU DANCE
TO WITHIN

Your stories and words have immense power that ripple out into the molecules of the Universe and commands them to create the experiences that you then encounter – which is why you should be careful what you wish for, or mindful of what you talk about. Your stories are the music that you dance to within. And just like music, you can change the tempo and notes any time you please; you can pause and listen and make new choices.

Could you change what you see as a low frequency pattern in your life song and change it to a higher vibration? Could you embrace the lows as the drumbeat of your soul? Yes – because your stories have rhythm, but you are the conductor! You can change the rhythm of your life simply by making the choice to do so.

A

M

J

STORYING

S

SOUTH

SOUTH QUARTER MEDITATION

RESTORYING

Make yourself comfortable and breathe deeply for a minute or two until you feel still and settled. With your mind's eye, imagine your Heart Centre, the place you came to for your previous Quarterly Meditations. How does it feel to be back here? Relax and breathe in the beauty and sanctity of your surroundings.

When you feel rested within your Heart Centre, find the central point and sit or stand there. Take a deep breath and look around you, reconnecting with the energies of each direction: first to the East, where the element of fire resides. Feel the warmth coming from the East; the energy of the rising sun, with its potential to burn up old stories and release you from self-limiting habits. Then turn to the South, where Water is in its element. Feel the generous ease and flow that water embodies, how it can resolve any feelings of restriction, how it can wash away your fears. Then slowly turn to the West, the element of Earth. Feel how the Earth holds you and nourishes you; feel how abundant and energised Earth is. Know that just by standing on the Earth in your bare feet, you can reconnect with her sacred spirit. Then turn to the North, and the element of Air; feel that freshness and clarity that can instantly give you a new perspective, feel the lightness of Air and know that you can mirror that lightness in your decisions and choices.

In this Quarter, you are facing the South of Summertime, the element of Water. This is the aspect of glorious abundance; the life-giving flow of energy and ripeness. Welcome the power or restorying at this time and see how it can enliven the flow of your life choices.

These four directions and their elements are your touchstones. Know that at any time, you can envision being in your Heart Centre and enjoy the equilibrium therein. Within the directions, over and above all elements and residing in your Heart Centre is the fifth element of ether; the essence and the mystery. The all-encompassing one-ness. Ether is of this world and not of this world. It is the essential element that enables transcendence into the cosmological realm. Your Heart Centre is filled with this bridging element of ether; feel how it moves you beyond this realm.

Continue to breathe deeply and envision yourself now leaving your Heart Centre and travelling upwards into the firmament of our Universe, deep into the cosmic realms. Follow the river of light up into the blue. How incredible it is to swim among the stars, looking down on the jewel that is Planet Earth. Allow yourself to travel beyond the Milky Way to the edge of the Universe, where you find a doorway, a portal between our Universe and the Multiverse or Cosmos. You are invited to slip through that doorway into the timeless, eternal realm where angels and archetypes reside. As you move into this new realm, you will see before you, as you have done before, the beautiful Cosmic medicine wheel mirroring the one in your Heart Centre. An archangel stands guardian of each of the four sacred directions – creating a blessed and safe space for you, a place where only the energies and guides that reflect your highest good can enter.

Come to rest in the middle of this beautiful Cosmic Temple. Notice how you feel residing here as your Universoul Self; relax in the harmonious energies that flow from all directions and anchor you gently in the centre of the wheel. Acknowledge the open door to the North and all the blessings that you have unlocked since meeting your Mentor from this realm. Bow your head to the open door in the East and your Mentor who beams love to you from this place.

Then turn to face the South and notice the doorway that is placed there. Watch as the door slowly opens and welcome whoever or whatever comes through, knowing they are sent as a messenger from your higher self. You may wish to take their hands or touch their being in an act of sacred connection and communion noticing any words, images, symbols, feelings, or colours that come to you as you interface in this way.

You are being invited to walk with this being, your guide to Universal Law, for the restorying quarter of Summer. They will support you in myriad ways; in your remembering, in your questioning, in your weaving – and you can always ask them for help or guidance.

Now your Mentor leads you back towards the Universal portal where you entered the archetypal realm. You follow, safe in the knowledge that this immortal being is always here in spirit for you. You begin to slowly and gently traverse the Cosmic realms, back down towards your Heart Centre, and come to rest there. Your Mentor has accompanied you and stands behind you with their hands on your shoulders. Your Mentor from the South greets your Mentors from the North and East.

Come back into your body now and rest in the blessings of your journey.

See page 364, Endnote 12 for links to the recorded version of this Meditation if you prefer to listen to it rather than read it.

RESTORYING

The threads of the new
Are woven from those that came before
But first they must be unravelled
To make new mythic tapestries
Will you welcome your own unravelling
As part of the dance of creation?
When you let go of that which no longer serves
You breathe new life into your weaving threads
Restorying is an act of destruction and creation
An eternal cycle of meaning-making
The seeds of the new are nurtured in the soil of the old
And we are reborn with the words of power we choose to speak.

Summer and light claim us. We dance through our worlds alive with the awareness of our power and sovereignty. Stories abound beyond words and we weave through our world, finding the lever points of change and transformation. Will we take that risk? Will we court the unknown adventure? Perhaps. The world awaits our choices and the molecules of the Universe configure and reconfigure, hanging on every word of power that we speak. We talk our walk, feeling-in to our creative potential.

Stories are so powerful; they are the fundament of our world. They enable us to navigate the choppy waters of existence by throwing us lifelines of meaning. The first story some of us may have heard is, 'In the beginning was the Word, and the Word was with God, and the Word was God.' Our first story was about a story: the Word. And since then, we have all heard so many different stories: fairy stories and fables, family stories and legends, news stories that some believe and others disbelieve, stories we tell ourselves about ourselves which become our own personal mythology, an invisible cloak around us that is hard to shake off. Stories are supremely powerful.

But ultimately, they are just stories and we can always tell new ones, if we choose. As we grow older, discernment allows us to align with stories that we resonate with most. Some now prefer, 'In the beginning was the Big Bang' or as Cosmologist Jude Currivan[33] suggests, 'In the beginning was the Big Breath'. Some people believe that we have been so misinformed by the stories of mainstream media that they align themselves with what others call conspiracy theories, and believe those instead. There are people who are so sure that their stories are the truth and that others' stories are not, that they will fight to the death to preserve them.

WHAT IS
REALITY
IF IT IS
INTERPRETED
DIFFERENTLY
BY EVERY
HUMAN BEING
THROUGH
THE LENS OF
THEIR OWN
PERCEPTION?

These are all stories we tell ourselves about the true nature of reality – how multifaceted reality is! Reality means something quite different to every one of the 7.8 billion people who are alive on the planet at this moment in time. Of course, this brings into question the nature of reality. What is reality if it is interpreted differently by every human being through the lens of their own perception? Does reality even exist? As Genevieve said in her 'Entering the Dreamworld' practice, "Is this life a dream? Are we walking through an imaginal realm, full of characters that we designed and created to dance with, before we were born?" The joyful fact is that the nature of reality evolves, transcends, mutates and alchemises in every moment, and what this does is offer us the opportunity to do the same with our own story lenses. Like reality, they can evolve too. We can wipe them clean and tell new stories about ourselves and the way we see the world whenever we choose. This is at the heart of restorying.

When we fully embrace our own sovereignty – by which we mean the knowledge that we are powerful, that we are the architects of our own reality, that we have authority ('author-ity', meaning we are the authors of our own story) – then, we can choose the stories we live by; those which empower us and others, those which change the trajectory of our lives towards abundance and joy, those that forgive the hurts of the past and focus on the potential of the Now.

Restorying is powerful – but choose your stories well. If you choose stories that are inauthentic, they will be your undoing.

MAY

THE 'DARLING BUDS' DELIGHT THE SOUL
AND HERALD THE CUSP OF SUMMER

MAY EARTH SIGNS

Many people will agree that May is the most beautiful month of all. Seeds that have been sown germinate and emerge in myriad delightful forms, the warmth of the sun giving each seedling the power to develop and thrive, cradled by the beneficent soil and nourished by life-giving rains. Everywhere you look there is beauty; the chestnut trees in full bloom, the splendid white stars of wild garlic flowers, the purple honesty, and the hawthorn swathed in pink-tinged white, appropriately called May blossom. The 'darling buds of May' delight the soul: just gaze at one for a while and notice how you feel. Their beauty opens a gateway to joy. Take time to stand and stare, and drink in the beauty of May.

The cuckoo sings his song, and all who hear him know he heralds the cusp of Summer. In the fields, newborn lambs and calves frolic in the sunshine, their gangly limbs catapulting them into ecstatic dance – in May, it seems, all creatures rejoice. The swallows grace the skies with their skilful flight and sweet chatter; the badger sets abound with cubs who tumble for the sheer joy of it; the fox cubs scuffle in the long grass, oblivious of all except play.

May is bountiful and bursting with life. May is creativity in full flow. It is emergent, dynamic, transformative, playful, fascinating. These qualities can be embodied in your life too if you dance around the Maypole and weave the threads of energy into your core.

TAKE TIME TO
STAND AND
STARE,
AND DRINK IN
THE BEAUTY
OF MAY

MAY COSMOLOGICAL SIGNS

TAURUS TO GEMINI

I HAVE

In this month you will experience one of the greatest paradoxes of our modern age. Taurus brings you back down into the physical world and the outer manifestations of your inner need for security, safety and wellbeing.

The Taurean, 'I HAVE' drives you to examine your stories about what you deem as success, failure, survival and abundance. Are you holding on to narratives of scarcity and victimhood or are you embracing the cornucopia of opportunities, adventures and manifestations that lay at your soul-tips when you flow with the cycles of life?

In this Quarter, you are asked to examine the contents of your narrative lenses and see what beliefs, thought patterns and emotional crutches you are holding on to so that you can release them, kick back and enjoy the blissful physicality of life that exists beyond competition.

You truly have everything you need, when you need it, and more – if you decide that this is the story you live by here on Earth.

EXAMINE
YOUR STORIES
ABOUT WHAT
YOU DEEM AS
SUCCESS AND
FAILURE

Phoenix Moon

– all is newborn and full of potential. Phoenix Moon gives rise to new life as energy continues to wax towards mid-Summer. Feel the abundance and celebration.

MAY SOULISTIC ARCHETYPES

SOLAR ARCHETYPE: LIFEFORCE

You are now in the lush and verdant South Quadrant of your Soulistic Wheel, a time when the archetype called Lifeforce is prevalent and visible all around. Lifeforce is the animating spirit that pervades our world; the energy that makes each being unique – take a look about you at the incredible diversity emanating from Lifeforce: the squirrel, the rose, the painter, the lemon, the dancer, the kitten, the oak sapling, the reader of this book… Diversity is reflected in every jewel of the sacred life story.

Lifeforce is the impetus of transformation. See how the kitten becomes a cat; the oak sapling transforms into a mighty tree. Transformation happens constantly yet is subtle and almost imperceptible moment to moment. But what you see transforming with your physical eye can also be seen by your mythic eyes on a metaphysical level. Mystery asks if you can see how you are transforming, too?

Robust as Lifeforce is, it can also be unpredictable. You may be feeling like you are stuck in an old story or unable to jump into the flow of life; you may see your friends and family busily enjoying life whilst you are uncertain of which way to turn; but this is also a natural quality of the energy at this time. A gardener can plant a row of peas in soil that he has carefully tilled; nourish them all with the same seaweed solution and the sun shines equally on them, as the rain also fairly shares her magical elixir – and yet some plants will be twice as big as others. The wise gardener knows however, that removing the weaker seedlings allows in more sunshine and energy to nurture the stronger seedlings. Mystery asks you to deepen into your feelings. Are there any blocking energies that you can remove at this time? What is stopping the sun (metaphorically speaking) from shining on you? Is there any barrier or concern that is diverting Lifeforce from flourishing? What can you let go of, that will allow Lifeforce in? Mystery asks if you can learn to surf the waves of your creative energy and your fallow times where you need to rest and recuperate? Can you accept that your Lifeforce ebbs and flows like the cycles of the moon, the sun and the tides?

LIFEFORCE
IS THE
ANIMATING
SPIRIT THAT
PERVADES OUR
WORLD

As with all beings and energies in our Universe, Lifeforce comes to be and in due course, he ceases to be. Lifeforce inspires new growth and is the energy behind every relationship and connection we make, but eventually Lifeforce will cease to be and we will have to face the 'mini-deaths' of our stories and relationships or the major 'deaths' of our lifetime(s). Therefore, in recognising the strength of Lifeforce at this time, you are reminded that being consciously alive is a privilege. Lifeforce asks but one thing from you: that you feel gratitude each day for the blessing of your life.

What makes you feel truly alive? Is it dancing till dawn at a festival? Is it lying naked in the warm sun? Is it facing your fears and jumping in at the deep end? Whatever makes you feel truly alive – just do it and build your inherent Lifeforce energy!

LUNAR ARCHETYPE: TRAJECTORY

As you continue journeying in the South Quadrant of your Soulistic Wheel, you are asked to pay attention to the mysteries that await you in the lunar realms of dreams and imagination. The archetype Trajectory resides in these realms and she guides the direction of your life path and orientates your evolutionary journey. A bit like the astrological sign of Sagittarius, the energy of Trajectory can often feel like an arrow shooting forth from your core self, into the unknown. It feels creative and exciting and a bit… challenging. Can you intuit any clues to your Trajectory from your dreams? (See the Entering the Dreamworld practice on page 118.)

Trajectory is intimately linked with imagination – the two work together to inspire your dreams and your creativity, within which the unfolding direction of your journey is held. You know when the muse of Trajectory is at work because of the feeling of excitement you get when you are on the verge of a new path or opportunity. You may then find yourself in the midst of choice-making, knowing that what you are doing serves your Soul Purpose, even when all around you are surprised at your actions or are counselling caution. But having got to the Southern Quadrant of your Soulistic Journey, you will, by now, be recognising synchronicity and intuition at play in your life, and you will find validation in your imaginative responses. It is then that the impetus from Trajectory's arrow energises you with possibility.

Trajectory weaves your lifeforce into a dynamic web of potential, and this is a wonderful thing. It is akin to abundance in that you may brimming over with exciting projects and ideas, but Mystery asks that you practice conscious choice to activate the energies that most serve your Soul Purpose. Then, Trajectory will focus your creative projects and also nudge you back onto your path if you become distracted on your journey.

Sit beside your altar, or in Nature if you prefer, and take some time to come into a state of contemplation. Reflect upon the Trajectory of your life thus far, and your hopes for the future. Draw the arc of your arrow of Trajectory. Start the arrow based in a symbol of where you are now and show its flight path towards a symbol of where you want to be. Pin it to your dreamboard and ponder it often.

UNIFICATION: INTUITION

As the energies from Above and Below combine in your Heart Centre, the hub of your unique Soulistic Wheel, they form the wonderful archetype of Intuition. Your Soulistic Wheel holds within it great healing powers and this entire journey is about accessing them, so that you can become wholly reconnected with your true self. This beautiful archetype, Intuition, that resides within you and without you, is your personal way-finder, your cosmic tracker and your Universal guide through the dreamweave of life, helping you to access the assistance and resources that you most need. How utterly wonderful that you have such support – but do you recognise Intuition when it arises, and have you learned how to dialogue with your Intuition?

THERE ARE
MANY PATHS
AND NOT ALL
OF THEM ARE
YOURS

You know that feeling? You KNOW that feeling. Your belly, your heart, your third eye, your very *being* converses with Intuition constantly and gives you a nudge when it arises – but your bossy brain is prone to ignoring the nudge! Try to recognise that *feeling* of knowing and relate it to the message you are being given by your wise soul. What is your quiet voice of inner wisdom saying to you? That is all that is necessary to connect with your Intuition, yet how hard it can be! So ask for guidance from your mentors, guides and guardians. Ask for help and it will be freely given. The key, as always, is to be able to read the signs that are 'writ large' despite the noise of the world story unfolding around you.

Intuition beckons to you, showing you the way to your own inner wisdom, your sense of integrity and right-knowing. So, as you can see, Intuition is a gift you really want to cultivate! Intuition shows you the way when all seems lost or if there are too many options to choose from. This sacred child lives within you, reminding you of your ability to practice discernment.

❊ Discernment is such a lovely word. Its synonyms are acumen, insight, understanding, perception, awareness, intuition. Get a calligraphy pen or brush, choose your favourite one of these words and write it in large lettering on a piece of paper. Embellish it with pattern and colour. Pin it to you dreamboard to remind yourself that discernment is a key part of your journey, as there are many paths and not all of them are yours.

MAY PRACTICES

VISION QUESTING

CRACKING OPEN TO A NEW STORY AND IDENTITY

Okay, so now we approach one of the oldest and deepest practices that we share with you in this book. It is not to be danced into lightly and indeed is one you may find yourself shying away from rather than running towards. If so, good – that means you are sensing into its power. Vision quests[34] have been used by indigenous cultures across the world for millennia as a mechanism to remove ourselves from our old story, humbly seeking a higher vision from Nature and the forces in our Universe, in order to inform the next chapter of our life purpose. And vision quests often sneak up on us when we least expect them.

You see, life moves in waves. We have periods of time when our focus is more outwards in the world, such as when we have children or start a new job, but then the wave that has risen falls back again, and we feel the pull to retreat inwards to integrate and harvest the wealth of our experiences in order to find new inspiration. These inward arcs of attention inevitably lead us towards transformation, and this is when we need to 'quest' in order to find a new vision to guide us into the next phase of our life.

Vision quests often come at pivotal moments and thresholds in our development, such as moving from childhood to adolescence or midlife to elderhood. They can also be as big or as small as you feel called to undertake. Indeed, each person must find their own way of questing that fits their personal circumstances.

What I would say is that the hallmark of any good quest is that it MUST take you well outside your comfort zone in order to crack open the outer casing of your old story and identity. "Everything we want is outside of our comfort

> VISION QUESTS OFTEN COME AT PIVOTAL MOMENTS AND THRESHOLDS IN OUR DEVELOPMENT

zone," entrepreneur Tim Ferriss once said, yet we resist leaving it with every breath we take. Humans are after all, creatures of habit.

The essential part of the vision quest is the knowledge that when you accept the quest, you leave your old life behind – you will come back as a new person, forever changed in some way. To do this, you need to let go and humbly seek your own 'death and rebirth' – the death of the old you and the rebirth into the new you. And there are no guarantees that you will succeed – yet seek you must. To refuse the quest is to know that it will stalk you until you finally face it.

You can undertake a vision quest in your garden or in the mountains, in your spare bedroom or the desert… you get to choose the scale and size of the journey you are willing to undertake. There are also many skilled and experienced organisations and wilderness guides that can help you should you wish to undertake a true wilderness quest.

Some key parts of any self-guided vision quest are:

WHEN YOU ACCEPT THE QUEST, YOU LEAVE YOUR OLD LIFE BEHIND

* Leaving behind the 'normal world' and entering into a liminal, imaginal space without technology or phones for a period of days.

* The night vigil – whether you sleep out for 3-7 days or simply take a 24-hour solo outside, it is important that you become friends with the dark.

* Fasting – abstaining from food for 24-72 hrs (we do recommend drinking water, however) and you must design this part of your quest based on your personal health situation.

* Taking minimal comforts, but ensuring that you are safe and warm (sleeping bag, tent, first aid kit, etc.)

* Ensuring that someone knows where you are and how long you will be out of contact for.

Once you have carved out enough time and space to undertake your quest, you must commit to it and prepare for it. Take small steps towards each element described above and undertake an avid journaling practice to explore your resistances and fears that come up as you approach the quest itself. You may find that parts of your old story and life start to naturally drop away. Good. This means you are truly on the path to transformation. Be gentle with yourself and grieve if necessary. This is all part of letting go, so you can let in the new vision.

If you find yourself paralysed with anxiety or fear at the thought of participating in a vision quest, then please seek out an experienced guide who can help you work through the process. Fear is completely normal and indeed expected as you approach a threshold practice such as this. I (Genevieve) host quests in the UK and the US on a regular basis because I have experienced their power in transforming our stories, time and time again.

Now plan your adventure. Decide on the amount of days, the location, whether you will fast or eat simple, sacred foods (please make sure you consider your health and wellbeing as foremost in this) and tell someone who can act as your 'watcher' where you will be and for how long. Then allow the quest to take you.

Once you become familiar with the vision quest practice that fits your style and circumstances, then you will find that this is an experience you can repeat again and again if you so wish, to continually find clarity and peace as you journey through your evolving story.

Here is an extract from my book *Tough Bliss: Restorying Life* recounting the first part of my Vision Quest[35]. This was a guided Quest, with much planning and preparation, but it does give you a taste of how deeply you can commit to this ceremony, if you want to:

> *When the time of my Vision Quest finally arrived, I found myself in a group of 13 fellow seekers. We came one by one to a beautiful valley on the edge of the ancient Anasazi lands in the southwestern*

I LEARNED
HOW TO
LISTEN, SEE
AND FEEL
MY WAY
BEYOND THE
BOUNDARIES
OF THIS
REALITY

tip of Colorado, close to the border of Utah. I was immediately enchanted by the landscape of my birth and ran joyfully into its embrace at every opportunity I had. In the day, the dry heat bounced off vibrant red, yellow and orange sandstone mesas. At night, we were enveloped in the deep dark of the desert, watched over by a million bright stars. I entered the process of coming home to the land, to my story and to my gifts.

One hot, arid afternoon, at the invitation of our guides, I set out to wander the land in search of answers. I was seeking a deeper truth, and like a hunter, I tuned my senses into the signs of tracks. Something in me knew that if I were to be considered worthy of finding the object of my search, then I would have to prove to the Universe that I had learned how to listen, see and feel my way beyond the boundaries of this reality.

I found myself following invisible energy lines that wove their way across the landscape into the distance – 'spirit paths' or 'fairy roads' my mother had called them when I was a little girl. Somehow, the memory of this inner GPS system had returned in full strength since coming back to Colorado. As I had known subconsciously as a child here, if you know what to look for and how to listen, the land, its creatures and the air itself will leave you clues as to your path forward.

A large desert yucca beckoned me, grabbing my attention to show me the place where I was to leave the main path and make my way through sage and Indian paintbrush plants towards a large, red rock. Reaching its base, I saw a ledge that, in my eyes, was sparkling with more than just the sun. Carefully, I scrambled up. On arriving at the top, I saw with a small gasp of surprise, a covered door into the rock with the top rungs of a wooden ladder peeking out. My heart started to beat faster as my intuition received information regarding the nature of the space I was being led to.

Slowly, using all my strength to pull back the heavy corrugated metal cover, I revealed the entrance and held my breath as old stale air escaped through the black hole at my feet. My breath caught in my throat in excited anticipation. I hadn't been into an 'Earth womb' since I was a small child and never alone.

Before my mind could convince me otherwise, I swung my backpack over my shoulder and tested the first rung of the ladder that led down into the darkness. It seemed steady and firm enough underfoot. Slowly and carefully so as not to fall, I descended into the black. I was gradually cloaked in cool, dark air that contrasted sharply with the hot desert wind above. I closed my eyes for a moment to allow them to adjust to the reduced light. When I opened them again, I was able to make out the smooth circular walls of the underground chamber I had been led to; a kiva, a place sacred to the indigenous peoples of this land, where we can speak to the voices beyond time.

As I asked permission to enter this sacred space, I thought I heard the whispered voices of the ancestors in my ears and had the impression of a welcome. Sitting down on the dusty dirt floor, I took a moment to prepare myself, contemplating the spiders' webs and faded paintings on the walls. I could hear the hum of the Earth like an intense pressure in my ears. I calmed and focused, the sound gradually clarifying into a regular rhythm. Consciously entwining my energy with the place, my own heartbeat slowed and synchronised to match that of the Earth. I was in her belly and I had a question. There was no need to ask it aloud; she could hear my heart.

Energy started to swirl around me in the darkness and I felt the air grow heavy with the essence of ceremonies that had been conducted in this place coming alive once more. Once a channel to the spirit world has been created, it is strengthened with each reconnection. I was here, now, tapping into centuries of focused ritual intention. The portal opened up quickly and a rising pulse started to move in the centre of my body. The energy whirled around me faster and faster, making me dizzy with its power. As I began to lose my ability to think clearly or attempt to control the course of events, I surrendered to the process. I felt safe and suspected that my question had been heard and received. After a moment, I started to wordlessly speak:

'I have come in humility. I have come for an answer to the question that has lain within my breast since before this life began. The eternal question that all human beings are designed to awaken to: Who am I?'

Thum, thum, thum, thum. The pounding increased to a crescendo pummelling my nerves. Then, softly, a female voice that was deeply familiar to me broke through the Earth orchestra and spoke:

'Star Seed. You are a Star Seed. It's time to remember. It is time to move beyond all human stories.'

I exhaled. At first my mind couldn't believe what it had heard but I knew the words were for me. My ego tried hard to tell me I was imagining things, but still, I knew the words were for me. My heart beamed out gratitude for the answer I had been given.

I now had a new question – one that may well take a lifetime to answer.

LUNAR BATHING

ILLUMINATED BY THE LIGHT OF THE MOON

The moon has been worshiped from time immemorial as a feminine presence in the firmament – with the sun, as the solar masculine. She has been known as Selene, 'the shining one', Artemis in Ancient Greece, and as Cerridwen in Celtic mythology. She has been prominent in great literature and poetry throughout the ages, due in no small part to her 'nocturnal predominance' as the nearest celestial body to the Earth. Luna (as she is also known) presides over the liquidities of the planet, be they the female menstrual cycle or the great tides of the oceans, and indeed the 'vapours' of our own mental health, hence the word 'lunatic'.

Due to the moon's axis and spin, her illuminated face is always turned towards the Earth, but the moon has a dark side which is perpetually in shadow. Contemplation of the moon invites us to explore our own shadow side, for the face we present to the world is often not the face that presides over our inner workings. Therefore, lunar bathing offers a wonderful opportunity to consider how best to bring this duality into balance.

Lunar bathing is most powerful when undertaken during this month's full Phoenix Moon, in itself a time for arising from the ashes of change, which may well be occurring as you undertake your Soulistic adventure. The metaphysical 'arising' that can be done at this time allows for the assimilation of your inner and outer facets – the face you show to the world and the one you keep to yourself. This can be a profoundly moving experience, so ask for help from your mentors (human and other-than-human) to make sense of the bigger picture that is unfolding.

Remember to journal this experience so that you can refer to it in due course. Very often the lessons from these practices do not reveal themselves immediately, as they take time to percolate through from the soul level to our consciousness. So, be patient and contemplate the process with an interested, open mind.

THE FACE WE PRESENT TO THE WORLD IS OFTEN NOT THE FACE THAT PRESIDES OVER OUR INNER WORKINGS

❋   Wait until the Phoenix Moon is waxing towards fullness, but check the weather forecast to see what night may work best for this practice. If it is a cloudy or wet evening, you may prefer to wait a night or two – no matter. If the Heavens are being particularly mercurial, lunar bathing can be undertaken on any clear, full moon.

❋   Dress up warmly and find a thick blanket to sit on. If it has been wet, you may also want to take a piece of canvas or plastic to put under your blanket. Prepare a flask of cacao or herbal tea to warm and temper your insides and remember to take your gifting bag with you.

❋   Go out into the moonlit night without a torch and allow some time for your eyes to adjust to the gentle luminosity. See how objects take on a different tonality and energy when bathed in moonlight. Feel how different the air is at night – it is not just cooler and fresher, but somehow denser, so that it almost caresses you.

❋   Go for a short walk, either within your garden or a little further afield to the local park, wood, heath or river. You are looking for somewhere with an uninterrupted view of the moon, where you can sit undisturbed. If you can't find such a space, then just sit where you feel safe and comfortable. Avoid light pollution if possible.

❋   Settle into your sit-spot and then make an offering from your gifting bag: a sprinkling of tobacco, or any other herb you might choose, in a circle around where you are sitting, for example.

❋   Take three deep breaths, slowly exhaling to centre and still yourself. Then tilt your head towards the moon and allow her light to bathe you; to connect you to memories of times past, many moons ago. Perhaps even lifetimes ago...

❋   Allow your thoughts to settle; do not examine them but let them pass like clouds across the face of the moon. Notice if any images come to mind, but do not analyse them. Just notice. Keep breathing deeply with your face to the moon.

❋ After a while you may find that as your mind stills, a different level of awareness replaces the chatter – an emptiness that is so full; a quietness that is loud. Enjoy this moment.

❋ You might like to contemplate what your 'shadow' characteristics may be; you can ask this question aloud: "What gifts am I hiding in the shadows? What attributes can I bring to the light and transform?" If any answers come to you, say them aloud, so you will remember them. Ask for help from your mentors to uncover your shadow aspects which you can then offer to the light of the moon. Remember that within all shadow resides the gift of light or illumination.

❋ When you are ready or your limbs are stiff, or something disturbs you, then it is time to pack away your things and head for home. As you walk back, what comes to mind? Are there any images, words or phrases that feel meaningful? Remember to write them down, along with the overall feeling of what you have just experienced.

Lunar bathing can be a powerful and emotional experience. If you are moved to work on your shadow energies, this may bring uncomfortable memories to the surface. Write about these; about your feelings and your reactions to them. How can you transform these energies or find hidden meaning and strength in them now they are remembered?

Even if nothing of note arose for you from your time in the lunar energy, just gifting yourself half an hour of silence in the fresh air will have done you so much good, on so many levels. Feel free to moon-bathe whenever you are called. All full moons have their own energy and lessons. This first taster is sure to make you want to experience it again.

Here is Genevieve's experience of lunar bathing:

ALL FULL
MOONS HAVE
THEIR OWN
ENERGY AND
LESSONS

I WAS
STUNNED TO
SEE NIGHT
BIRDS AND
SMALL
ANIMALS OUT
ON THE ROCKS
AROUND
OUR HOUSE
ENJOYING
THIS
ENCHANTED
MOMENT

THE LIGHT OF THE MOON

I woke up this morning with the light from a full Virgo moon streaming across my face as I lay in bed. It was magical. Mystical. And so very natural. I imagined it was how countless numbers of our ancestors would have awoken in times past.

And as my eyes adjusted to the almost-dawn light in my bedroom in the mountains of Colorado, I was stunned to see night birds and small animals out on the rocks around our house, also enjoying this enchanted moment.

Instead of getting up and sitting down to do my emails (as is my habit these days), I left all the lights off and drew myself a bath. I soaked in the moonlight that beamed itself right into my bath-tub and I set some intentions – for full moons are a great time to release the past and set new visions for the future.

The voices of the mountain told me that whatever I let go of in the bath would drain away as soon as I let the water out. So, I meditated. I allowed old stories, fears, beliefs, and identities to come up and float around me in the water. I honoured the part they had played in my life so far and I told them that it was time for them to go.

I looked kindly and lovingly on my body that has carried me through this life with good health and massive resilience, and I allowed every scrap of self-judgement that I could ever remember feeling towards my body melt into the soft warm waters.

Then I went to the core. I went to the root of the most fundamental mythology that I have based my entire existence on. The myth of what it means to be human. I allowed every old story about 'how I should be and what I should do' wash away from my ecosystem. I let it go. In full.

I was struck with the power of my choice in this micro-moment of magic on the moonlit mountain. I chose to become a citizen of Earth. I chose to remember that I am interconnected to all life in the Universe and live from that place. I chose to forge into unknown territory and fully embrace the adventure of a life well lived.

And then I rose and let the bathwater drain away into the Earth, stepping out naked into the moonlight of a new dawn and a new day.

MAY STORYHACK

GENEVIEVE GUIDES YOU IN THE GENTLE ART OF RESTORYING YOUR LIFE...

COME-UNION

DANCING UNITY ALIVE

I CHOSE TO REMEMBER THAT I AM INTER-CONNECTED TO ALL LIFE IN THE UNIVERSE

I have this happy memory; a memory from a time in my younger life when there weren't many things to be happy about. It was a flash of colour. A dance of DNA woven in ribbons. It was a 'coming in' to a moment of unity amongst a sea of duality. I was about eight-years old and it was May Day and we were dancing around a May Pole in my school. I didn't have many friends. I was too 'weird' and often felt overwhelmed, which the other kids mistook for shyness. In truth, I found everything too loud and it hurt my nervous system, but I didn't have the words to describe this back then. So, I sought solitude and the company of the rare individuals who held the quietness in their soul that I found soothing.

THE GIFT OF
TIME AND
EXPERIENCE
ALLOWS US
TO WEAVE
INTELLECTUAL
AND
EMOTIONAL
CONTENT
INTO THE
FABRIC
OF OUR
FORMATIVE
EXPERIENCES

Yet I also craved to belong. Like many young children, I looked to those around me for guidance as to how the world worked, yet I found very little to go on. My instinct told me that everything was alive and connected, yet hardly anyone I knew acted as if this was the case. Occasionally however, something would happen that would give me cause to validate my inner wisdom. The May Day Dance was one of those occasions.

From the outside, it was a gaggle of young children winding coloured ribbons around a hastily erected pole in the schoolyard. On the inside however, it was an enactment of universal truth. For me, as I danced in and out of the other ribbon strands that my classmates held, I saw the fabric of the Universe itself being woven like a story of evolution in play. For me, the ribbons were separate beings that surrendered their air-born freedom into the weave of a collective creation. In dancing around the pole, I stopped being the 'lonely American kid' and became one with the come-unity of dancers, expressing joy at creating something together that we could not have done apart.

This may sound very 'high-brow' and well thought-out so many years later as I write these words, and although my eight-year-old-self sensed something special, I could not have articulated it in this way. The gift of time and experience allows us to weave intellectual and emotional content into the fabric of our early formative experiences. All I knew was that dancing in this way made me feel alive and part of something bigger than my eight-year old body.

As a child, I craved Unity. I longed for deep connection with the world around me and sought it in the moments when I felt safe to do so, often with the other-than-human world which I trusted far more than the human one. The dance of the May Pole in the ancient Celtic calendar was a celebration of Spring: of fertility, new life and new lover(s). In dancing it, we come into union with the separate parts of ourselves – male/female, light/dark, conscious/unconscious. We literally dance unity alive and emerge from our come-union anew. We celebrate the joy of being alive.

What seemingly separate strands of your life story would you like to weave together into a new creation of some kind? Where are you feeling alone and separate? How can you come into a deeper connection with the flow of life all around you? How can you stop and simply celebrate the joy of being alive more often? All of these questions and more will open up as you dance around the 'May Pole' of your future. It is up to you to take the separate strands and weave them into a beautiful new story that inspires you and moves you into the future.

JUNE

A TIME OF HEALTHFUL VITALITY
A TIME OF OPPORTUNITY AND ADVENTURE

JUNE EARTH SIGNS

Light energy is at its zenith now. In June all beings are bathed in light and recharged with solar energy. The lengthening days provide the opportunity for the maturation of growth, a true burgeoning that is glorious to behold. The bees, laden with pollen fly back and forth to the hive, making honey for their winter stores; the fledgling sparrows dare each other to take flight to the opposite branch where a beak-full of caterpillars awaits, the bravest launching first into unknown territory. The peach blossom has set and tiny, fury fruit emerges. What a fecund time June is.

In the long days of Summer the field grasses begin to flower, giving a gauzy quality to the landscape; the cow parsley and ragged robin in the verges reach out into the lanes and caress passers-by; the swifts screech on high, a true sound of Summer, the arc of their inky-black wings scything the bluest of skies. In the woods, the fawn lays camouflaged in the long grass awaiting his mother's return, bathing in the dappled warmth, resting but alert. And on the heath the adder basks on a granite outcrop, flicking the air with its tongue, sensing what is close. It is summertime, and the living is easy, yet in the middle of June, the cuckoo changes his tune, a portent of transition.

The Summer Solstice arises around 21st–22nd June (the exact date is determined by the moment when the geocentric longitude of the sun is equal to 90 degrees) marking the longest day of the year. It is a time to celebrate the healthful vitality and energy that is unmatched at any other time of the year. It is a time to dance and make merry. Like all of Nature, we humans can also be up with the lark and then dancing in the moonlight and still not feel tired. June is the month of opportunity, where we have the energy to nurture the seeds of our intentions into fruition.

JUNE IS THE MONTH OF OPPORTUNITY WHERE WE HAVE THE ENERGY TO NURTURE THE SEEDS OF OUR INTENTIONS INTO FRUITION

JUNE COSMOLOGICAL SIGNS

GEMINI TO CANCER

I THINK

In June you move from the depths to the heights. Gemini brings you to the vastness of the mind and the purity of your soul's visions as they manifest across the eons of time and space.

Thinking can be either liberating or distracting depending on its intention and context, so in this month choose your focus well. The essence of your higher mind is the ability to switch it off as needed and find moments of sacred pause, where you can sink into the silence and breathe.

If you can let go of your human compulsion for 'more, better, higher, bigger' then you can become the chalice through which the vast mind of the Universe thinks. This is when the real adventure begins.

BECOME THE
CHALICE
THROUGH
WHICH THE
VAST MIND OF
THE UNIVERSE
THINKS

Soaring Eagle Moon

– the warmth of June's long days delights the soaring eagles high up on the thermals, as they gaze down upon creation, seeing the bigger picture. See like the eagles – take a higher view of everything that is happening in your life and life on the planet.

JUNE SOULISTIC ARCHETYPES

SOLAR ARCHETYPE: LEAP

If you started your Soulistic Journey around the Winter Solstice, then you are at the mid-point of your adventure; but no matter when you set foot on this path, you are now at the mid-point of the year – a time to take stock; to contemplate all you have experienced in the seasonal flow of the year. You have come a long way from the darkest days of winter; you have hibernated and ruminated, imagined and walked new paths and made creative intentions. Now the seeds that you sowed have germinated and are growing strongly. But, as every good gardener knows, those seeds need tending. They need to be coaxed by the playful energies of life so that they will mature and fulfil their potential.

Likewise, you are also asked to tend to the intentions you sowed earlier in your Soulistic Wheel, especially if you have lost faith in your decisions or if self-sabotaging behaviour is making you cautious about taking risks or 'leaping off the cliff' into unknown adventure. So, if you are being invited to make a Leap of faith at this time, for courage, look at Nature and see how the other-than-human world takes 'Leap' in its stride.

Have you ever watched a fledgling bird leave the nest? That little ball of fluff and feathers is coaxed out of his comfort zone by a parent (often tempting him with a juicy caterpillar as a reward); he will peep out of the nest and look around seeing the big wide world for the very first time, taking in the colours, sights and sounds of an environment that is entirely new to him. And then, all of a sudden, this little bundle of energy will Leap into the unknown and miraculously, he will take flight! He does not fall, he does not fail, he does not need a net to catch him. That is such a life-affirming metaphor for how you, too, can nurture the seeds of your intentions. Take a Leap of faith that what you sowed in the unfurling of your journey will take root and mature into healthful and sustaining ventures.

Leap is an incredibly vibrant and dynamic energy; full of excitement, of change, of the passion of fulfilling dreams. Leap is a heart-stopping moment in time. 'Will you? Won't you? What is stopping you?' Leap can be likened to the universal archetype of The Fool – he who will gleefully Leap off the cliffs of the known into the ocean of possibility without a second glance. Paradoxically, The Fool is no fool – he knows that to stay static and cautious is to risk everything; for it is not the Leap that is dangerous but the entropy of staying in your comfort zone.

So, the Mystery of this archetype is to ascertain why you are clinging on to that which no longer serves you, and the Wisdom of this archetype asks you to be courageous in moving towards your new realities and stories. Leap reminds you to trust that all is always well when you follow your inner sense of destiny.

How are your seeds of intention growing? What can you do to nurture them? Do you need support, as a pea shoot needs a twiggy stick to hold it upright? Then ask for help (with focused intention) from your guides and mentors, or friends and family, and notice how and when help is offered to you. Your seeds will need watering and tending. This is an ongoing practice from now until harvest time. Nothing will survive the drought of neglect, not even the best-laid plans.

LUNAR ARCHETYPE: SPARK

As you journey through the Southern Quadrant of your Wheel, you may notice Sparks of energy flying off you like fireflies in the warm night air. You are so energised by the long days of sunshine that it is almost impossible to stay still; instead you are busy, busy, busy, 'making hay whilst the sun shines.' The energy of Spark may express itself spontaneously through dance or music-making and as you frolic, your imagination kindles the fires of inspiration. As my friend Lynn once said to me (Lorna), "I'm sure I'm solar-powered – there's no stopping me when the sun shines."

But you may not be sparking on all cylinders, and instead you may feel listless, tearful and lost; or you may be finding it difficult to generate a sense of excitement or interest in anything. If this is how you are feeling, don't angst about it; instead, accept that the ebb and flow of your emotions will fluctuate like a wave on the ocean, and trust that your Spark will reignite. Presence with what is occurring in any given moment and patience with the flow of the creative process is often the key to all our conundrums. So, don't push it, but allow Spark to flare when she is ready. Spark instigates and she will fire you up at precisely the right moment, igniting your passion for life.

In fact, your own unique Spark is an energy that has been with you since before you were born, catalysing your entry into human form. So do not doubt her appearance in your life. Spark is the lightning rod that fertilises the soil of your dreams and causes your imagination to flare into the most vibrant adventures before your very eyes. Spark will actually jolt you awake, like an electric shock, when you have been dallying too long in the illusion of the world and not paying enough attention to the inner adventure you were born to experience. Your inner spark illuminates your path.

On the Summer Solstice – usually celebrated on June 21ˢᵗ – go out into Nature and find a place where you can watch the sun set, on this, the longest day. Watch as that ball of fire sinks below the horizon marking the transition from one season to the next. Tomorrow the night will be imperceptibly longer. Stay up late dancing around a Solstice Fire, watching as the Sparks dance into the night sky, and mark the seasonal transition by making an offering from your gifting bag to the flames. This can be anything from a found item of wood to a nub of incense or a written note about something you no longer wish to hold on to.

SPARK IS THE LIGHTNING ROD THAT FERTILISES THE SOIL OF YOUR DREAMS AND CAUSES YOUR IMAGINATION TO FLARE

UNIFICATION: BLAZE

How much magic there is afoot in these brief summer nights when no sooner does it get dark than the light seems to emerge on the Eastern horizon once again. There is a bewitching alchemy that pervades the very air we breathe in this transitional time of the Summer Solstice, which is palpable; spend some time out in the woods at night in June and you'll feel it too. It's like your own personal version of *A Midsummer Night's Dream* where fairies mischievously create disorder from order and things seem to vanish and reappear before your very eyes! This is how Blaze moves amongst us.

The energies of Above and Below have merged in your Heart Centre, the hub of your unique Soulistic Wheel, and created the archetypal energy called Blaze. Blaze takes the volatile energies of its parents and transforms it into the very stuff that miracles are made of. The old term, 'blazing a trail' comes from this archetype: you can literally make things happen as if by magic if you deepen into the energetic quality that surrounds you at this time. But blazing a trail is akin to a comet sparking through the night sky. The energy is quite fleeting, and you may miss it altogether, so be prepared for it, look out for it. Its emanation is in inspired action, epiphany, creative expression and synchronicity.

Now that you have leapt off the cliff into the sea of possibility, and you have been ignited by the spark of imagination, you can blaze a trail blessed by this forward momentum. Blaze carries you in its wake once you have said 'yes' to the adventure of your life and harnessed the power of courage – it literally 'blazes the way'. Blaze takes your hand and leads you forward in the dance of inspired action.

The Mystery of this time is what may be holding you back from blazing your trail? What do you need to let go of so that you can take action? There is great liberation in the combined wisdom of Leap, Spark and Blaze; but you can also get your fingers burned, or at least, get very hot under the collar if you repress the energy or divert it into old patterns of behaviour that you know no longer serve your Soul Purpose. The choice is yours.

Come to your altar, or to a favoured place in Nature if you prefer, and contemplate all the people you have known who have 'blazed their trail' – and if you don't know anyone personally, there are plenty of people in the public eye who have done so. What qualities do you admire in them? What is the common factor that underpins their journey? Ponder on these questions, for they may open a door for you that leads to great fulfilment.

JUNE PRACTICES

SIT SPOT

THERE IS A CLOUD FLOATING IN THIS SHEET OF PAPER...

June is such a glorious month; it has the longest, warmest days of the year, wildflowers are in full bloom and the air is heady with their scent and that of newly-mown grass – and sun cream! June is a time when memories are made, for there is something in the kinetic energy of these magical days that stays in our subconscious, so that in the middle of Winter, a scent or a sound or a glimpse of the sun can take is right back to June.

In order to make memories of any sort, a different kind of focus is required which is one of 'being relaxed in the moment' – because it is only then that you truly notice the world going on around you and deepen your experience of it. This practice facilitates just that; it is one of the best and perhaps my (Lorna's) favourite of all the practices we advocate in this book: finding your Sit Spot.

TO MAKE MEMORIES OF ANY SORT, A DIFFERENT KIND OF FOCUS IS REQUIRED – ONE OF BEING 'RELAXED IN THE MOMENT'

TRANSFORM
FORM THE
MUNDANE TO
THE MAGICAL

Your Sit Spot can be in your local park, in your garden, by a river, in a woodland, in a meadow, overlooking the ocean – but it should be outdoors, not in a building. It is an opportunity to reconnect with the other-than-human world, as well as reconnecting with yourself. All you need to do is sit in your Sit Spot. But, the key to this practice of transforming from the mundane to the magical is to repeat it at the same time every day for a week or more, if possible. If you do this, what happens is astounding.

When you first approach your chosen Sit Spot, do so with mindfulness and reverence. You are coming into another being's home territory, albeit an ant, a pink campion, a bullfinch, an oak seedling, a stoat, or a centipede. Be slow and gentle in your movements, assuring all beings that you come in peace. This is important, and you can even say it out loud – "I come in peace" – because it will set the tone for your visit. Then sit. Sit for at least 15 minutes and observe what is going on around you, and what is going on within you.

Notice how your breathing changes after a while, how it deepens and slows; notice the external sounds, smells and breezes. Sit still and be quiet. After about 15 minutes of doing this, the natural world seems to accept that you are not 'the enemy' and it begins to carry on its business as if you are not there. A robin may alight on your foot; a bumble bee will come close to sip the nectar from summer blossoms, a fish may jump for a flying insect if you're near water… Observe.

Observe too how you are feeling. Is your mind still busy with thoughts of work emails and the like, or is your mind now as loosely relaxed as the world around you? For this is the key: other beings in Nature are not stressed (unless they are forced into chaos by external influences like a flood or drought). Does the bee seem anxious to you? Does the goldfinch on the thistledown appear stressed-out and deep in thought? No. Creatures have this incredible ability to live in the moment – and in reality, that is all there is: the past has gone, the future hasn't happened yet, there is only this moment, and this one… So, be like the bee or the goldfinch and relax into this moment.

After a few days of going to your Sit Spot, you will find that relaxing into this moment becomes easier; and you will find, too, that your creature friends don't mind you being there at all. They accept you as you are, and their lives encompass yours. One day, you may like to approach your Sit Spot as if you are an ant: see how tall the grass is, how the dandelions look like giant satellite dishes orienting to the sun; see how ant perspective makes the world far bigger, and how living in one square meter offers a lifetime of adventure. Then one day, approach your Sit Spot as if you are a bird. Imagine yourself flitting from branch to branch or flying overhead – how different your Sit Spot looks now! From a birds-eye view, your Sit Spot is nestled into a wider ecosystem where every single being is interconnected; from a birds-eye view, your Sit Spot is cradled by the undulating soil and tree roots, which themselves are nestled into the rock strata, the river and the four winds. Then another day, come to your Sit Spot as if you are a badger or fox. What lays beneath the ground, and where does that trail of flattened grasses lead?

As you become more and more curious about this place, which when you first arrived seemed only three-dimensional, you will see that it is infinite, multi-dimensional, interconnected and abundant. As Chickasaw poet and writer, Linda Hogan[36] has explored in her books, you are now using your 'vocabulary of the senses'. What do other-than-human beings say to you? What is their vocabulary?

Your Sit Spot is truly wondrous and you will see it anew every time you visit: the hues of greens and golds at various times of the day will intoxicate you; the sounds will enchant you; your mind will become timeless and transcendent – you are ant, fox, badger, bluebell, web-spinning spider. You 'inter-are' with all that is, your Sit Spot reconnects you with the Cosmos.

Here, the venerable Buddhist teacher, Thich Nhat Hanh explains the concept of Interbeing[37]: "If you are a poet, you will see clearly that there is a cloud floating in this sheet of paper. Without a cloud, there will be no rain; without rain, the trees cannot grow; and without trees, we cannot make paper. The cloud is essential for the paper to exist. If the cloud is not here, the sheet of paper cannot be here either. So, we can say that the cloud and the paper inter-are."

IN YOUR SIT SPOT YOU USE THE 'VOCABULARY OF THE SENSES'

If you are able to see the cloud floating in this piece of paper before you, then you have grasped the concept of Interbeing, and when you go to your Sit Spot, the magical realm of Interbeing unfolds before you. It changes you forever, because herein lies one of the greatest lessons humanity needs to learn: 'What we do to the Earth, we do to ourselves.' Therefore, if you treat the Earth and all her beings kindly, you are treating yourself kindly too.

With kindness, love and compassion we can live lightly on this Earth.

IF YOU TREAT
THE EARTH
AND ALL
HER BEINGS
KINDLY, YOU
ARE TREATING
YOURSELF
KINDLY TOO

THE SACRED ART OF PLAY

"YOUR IMAGINATION IS THE PRELUDE TO LIFE'S FUTURE EVENTS." – EINSTEIN

You are at your most potent when you are playing: playing with opportunities; playing with the unknown; playing with potential. The art of play opens up new areas in your brain and nervous system. You naturally relax and stop assuming (or pretending) that you 'know' everything …or anything. You enter into the mystery of life and 'see what happens' when you try new things and use your imagination.

The sacred art of play is intrinsic to your Soulistic practice because it is a relatively safe and innocuous way of bringing yourself out of comfort zones and into the fertile territory of creation. Whether the door into this is through your children or you own inner child, it is essential that as 'adults' we un-learn our seriousness and start to engage with joy as a major factor in our physical, mental, emotional and spiritual practice.

Play has several distinguishing elements that you can consciously create in short bursts, allowing you to find the 'juice' in any learning edge that you might be undertaking. I (Genevieve), at the time of writing this, am learning how to meditate again in ways that give me direct access to the streams of universal wisdom that I am seeking (many of which we have woven through this book!) My practice here is one fundamentally based on play and as such, has a few key elements that I want to share with you.

UNLEARN AND UNRAVEL THAT WHICH YOU THINK YOU KNOW

In order to truly play without boundaries, all your habits and barriers that prevent new exploration must be unravelled. I have had to untie all my preconceptions (of which there are many) regarding what a 'good' meditation practice looks and feels like in order to find my own practice that leads me deeper at this stage of my life. The practice I developed in my twenties is no longer applicable and yet I found that I was beating myself up for not being as consistent as I once was, even though the entire shape of my life has altered irrevocably! The trick here is to consciously let go of anything and everything that no longer fits, even if you don't know what will take its place. After all, in play, we rarely have an outcome in mind when we begin.

ENGAGE YOUR IMAGINATION AND THEN LET IT LOOSE!

As Einstein is credited with saying, "Your imagination is the prelude to life's future events." Your imagination is a super-power. One that you may only be using at half speed. Your imagination is the doorway into the mythic, arche-typal, mystical realms and allows you to move beyond the stories that keep you chained to your current life and identity, into unchartered waters where anything can (and often does) happen.

My imagination is turning-up all manner of insights and epiphanies in my new meditation practice that now naturally fits with my current lifestyle and future vision. It has led me into new areas of esoteric study and tantric wisdom and has forged new connections and friendships with the other than human realm – none of which would be possible without a fully-functioning imagination.

YOU ARE AT
YOUR MOST
POTENT WHEN
YOU ARE
PLAYING

FOLLOW YOUR JOY INCESSANTLY

It's an ancient and almost clichéd saying to 'Follow your joy' but boy, is it powerful! When was the last time you did something just for the joy of it? I woke up a few days ago with emails aplenty, a 'To Do' list longer than a page of A4 and multiple people all asking for my attention on the various apps (too many) on my smartphone. Yet, instead of engaging in what I 'should' have done to please others, I made myself a blissful cup of cacao and went to my copper meditation pyramid to rest. Why? Because I wanted to. Because it felt rejuvenating. And because I knew that if I started on other things, I would miss the joy of being quiet and contemplative first thing in the morning when my energy is at its best. I did it for the simple joy of having freedom of choice. Joy is the rocket fuel that charges play and transformation. Find yours, follow it and then play in the field that it creates.

'FOLLOW YOUR JOY' – BOY, IS IT POWERFUL!

Our recommendation is that you connect to your inner child (and inner mischief maker) and engage in potent play as often as you can this month and beyond. The more the better. Of course, there are ways of making any task or job 'playful' and then again, sometimes you just have to throw schedules and targets to the wind and run off into the woods for the day. Perhaps that time is now…?

JUNE STORYHACK

GENEVIEVE GUIDES YOU IN THE GENTLE ART OF
RESTORYING YOUR LIFE...

STORIES FROM THE SOUL

OUR WHOLE EXPERIENCE ON EARTH
IS JUST A SERIES OF STORIES

One of the basic cognitive patterns we learn from the moment we are born is how to make meaning of the things that happen in our lives. 'This' object held in front of my nose by my mother means 'that' to me. This colour is called 'yellow'. This animal either means 'love' or 'fear', depending on my culture, my family's beliefs and my personal preferences. Our human software is programmed by our families, our culture and the rules of the society in which we live.

Our human ability to 'make meaning' from the things that surround us and happen in our lives has led to language, art, social structures, political systems, trade... the list goes on and on and yet, where do these 'meanings' come from? Who decides which person's meaning is better than another's? Let's face it, wars are fought over whose meaning beats whose, to this day. We could even look at this from a level higher and say that all human systems of belief on the planet are really just a form of 'story'. By story, I'm referring to an understanding – a meaning – that someone or a group of people have formulated and agreed upon at any one time, to explain something that they saw or experienced. So, from this perspective, the whole of our human experience on Earth is just a series of... stories.

What is the dictionary definition of a 'story'? *'An account or recital of an event or a series of events, either true or fictitious'*. Or the dictionary also states that

**WHY IS IT
THAT SO
MANY OF
US ACCEPT
CULTURAL
STORIES AS
TRUTH?**

a story is, *'An anecdote'*. It goes further to say a story can also be, *'A lie'*. So, if stories can be either someone's 'anecdote' or 'opinion' or even someone's outright 'lie', why is it that so many of us accept these cultural stories as 'truth'?

This leads me to my next question which is, *'What is truth?'* In (very) simple terms, new physics tells us that whatever stories we believe with enough conviction, work in alignment with the particles in the Universe to create the experiences we end up having in our lives. That becomes our truth. Therefore, if we believe that the world is a good place then we will generally experience it as good. The reverse is also true in that if we fear that the world is bad, then guess what? Bad things happen.

So, all of this got me musing… When the first person made the first meaningful story, did it come from their mind? Their heart? Or from a place beyond them? I know that when something feels meaningful to me, it seems to come from beyond my conscious mind. When my intuition is in play, I don't formulate thoughts, I just 'know' yet a part of me is 'observing' this intuitive process, smiling when I connect the dots. This deep inner knowing comes from beyond the human stories I tell myself; it is a voice that is me and not me, connected to a vast web of knowing.

I believe my human storyteller works within the imaginal realm of the soul which in itself is a facet of me that watches, guides and loves unconditionally as my storyteller makes things up and then sees what happens as they unfold into reality. My soul is the part of me that holds the silence that I reach when I finally get my mind to shut up in meditation or yoga. It is the all-seeing part of me that is beyond even the 'knowing' of my intuition.

Lately I have begun to dive even deeper; I have been considering the question: 'Which part of 'me' do I want to put in charge of creating my stories?' And, 'What would happen if the human storyteller suddenly started taking its direction from the muse of my soul instead of the programming I received as a socialised human child?' Well, I can tell you, I have tried this, and things certainly got interesting when I gave over control of my life to my soul! Things happened that my human mind very much did not expect.

With my soul in conscious control I suddenly found that:

- Everything I thought was important, suddenly was not

- The things that I assumed were giving me security were shown to be paper thin and even complete and utter illusions

- All my well laid plans? Down the toilet!

- All thoughts of even making plans? Down the toilet!

- All my old fears and stories based on lack and separation began to clear

- That deep space of quiet, potential and love became more and more present and then always present

- My connection to all of life and the deep joy that comes with simply realising that I am alive, became the very source of my daily consciousness

- My ability to function in the normal world was actually enhanced as it started to come from a deep place of 'soul-being', not conscious human story-led 'doing'

- My real purpose on this Earth rocketed into my awareness – to be me! Me, in all my glory, all my madness, all my beauty. Me. It's that simple.

So, what stories am I now creating from my soul? Well, the truth is that some of my life narratives are still beyond my conscious awareness, but I spend each day simply flowing with whatever creates joy in my life; whatever gives me peace inside and allows me to help those around me in accessing the same for themselves. This doesn't mean that I have retreated from the world and am now meditating on a mountainside. Far from it. In fact, today, I even spent an hour cleaning up a washing machine-related tsunami in our utility room with a smile on my face and giggling at the 'story' I would tell about it later. I have found joy in the small challenges of life. I have found a deep cosmic sense of humour.

Things have become so much more fun, and light. I play with every moment and every person I come into contact with. Most importantly, I am playful with myself. I know that from this place, I really can 'have it all' and yet most of the 'all' is no longer important to me. What has become important are the stories I accept, the stories I tell and the stories I enact in my life. My soul muse guides these; guides me from a place beyond stories. Beyond human meanings. A place of love, full of the joy of being alive as a privileged human on the planet at this time of change.

What I choose to create from here on in and whom I choose as the actors in my human story will largely depend on whether they can co-create with me, so that joy, love and peace suffuse the world. It is a cause greater than my human self.

YOU CAN
CHOOSE TO
RECREATE
YOUR STORIES

Ask yourself, what are your stories? Where do they come from? Do they give you and those around you joy and love? You can choose to recreate your stories – go ahead; give it a try. Dance and play with your soul muse.

JULY

THE GREAT TURNING HAS BEGUN
BRINGING A QUALITY OF EASE AND JOY

THE GREAT
TURNING HAS
BEGUN

JULY EARTH SIGNS

In July there is a turning point. Growth is approaching its peak until a threshold is reached where the growing slowly subsides and the maturation begins. The change is imperceptible, just as the diminishing light is, but change is happening, nonetheless. The great turning has begun. In July, the cuckoo flies away.

Summer blossom is abundant at this time and the world is awash with colour, yet even so, the first signs of maturing and mellowing appear as fruit begins to form from the blossom and slowly ripens. Raspberries and blackcurrants are so abundant they fall to the Earth where even the blackbird cannot feast upon them all. The embryonic plums begin to fatten, and the bean pods lengthen. Towards the end of the month, we can see how the hedgerow flowers of sloe and blackberry have transformed into tiny jewels of fruitful promise, and the floriferous honeysuckle perfumes the night air so sensuously that moths and humans alike swoon in its delightfulness. Nature's abundance is glorious to behold.

There is a quality of ease in July – all the busyness of Spring and early Summer now gives way to maturing, ripening and mellowing, a process that is informed by the warmth of the sun and the gentle summer rains. What a lovely time of year. There is not much to do except watch and wonder at the magnificence of maturation, at the transformations that are taking place in front of your eyes as flowers become fruit, as tadpoles become frogs, as choppy seas become millpond calm. July is joyful. Relax in its charms and enjoy the maturation of your own intentions.

JULY COSMOLOGICAL SIGNS

CANCER TO LEO

I NURTURE

Having gathered valuable information from your 'month of mind', you can – if you are able to maintain your sacred perspective – harvest your learning and weave together a new way of thinking, feeling and acting from a place of soul nurturing.

Make time and space to do your deep inner work and engage in the activities and studies that replenish your energy and your emotional bank account. It is possible to conquer your 'people pleaser' archetype stage by stage, by speaking loving truths to those around you and setting new boundaries around your own evolving being.

This is the time to tend all your loving and mutually beneficial relationships with the human, other-than-human and cosmic realms, thereby expanding your stories of what you come to know as family.

MAKE TIME
AND SPACE TO
DO YOUR DEEP
INNER WORK

Joyful Moon

– a time when the activities of Spring and early Summer culminate, and a slow maturing towards fruition begins. Life takes on a timeless quality as Nature's transformation cannot be rushed. An air of ease abounds, indeed, 'the living is easy'. It is time to relax and enjoy this bounteous season.

JULY SOULISTIC ARCHETYPES

SOLAR ARCHETYPE: FREQUENCY

Your journey through the Southern Quadrant of the Soulistic Wheel is coming to its culmination. As you walk your path of adventure, you are likely to feel 'in sync' with the pulsing Universal rhythm of life; a Frequency that is your birthright and can be heard in the beat of a heart, the breathing of a loved one, the ceaseless tides... As you journey, does your Frequency feel aligned to that of the natural world – do you notice what is happening around you and does it confer its wisdom to you? Or do you feel out-of-step, always in a rush to catch up, constantly on the back foot? If this is the case, now is the time to down-tools and rest. Take a holiday from everything, including your Soulistic Journey, and relax. Take a breather, don't try so hard.

It sounds easy, but going with the flow does take practice, and the flow itself is a type of Frequency: sometimes it ebbs, and sometimes it is in full spate. Often, if you feel out of step with everything it is because you're actually wading upstream, going in a direction that creates logjams and barriers, and that way, life becomes difficult. John Lennon wrote a wonderful song called Tomorrow Never Knows, in which he suggests you, 'Turn off your mind, relax and float downstream…' Give it a go and see if, by going with the flow rather than against it, you can tune in to your own subtle energetic Frequencies.

Frequency is a fractal pattern that pervades the Universe and connects the microcosmic molecular realms with the macrocosmic interplanetary realms. Fractals are sacred geometric patterns that are fundamental to all life. For example, the helical form of your DNA also reflects in the spirals of galaxies. In this way, you can see your incontrovertible connectedness with all that is, and take solace in the fact that you are truly one with creation.

Frequency is powerful yet subtle, an energetic quality that supports the entraining of molecules in the sacred harmonics of life and death, which can be seen to greatest effect in the fluid changing of the seasons or the circadian rhythms of night and day. But death is not to be feared, for Frequency always brings rebirth: as day follows night or Spring follows Winter. Frequency is the great connector, the great weaver of notes into the symphony of creation, and if you are able to switch off your mind and relax into your body, you can feel life pulsing through you, and you can see it pulsing through the natural world, too. Know that you are kin.

So, Frequency's gift is to show us how to listen to the different pulsing energies of every being on Earth; it speaks in a language beyond words, a language of knowing and trusting, a heartfelt at-oneness that sings you awake at dawn, ready for a new day.

It's time to switch off your mind, relax and float downstream. Literally, in a boat if you can. There is nothing quite like floating on water – it is the most joyful thing. So, see if you can find a boat of some kind – even a lilo on a swimming-pool will do – and 'float downstream…'

LUNAR ARCHETYPE: BLOSSOM

In observing the exquisite abundance of Summer, you may have noticed that the natural world has perfect timing: swallows know when to return in Spring, blossom knows when to unfurl in Summer, fruit knows when to ripen in Autumn. It is no coincidence that the verb 'to blossom' is synonymous with success, perfect timing and thriving! You may also have noticed that you are blossoming too. That is because the conditions are ripe and potent for the maturation of the intentions you set, earlier in your Soulistic Journey.

How is your own personal blossoming showing up in the world right now? Are you fulfilling a long-held dream? Has your new business started to take off? Have you rekindled a relationship you thought had died? Or are you beset by judgment and self-deprecation where you cannot see the point of anything and where you find no joy in your journey? Mystery invites you to look honestly at yourself and ask why you struggle to see the beauty in the world.

Sometimes, when you see another person blossoming, able to manifest all that they intend, seemingly able to make all things come into being in multiple facets of their life, it can make you feel as if you're a victim to fortune, and that life has not been fair to you. But remember that Blossom is about timing. Wisdom invites you to consider whether your blossoming is just taking its own sweet time; whether, in fact, you are on the cusp of unfurling. Can you take comfort in that? Rest assured that when the time is ripe, Blossom will open her loving arms and welcome you into the erotic dance of plenty. She will flaunt her full, voluptuous exquisite form, tempting you to forget all your inhibitions, your self-doubt and judgement, and do the same. Are you ready to dance your intentions into fullness, so that they can flourish, prosper and mature?

Blossom is the true celebration of Summer – how can it be otherwise? Look as she waves her flags of colour, inviting you to behold her gorgeousness. Blossom is the physical emanation of Earth's everlasting generosity. She is the high noon sun and the blessed full moon. She is all. When you look at her beauty, you rise in love for yourself, because you know in your heart that we are all one, rooted in the same Divine heritage; we are the multidimensional Blossoms of life.

Go out into the garden and pick yourself a bunch of Summer flowers. If you don't have a garden, treat yourself to a bouquet of flowers from a florist – if possible, ones that have scent. Revel in the sheer beauty of each form; the shape, the colour, the smell, the leaves, the overall effect. Can you see Heaven in a [wild] flower, to paraphrase William Blake?

BLOSSOM IS
THE PHYSICAL
EMANATION
OF EARTH'S
EVERLASTING
GENEROSITY

UNIFICATION: ECSTASY

Frequency and Blossom merge in your Heart Centre, the hub of your unique Soulistic Wheel, and create the exquisite archetype of Ecstasy. Ecstasy is such a powerful energy because it reminds you that anything and everything in your wildest imaginings is possible, if you have the courage to dream beyond the doors of perception.

Dreaming beyond the doors of perception is about engaging your imagination in all that you do. Imagination is playful and boundless, pleasurable and creative – but if you are experiencing shadow, it can also be horrifying and scary. You have a choice to step into the light if that is the case for you – you can relinquish the shadows and swim towards glittering enlightenment, but that must be your chosen trajectory.

Imagination allows you to think outside the box and 'download' new ideas into being. Imagine the Ecstasy of creation on that level! Imagine what is possible if you truly believe in it – and that is all you have to do – believe. There's an old saying: 'seeing is believing' – but in fact, the opposite is true: 'believing is seeing'. You have to truly believe in yourself to see the fruits of your labours, and in that moment, Ecstasy is yours, because you are fulfilled. Allowing yourself to experience true Ecstasy is freedom incarnate. Ecstasy liberates on every level.

Ecstasy dances us out of the cage of our habitual 'rights and wrongs' and into the imagination. It is a space where we can be spontaneously mischievous and endlessly inventive – for this archetype leads us to the 'other-than-human' realms where we can commune with the fairies and the fireflies, the dragons and the devas, the angels and the animals. Ecstasy encourages you to frolic with the hidden ones and stop being so serious!

How about a bit of frolicking? How about letting your hair down in whatever way you enjoy most? You may not have done so for a while, so give yourself permission and get out of your head and into Ecstasy. Trance-dancing is a great way to do this, as is music-making or singing. Festivals are held in the Summer for this very reason, so get yourself off to a festival or a gathering of like-minded souls and explore the multidimensional nature of your true being.

JULY PRACTICES

WILD SWIMMING

FEAR IS SIMPLY A PART OF THE INITIATION

As Summer sinks into our hearts and bones and the plant kingdom struts its stuff, we approach the time of glorious abundance and playful gratitude. In the warm days of July, there can be no more exhilarating a practice than that of wild swimming[38]. Beings of form have been doing it for millennia and it truly is one of the most liberating of all the practices we offer in this book.

Ever since I (Genevieve) first swam naked in the warm Mediterranean ocean in my teens, I have been a firm advocate of wild swimming whenever and wherever possible. Wild waters such as the ocean, a river, a lake or a cold mountain stream are living energetic beings. They have an essence, a spirit and a consciousness that requires respect and prayerfulness if you are to fully benefit from their healing powers.

A few days ago, my friend Donna and I decided to get up early on a warm, balmy day and walk down to Swallowhead Springs in Wiltshire where we live.

ECSTASY DANCES US OUT OF THE CAGE OF OUR HABITUAL 'RIGHTS AND WRONGS' AND INTO THE IMAGINATION

Swallowhead is special in that it is the confluence of two underground springs that flow into the powerful and sacred Avebury landscape. Not only do these waters weave around the Michael and Mary ley lines but they wind their way into the seasonal Kennet river that flows around Silbury Hill and onwards across the land, passing close to Avebury Stone Circle itself.

Swallowhead Springs are guarded by a powerful Grandmother Willow tree and over the years has had many passing souls stop, say their prayers and pay their respects. We arrived to see both the Springs in full flow (rare for this time of year as the waters dry up as Summer progresses), and my breath caught in my throat as I beheld the beauty of all that resides there.

THE 'OTHER-THAN-HUMAN' WORLD IS PATIENTLY WAITING TO BE ACKNOWLEDGED BY US IN ORDER THAT WE MAY LOVE EACH OTHER FULLY

Picking our way down the sodden, nettle-filled slope, we arrived and made our way through the mud and water plants to the source of both the Spring heads. Carefully offering a 'prayer mix' from my gifting bag (my own alchemical concoction of tobacco, flowers and charred earth) to show reverence to the spirits of the waters, I was joined by a multitude of fae, elementals and plant spirits. I felt joy well up through my spine and knew we were being welcomed.

Making my way back to Grandmother Willow herself, I laid some more prayer mix in a hollow in her trunk and hugged her in gratitude. She returned my embrace and I distinctly felt the winged arms of her long, trailing branches wrap around me in etheric form. The 'other-than-human' world is patiently waiting to be acknowledged by us in order that we may love each other fully.

Taking a seat with Donna, back to back on the stones that span the flowing waters, we tuned-in to the energy of the morning. It was exquisite; definitely the quintessence of the Garden of Eden. As I opened my eyes, I saw a fresh clump of watercress that had separated from a colony further upstream, was flowing with the current towards us. The fae told me that it was a gift. Plucking it like a precious jewel from the clear waters, I looked at Donna in childlike awe and picked a glistening leaf for each of us to eat. It was like nectar of the gods, as only wild, fresh foods, eaten as they are gifted from Earth Mother are; the flavour powerful and yet subtle. After eating a leaf each, I placed the clump, roots intact, back in the current of the Spring waters to flow towards its eventual resting place, where it would root and grow into a whole new community. Thus, is the nature of abundant life on Earth. When we are gifted and take only that which we need, the rest flows on to nurture others in our Gaian community.

Then I was overtaken by the urge to immerse myself in the waters. Yes, the water was cold, yes people might see me naked as I hadn't brought any swim-suit or towel, but as soon as the urge took me, I knew I would surrender to it. The siren call of the water was too much on this gloriously sun-drenched, magical morning.

Looking at Donna, she knew what I was thinking before I said it and started laughing, offering to hold my clothes as I stripped them off. Tentatively, I made my way into the centre of the flowing waters which were bitingly cold but more refreshing than anything else could be in that moment. I worked up my courage and then dunked myself down, submersing myself in the healing water to the delight of the water fairies and Donna's dog Mylo, who joined me. The cold made me gasp as I came back up. My naked skin instantly warmed in the sunshine, but the alchemy of the elements far outstripped any fear of being seen by other humans. I felt clean from the inside out and blessed by the Earth herself. It was like a baptism in Nature.

After playing in the water with the dog and fairy kingdom for a while longer, I finally pulled myself away and, drying myself on my t-shirt, managed to get back into my clothes without too much mud being transferred to them in the process.

We invite you to enjoy the liberating bliss of wild swimming, which can be done anywhere there is a safe body of water to do so. In fact, there are apps and social media groups dedicated to this practice. It requires that you engage your sense of adventure and of courage to immerse yourself in cold waters – and of course a willingness to engage with the intense feeling of bliss once you have done so. Be reverent, show respect and acknowledge the spirit of whatever water you decide to get to know. Then enjoy every moment and know that fear is simply a part of the initiation of wild swimming!

EVERYTHING
IS MEDICINE

THE MEDICINE WALK

SEEING WITH MYTHIC EYES

I (Lorna) first came across the phrase, 'Everything is medicine', in a thought-provoking book, *Sacred Science*[39], by Nick Polizzi. 'Everything is medicine' is a precept at the heart of shamanic healing; in essence it means that everything you encounter in life has exactly the right meaning and healing that you need on your spiritual journey at that moment in time. The medicine is administered by your ability to see the symbolic roots of what you experience.

This can be hard to comprehend, especially for those who are living with a life-threatening disease, or who are going through a relationship break-up, or who are unemployed or grieving. How can any of these things contain within them any healing energy? The answer is in your attitude to what you encounter in life. Every facet of your journey contains a 'shadow' (or mystery) and a 'gift' (or wisdom) – it is up to you to discern these aspects and to embody the medicine they offer. I can speak from personal experience here, having been diagnosed with breast cancer twice in the last 15 years.

Cancer is a scary word that we immediately link to pain, suffering and death – these are the shadow aspects of cancer and they can be a gruelling learning curve; but cancer also gives us the opportunity to encounter some incredible gifts. When I was having chemotherapy, I received a get-well card from someone called Linda. I couldn't think of anyone I knew called Linda. I racked my brains for a long time, then it dawned on me that it must be Linda from the Post Office, a woman I chatted to when I had to send off parcels of magazines, but whom I didn't feel I knew that well. I understood at that moment that many more people cared about me than I realised – I felt unconditionally loved, and that was very healing medicine.

This was one of the many gifts of my cancer experience – unconditional love – but there will be people reading this who recoil from such a statement. How can cancer offer any gifts? That's okay, because everything is medicine. Even a strong opinion or judgment is medicine, if you choose to contemplate why you feel that way.

Before I was diagnosed with cancer, my younger sister Clair, passed away from the same disease. She was only 33 and had two young children. At the time, it was a massive tragedy and our family grieved for years over her loss. But, for me, two gifts arose from the shadow of her death. The first was that my mother spoke openly to me about her feeling that Clair had *chosen* to come into her bodily incarnation to experience certain aspects of her own journey; that she intuitively knew her destiny and chose it anyway. In speaking candidly about this, Mum opened the door for me to be able to speak about Clair's death and how it affected me; and as I did so, I became less afraid of my own death and really quite interested in our cultural fear of death – death as failure – despite the fact that we will all experience it.

The second gift came when my father passed away from cancer, quite recently. His death was incredible, not least because of the dignified and fearless way that he surrendered to it, having healed on many levels from the medicine of Clair's passing.

Everything really is medicine if you choose to dive into the mystery and wisdom of the experience – if you choose not to go there, the window of opportunity will close to you, but another will present itself, again and again, until the lesson is learned. It is up to you how long that takes. So, this practice, The Medicine Walk, offers the opportunity for you to see things in a different way – to see with mythic eyes. Seeing with mythic eyes is about looking for the deeper mythic or symbolic aspects of that which you encounter.

Go for a walk and be open and observant as you do so. What do you encounter on your way? If you bump into a neighbour who is moaning about something, can you practice compassion in your response rather than irritation? Perhaps your medicine is about being compassionate towards yourself too? If you see a sign in a shop that catches your eye, stop and pay attention. Why were you

A STRONG
OPINION OR
JUDGMENT
IS MEDICINE
IF YOU
CHOOSE TO
CONTEMPLATE
WHY YOU FEEL
THAT WAY

drawn to it, and what could open up for you if you took action? If you see a cat curled up in the sunshine and you feel a surge of emotion in your heart, ask yourself why? Are you feeling unloved? Do you need to rest in the sunshine – or are you just missing your beloved cat and have an urge to connect with an animal familiar again? If on your Medicine Walk you encounter nothing of interest whatsoever, what does that say to you?

You see, everything really is medicine!

JULY STORYHACK

GENEVIEVE GUIDES YOU IN THE GENTLE ART OF RESTORYING YOUR LIFE...

TRUST THE 'IS-NESS'

THE WORD 'MIGHT' IS MY VERBAL HINT THAT I AM MAKING UP A STORY

I woke up one morning, sweating and racked with anxiety. I had been having bad dreams. Different dreams all night long that all had a common connecting factor: they were laced with the emotion of fear. Fear of losing the people I loved; fear of not stepping up in my career and fulfilling my true purpose; fear of physical harm coming to myself in a variety of forms. Dream after dream had hit me via my unconscious mind and I woke up feeling like I had been beaten with clubs all night – rather than the truth, which was that I had been sleeping in a soft king size bed with my loving partner.

Breathing deeply for a few moments, I managed to calm my racing heartbeat and slowly acclimatise to my surroundings. I gradually saw the truth once more that none of the things that I had dreamed of were actually happening (at least not in this dimension of the Universe); that I was physically safe and healthy and that I still had freewill and a choice in how I would be showing up in the world today. Phew! Panic over. For now.

As I was brushing my teeth later that morning, I found myself thinking about how often as human beings we choose to view the events of our lives through the lens of worry and fear. Our tendency for 'story making' can create something from nothing at the drop of a hat and fashion a compelling illusory movie of our future that is so believable, we can spend hours if not days engulfed in its fury. I've lost count of the times that I had done this to myself, worrying about 'what might happen' or 'what that person might do' or 'whether I had ruined my reputation by saying something that might be misunderstood'…

The word 'might' is key. 'Might' is my verbal hint that I am making up a story. 'Might' is a subtle clue that it hasn't actually happened, otherwise it would be 'did'. It isn't happening now because if it was it would be an 'is'.

*Past – That **did** happen*

*Present – This **is** happening*

*Future – That **might** happen*

The past can also be tricky if you are in the habit of attaching a 'might' to the 'did': That **might** happen again because it **did** in the past… but as soon as 'might' enters into the fray then I know I am making something up. It's an interesting exercise to start to notice the language with which you narrate your life.

Now, there is nothing inherently wrong with making things up. In fact, as a storyteller by nature and calling, I believe that this ability is one of our most powerful tools as a human being in manifesting change and progress within our lives – suffice it to say that I believe our ability to create stories is our ability to create life.

The important thing that clarified this for me, as I spat my toothpaste into the sink, is that it is crucial where my story is created from. When we create our future 'might,' from a place of worry and fear, then we energise the story to unfold within that mindset and emotional vibration. However, when we run exactly the same story-making process from a different place, say one of love, humour and trust, then our future 'mights' manifest in a very different way.

I want to say a few words here on trust. For me, trust is a process of letting go. Of relinquishing any human 'control' I might want to have over a situation in favour of a higher purpose or common good for all. Trust expands for me in three nested circles; all of them having various flavours and shades in the way they are experienced and seen:

- ❈ **Personal Trust** – trust in myself, my own integrity, my honesty (to myself and others) and my ability to roll with the punches and deal with pretty much any life challenge or lesson that comes my way.

- ❈ **Collective Trust** – trust in others, and in the basic goodness of most human beings. Trust in the common good, shared human values and ethics like love, respect and service. Trust of those in my life (human and non-human) and that what I put out to them I receive back in return: karmic relating. Trust in the power of Love.

- ❈ **Universal Trust** – faith in a universal consciousness and energy that is far greater than my human brain can comprehend; yet my human heart can sense. Trust that I will always be spiritually safe no matter what the external circumstances. Trust that I am an eternal soul in human form and that I am here to experience life in all its forms.

Just thinking about the different forms of trust immediately helped me to see my disturbing dreams of the night before from a new place, and more

START TO
NOTICE THE
LANGUAGE
WITH WHICH
YOU NARRATE
YOUR LIFE

importantly to feel differently about them. The contraction in my solar plexus relaxed and I was able to smile with a wan sense of humour at the turmoil I had put myself through with my 'mights'. Trust was my deep ocean, and worry was just the waves that crashed across its surface. When I find myself drawn into their power, and rolled and tumbled by their might (see what I did there!), I just have to remember to take deep breaths and dive beneath the surface of the noisy 'worry story' into the quiet, calm depths of the bigger story of trust.

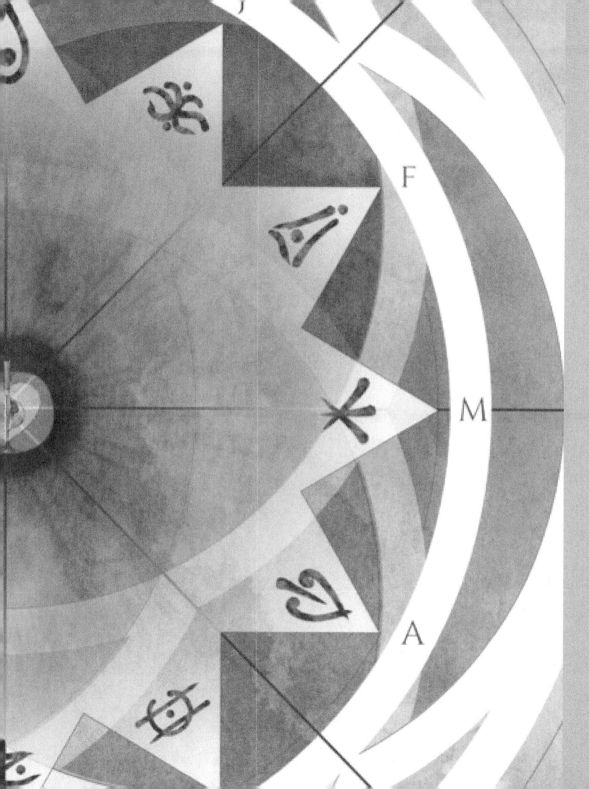

F

M

A

W
E
S
T

257

WEST QUARTER
MEDITATION

REUNION

Make yourself comfortable and breathe deeply for a minute or two until you feel still and settled. With your mind's eye, envision your Heart Centre, the sacred space within, your portal to other realms. Has anything changed since you were last here?

Once you have rested in your Heart Centre and feel comfortable, find the central point and sit or stand there. Take a deep breath and look around you; first to the East, where the element of fire resides. Feel the warmth coming from the East; the energy of the rising sun, with its potential to burn up old stories and release you from self-limiting habits. Then turn to the South, where Water is in its element. Feel the generous ease and flow that water embodies, how it can resolve any feelings of restriction, how it can wash away your fears. Then slowly turn to the West, the element of Earth. Feel how the Earth holds you and nurtures you; feel how abundant and energised Earth is. Then turn to the North, and the element of Air; feel that freshness and clarity that can instantly give you a new perspective, feel the lightness of Air and know that you can mirror that lightness in your decisions and choices.

In this Quarter, you are facing the West of Autumn, the element of Earth – the solid, life- manifesting matter of our beautiful planetary reality. This is the aspect of unity and one-ness. Welcome the blissful unifying perspective that lays in the West.

These four directions and their elements are your touchstones. Know that at any time, you can envision being in your Heart Centre and you can reconnect with these energies for sustenance. Within the directions, over and above all elements and residing in your Heart Centre is the fifth element of ether; the essence and the mystery. The all-encompassing one-ness. Ether is of this world and not of this world. It is the essential element that enables transcendence into the cosmological realm. Your Heart Centre is filled with this bridging element of ether; feel how it moves you beyond this realm.

Continue to breathe deeply and feel the magnetic pull of Earth drawing you towards the West. Envisage yourself now leaving your Heart Centre and travelling upwards into the firmament of our Universe, deep into the Cosmic realms. How freeing it is to swim among the stars, looking down on the twinkling blue jewel that is Planet Earth. Allow yourself to travel beyond the Milky Way to the edge of the Universe, where you find a doorway, a portal between our Universe and the Multiverse, the Cosmos. You are invited to slip through that doorway into the timeless, eternal realm where angels and archetypes reside.

As you move into this realm, you will see before you the familiar Cosmic medicine wheel; a mirror of the one in your Heart Centre. An archangel stands guardian of each of the four sacred directions – creating a blessed and safe space for you, a place where only the energies and guides that reflect your highest good can enter.

Come to rest in the middle of this beautiful Cosmic Temple. Notice how you feel resting here as your Universoul Self; relax in the harmonious energies that flow from all directions and anchor you gently in the centre of the wheel. Now, acknowledge the open door to the North and all the blessings that you have been gifted since you met your Mentor from this realm. Bow your head to the open door in the East and to your Mentor who beams love to you from this place. Turn to face the South and greet the Mentor who has been walking with you for the last few months – they nod in acknowledgement of all that you have realised. A flash of joy in their eyes tells you it is time to turn westwards. You move around to face the Westerly direction of the Cosmic wheel and feel benign power pulsing through the doorway. It calms and recalibrates you. You feel your ancient DNA reawakening and aligning to the Universal codes of life.

Watch as the door slowly opens and welcome whoever or whatever comes through, knowing this is a gift from your higher self. You find yourself walking towards their energy, drawn by their light, allowing yourself to be submerged in the blissful frequencies they embody. Your Mentor from the West embraces you, for you are as a child returning to the only home you have ever truly known. A symbol appears in your heart. Acknowledge it and remember it, for it will guide you through this Quarter of reunion.

This teacher will walk with you for the next three months, a guide in Unity for the reunifying quarter of Autumn. They will support you in myriad ways; in your remembering, in your questioning, in your weaving – and you can always ask them for help or guidance.

Your new mentor invites you to move up and outwards from the Cosmic Temple towards the Universal portal where you entered the archetypal realm. As one, you begin to slowly and gently traverse the heavens, back down towards your Heart Centre, and come to rest there. You greet your Mentors from the North, South and East as a unified being with your Mentor from the West.

Come back into your body now and rest in the blessings of your journey.

See page 364, Endnote 12 for links to the recorded version of this Meditation if you prefer to listen to it rather than read it.

REUNION

Reunion is all that remains
When separation falls aside.
To allow this, you must confront your demons of illusion
And embrace them.
For all is one at its core
The golden thread weaving through the many;
Diversity dancing in spirals of unity
Fractal stories stemming from source.
Now is the time to find your wholeness
To drop the masks of persona
And reveal your naked beauty
So that everyone and everything else
Becomes your sacred reflection.

And then from where we began, we come full circle once more. The ending of one story and the beginning of a whole new alchemical cycle of evolution beckons us into the void of death and life. We see everything that we cling to keeping us separate from the Cosmos and we are invited to release it all. Will we surrender our soul to creation? Will we make the choiceless choice that eternally liberates our life? There is a part of us that knows we will, the only question that remains is, When?

Have you ever experienced reunion? Can you remember what it feels like to meet your beloved brother or mother again after years of not seeing each other? Or seeing your lover again after an enforced separation due to work or travel? It is a marvellous feeling; one that is hard to describe but it is akin to a feeling of wholeness, completeness, of true wellbeing, of love.

On your Soulistic Journey, however, the reunion we are talking about is a reconnection with your true self, your Divine Soul; how full of wonder it is to reunite with the source of your own being. This is the 'holy grail' of your journey, the holy chalice, the alchemical 'gold'. For, in coming full circle to greet yourself again at the end of one journey and the start of another, you are encompassing all that you have been, all that has brought you to this point in time; you are acknowledging that every step you have taken, whether fraught with difficulty or full of ease, has made you the wise and soulful being you are.

Reunion is about acceptance of your stories, your journey, your struggles; it is about surrender to the mystery of the dance and the unfolding spiral of your path. Reunion is about the yin and yang of your emerging self, coalescing into unity. It is a joyful state of open heartedness.

Reunion transcends the myth of separation, allowing you to see yourself – perhaps for the first time – as a facet of the holographic Universe. You are a perfect microcosm of the macrocosm. You are Divine. When you deepen into the quarter of reunion, anxieties and worries dissipate as you accept that you are exactly where you need to be at this moment in time; and what is more, you trust that you are facing in exactly the right direction for your continuing journey.

Reunion is a homecoming and a reconciliation – with yourself.

REUNION TRANSCENDS THE MYTH OF SEPARATION

AUGUST

REST IN THE GOLDEN DREAMTIME OF AUGUST
AS ALL OF NATURE RIPENS

AUGUST EARTH SIGNS

There is a pause in August when all of Nature takes a long, deep in-breath allowing the process of 'ripening' to occur. The trees sough and susurrate in the warm southerly breezes. The birds no longer sing; they are exhausted from the activities of Spring and Summer and need to moult, rest and replenish. The heat of long August afternoons drives all but the hardiest of creatures into the shadows, to find respite; a place to linger and luxuriate.

In August, the turning of the seasons becomes obvious; Earth's creatures know that the nights are lengthening and that this period of quiet precedes another bout of activity as winter preparations begin. So, in August, all but the busy bees and the even busier human beings, down tools and rest, waiting for the Autumn energies to take hold. The light becomes warm and golden, losing the brilliance of early Summer, aiding the slow ripening that is taking place. The starry nights reveal their magnificence to all who lay on the warm ground and gaze upwards in awe.

At rest in the in-between space of August, the first thud of an apple falling to the ground alerts the blackbird that feasting is about to begin. A badger finds a cluster of sweet, low-hung blackberries and knows the seasonal abundance will soon be forthcoming. The kingfisher takes a beak-full of fry to his nest knowing that soon enough, the waters will rise. All is well in the glittering dreamtime of August.

ALLOW THE
PROCESS OF
RIPENING TO
OCCUR

AUGUST COSMOLOGICAL SIGNS

LEO TO VIRGO

I SERVE (INNER)

Unlike the classic image of the male lion, proud and sovereign over his realm, the cosmological energy of this evolving archetype builds on the nurturing phase of Cancer and asks you to consider how you might best serve your soul's evolution.

So many of us are drawn away from our personal Soulistic quest by the seductions of outer world success and renown, yet often these are merely tests along the path of true adventure and commitment.

You are the centre of your Universe and as such, you are called to turn your focus inwards towards the heart of every story and experience you find yourself living. Once you are able to move away from the noise of the outer world, you can begin to 'serve yourself' by saying no, compassionately, to anything that might distract you from your quest.

CONSIDER
HOW YOU
MIGHT
BEST SERVE
YOUR SOUL'S
EVOLUTION

GOLDEN MOON

– all turns golden as the nights begin to lengthen and the sun's rays burnish the fruits of the forest. Gold is the ultimate reflection of Nature's alchemical transformations.

AUGUST SOULISTIC ARCHETYPES

SOLAR ARCHETYPE: CHOICE

Here you are in the Western Quadrant of your Soulistic Wheel. A time when all your choices over the last few months will be maturing and ripening. Now is a time to reflect on the choices you made with a discerning eye and ascertain what is working for you and what, if anything, is not. Choice is a constant state, an all-pervading archetype which accompanies you throughout your life. Sometimes your choices seem insignificant: What shall I wear today? Where shall we meet for lunch? – and sometimes they seem epic: Shall we become business partners? Do I want to stay in this relationship? Choice creates the momentum and landscape of your life.

Choice can be a trickster, who comes masked and disguised, empowering or distracting you depending on how you engage with him. Choice can present you with a confusing cornucopia of options, and it is up to you to find your truth amongst the distraction of variety; or truth can be so concealed that you think there is no Choice at all. However, once you remember your sovereign power of focus and discernment, Choice becomes your ally once again.

The key to discernment is the recognition of authenticity, which in itself is more of a feeling than an intellectual decision. Authenticity is a gut feeling about something which will always point you in the right direction. So, if you have a gut feeling about something, or if your heart feels something that your head disagrees with, it's usually wise to listen to that deeper inner instinct.

The wisdom of Choice then, is to remind you of your authentic path through the vast Cosmos and empower you to choose that which leads you on the path of your Soul Story. The good news is that nothing is ever a waste of time, and there is no such thing as a mistake or a wrong turn, only an opportunity to learn important lessons. So, your choice-making may be circuitous, but if you become adept at listening to your inner wisdom, then you will begin to discern wisely that which is healthful for you.

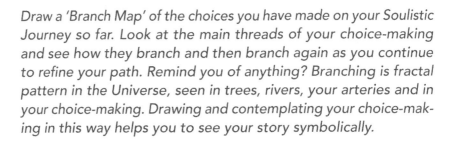

Draw a 'Branch Map' of the choices you have made on your Soulistic Journey so far. Look at the main threads of your choice-making and see how they branch and then branch again as you continue to refine your path. Remind you of anything? Branching is fractal pattern in the Universe, seen in trees, rivers, your arteries and in your choice-making. Drawing and contemplating your choice-making in this way helps you to see your story symbolically.

LUNAR ARCHETYPE: INFINITY

You are now navigating the languid waters of the Western Quadrant of your Soulistic Journey, at a time when the natural world takes a deep breath, before the busyness of Autumn. Because you are reading this, you will have committed to your Soulistic Journey in a profound and life-affirming way. You have set intentions and they express themselves through the Infinity loop that embodies timeless wisdom. The Infinity loop is the path that each intention takes: you make an intention, you follow its trajectory and flow, you dance with its frequency and balance its energies as it manifests in your life, and eventually, you arrive back at the point you started, a different person, full of wisdom and authenticity, and you understand yourself in deeper and wiser ways.

There is a beautiful poem by T S Eliot, taken from *Four Quartets: Little Gidding*[40], which perfectly encapsulates the Infinity loop. It is a long poem, so we will not quote it in full, but the extracts below, taken from verse five, perfectly express this archetype:

> What we call the beginning is often the end
> And to make an end is to make a beginning.
> . . .
> We shall not cease from exploration
> And the end of all our exploring
> Will be to arrive where we started
> And know the place for the first time.

How perfectly Eliot expresses the fact of time not being linear, as we have been taught, but cyclical and revealing. Time is infinite and Infinity is the eternal and endless loop of creation. Infinity's wisdom is that she invites us to see with mythic eyes in deep time; practices that are both enlightening and consoling. To see with mythic eyes means to look beyond what is presented to you in the moment and recognise the embodied deep meaning which is usually revealed through patterns of thought or behaviour, symbolism, intuition and contemplation.

An awareness of deep time allows you to see the Infinity loop within a given situation; deep time reveals how life always follows death and how all crises are part of an energy of transformation where creation follows destruction. Cultivating these abilities – seeing with mythic eyes in deep time, allows wisdom to prevail in all you do.

Infinity herself persists when everything else changes shape and form. She is the eternal keeper of wisdom and power, the silent space behind all things, revealing Cosmic law. When you are at the crossing-point of the infinity loop you will experience balance and integration, but the mystery of Infinity is that chaos will dissolve all temporal form so that creativity can arise once again. The wisdom of Infinity is to trust that through this dynamic energetic flux, your path arises renewed.

Infinity unites you with your Soul Purpose, as you walk the loop and turn back on yourself; this is the point where you know yourself anew, and the point at which you begin the journey again. It happens in a nanosecond, yet it is not a treadmill; it is the eternal path without destination.

When you stop, relax and breathe deeply, the scales of daily life drop from your eyes, allowing you to see more clearly the depth of your deep time story. Why not take a breather like the natural world is doing at this time? If you can, lay out in the golden August sunshine and just breathe and contemplate Infinity and

INFINITY IS
THE ETERNAL
KEEPER OF
WISDOM AND
POWER

COSMOS
ENCIRCLES
THE DIVINE
MICROCOSM
AND
MACROCOSM
OF WHICH
HUMANS ARE
THE MID-WAY
POINT

how it expresses for you.

UNIFICATION: COSMOS

The powerful archetypes of Choice and Infinity merge and give birth to all-encompassing Cosmos. Almost beyond words, Cosmos conveys the multidimensional, holographic nature of reality as we experience it. The Hubble Telescope has been able to beam us images of the Eagle Nebula in the constellation Serpens. This nebula is so-called because it looks like an eagle with its wings unfolded, yet it is thirty trillion kilometres high (one thousand times the diameter of our entire Solar System). We just cannot comprehend something that big and yet the computer image looks just like an eagle. Similarly, electron scanning microscopes have given us images of some of the smallest things in the Universe: of atoms, viruses and bacteria, which in turn remind us of bears and trees and constellations of stars. Cosmos encircles the divine microcosm and macrocosm – of which humans are the mid-way point. How mind-blowing is that!

The microcosm/macrocosm essence that is Cosmos is home to all the holographic in-form-ation necessary for biodiversity to thrive. Cosmos creates new potentialities through imagination, choosing life in alignment with the trajectory of each story. Cosmos, weaves the world around you and shows you how to do the same; a powerful ally in your journey:

> *Remember, you are a child of a miraculous Cosmos, and so you are able to reflect miracles in all you do. What is the most miraculous thing that has ever happened to you? Write a story, poem or song about it.*

AUGUST PRACTICES

STAR GAZING – COSMIC COMMUNION

COMMUNICATING WITH THE LANGUAGE OF LIGHT

Years ago, when I was travelling in Egypt for the first time (in this lifetime any-way), I (Genevieve) learned about the nature of stars. Ever since I was born, I have been fascinated by these celestial guardians of the skies. As a small child, whenever I felt lost or alone, which was often, I would look to the sky (night or day) and seek familiar constellations – or our sun, which is also a star – to bring me comfort.

I talked to the stars and they talked back to me, or so I imagined as an open-hearted child. Indeed, they would even sing. As I stared up at them, I would hear ethereal melodies streaming forth from the stars like harmonies of light, caressing me and bringing me a deep sense of home and peace.

Like many on Earth, I have always known that my soul comes from the stars, and to the stars it will return when my work is done. I thought I knew how to commune with the stars – that was until I journeyed to Egypt in 2014. On this trip sailing down the Nile, the stars started to speak to me in a whole new way. It was here that I started to dream of the stars.

During this trip, certain constellations came into my dreams at night as the boat we stayed on gently rocked with the current of the ancient Nile river. When I awoke (always before dawn with the distant call to prayer streaming forth from the mosques), I would go up on deck, wrapped in a blanket, and stare at the dawn sky. Inevitably, the constellation that I had been dreaming about would be hung in the sky, fading gently with the morning light.

MY SOUL COMES FROM THE STARS AND TO THE STARS IT WILL RETURN WHEN MY WORK IS DONE

And as it disappeared, I would commune with it for its teachings. One night, the star Aldebaran (the eye of the bull in the constellation of Taurus), dropped down from the heavens in my dream, and landed in my lap. On waking, I went up on deck with my smartphone star-map app in hand, and found that yes, Aldebaran was there, just dropping below the horizon. Aldebaran taught me of the informational flows of Cosmic law and the libraries of galactic history. By breakfast time, I was stunned by how much I had learned.

Star gazing is an ancient practice, core to humankind since our early days as a conscious species. Each of us communicates with this celestial consciousness in our own way and through the lens of our unique story. In my story lens, the stars are vast fields of Cosmic consciousness that can be dialogued with to discover the energies they hold and the lessons they teach. For me, communication comes in the forms of images and feelings instead of words and often I find myself taking days, if not weeks, to process the information that a star or a constellation has given me. Indeed, it was this type of communication that we used, when we wrote the evolved forms of the twelve zodiacal constellations in the Cosmic Signs sections of this book.

If you wish to practice this form of other-than-human communication, find a clear night when the stars can be seen, with as little light pollution as possible. A fun thing to try is wild camping or night walking without the light of a torch, so you can really come into relationship with the stars and their energies. I find it conducive to wrap up warmly and find a comfortable place to sit where I won't be tempted to move and distract myself. Once settled, I scan the night sky and see which star or star cluster repeatedly draws my attention. Once I have found the area of the sky wanting to connect with me, I get my star-map app out on my phone and see if I can identify the constellation (if I don't already know it).

Then (after putting my phone away where it won't distract me again), I relax and start to breathe deeply, focussing my outbreath towards the star(s) as a gift of connection and communion. Due to the nature of light and how it appears to the human eye, often it will seem as if the stars are breathing back to me and shimmering in their own frequency of connection.

Just like I did as a child, you may feel like tuning-in to the stars by 'singing' to them (this can be a hum, a drone or wordless harmony), then wait for the cosmic melodies to come back from them. You have to be patient (especially if you have a strong mind and ego that tells you all of this is bullshit). But after a few attempts, most people I have done this exercise with, will experience some kind of vision, feeling or sound.

Wait and engage your imagination. As you know from the foundational practices in this journey, your imagination is your primary tool of sensing beyond the human world. It is a vital instrument in speaking with our star cousins; rarely will they speak in words, so you will need to become practiced in the art of translating your own inner feelings and any impressions you receive, no matter how abstract.

There is no right or wrong way to do this so get any performance anxiety out of your head right away! You are learning to communicate with the language of light – and that is a whole new thing for most people. Breathe in the star light and make it part of your imaginal body. After all, we are all made of star dust, as Carl Sagan would say. Now you get to remember it.

BREATHE IN THE STAR LIGHT AND MAKE IT PART OF YOUR IMAGINAL BODY

DAILY ALCHEMY

HARNESS THE POWER OF CHOICE

Alchemy is more than a medieval occult practice or something to be found in children's stories such as *Harry Potter* – albeit there is a lot of truth to be found there! True alchemy is a practice of inside-out transformation, one that moves us from a sense of separation and inferiority to unity-based interconnection with all of life. Here is what I (Genevieve) have to say about alchemy in my book, *Tough Bliss*:

"Stepping fully on to the realisation and path of unity conscious-ness is a form of alchemy: the ancient art of transforming base metals to gold, or lower forms of consciousness to higher forms. For me, this alchemy is hard to put into words or a (simple) step-by-step process. Each of us experiences alchemy in our own unique way, dependent on our soul's vision, mission and story. Alchemy, for me, is the realisation of our unity with all of life and the nature of true unity dictates that there is nothing outside of ourselves. 'Me' merges completely with 'we' and we start to reach the stages of non-dual awareness where the story of interconnection comes alive in the cells of our being."

MAGIC IS OUR ABILITY TO CO-CREATE WITH THE NATURAL FORCES OF LIFE

The practical process of living alchemy becomes a daily choice – to consciously breathe into and let go of anything that we have outgrown, creating space for new understanding, experiences and opportunities to emerge. It takes constant bravery to live in an interconnected world, where there is no-one or no-thing to hide behind when life becomes challenging. We understand that 'magic' is our innate ability to co-create with the natural forces of life; both chaos and order.

Daily alchemy can be practiced in several physical and non-physical ways such as:

❀ Taking action towards something that feels right even though you can't quite see how it will be successful in the long term.

❀ Realising that there is nothing inherently wrong with you or the world; that your life experiences are catalysts to prompt you into action on behalf of 'we' instead of 'me'.

❀ Being guided by magical, synchronistic events and 'lucky' opportunities.

❀ Living mythically by witnessing potential plotlines, archetypal influences and quests, as they appear in your life and the wider world.

✳ Developing the ability to be creative in discomfort, challenge, conflict and chaos: holding both dark and light without judging them as right or wrong.

✳ Entering a heightened sense of interconnection and communion with the all human and non-human beings.

✳ Love (in all its forms) becoming the core driver for your decisions.

✳ Experiencing 'God' as a verb rather than a noun.

Why not start to look for all the areas in your life where you feel you are still working with 'lower' energies or emotions. They are often areas where you feel separate or at the mercy of a force outside of yourself. Start here. Work consciously with these situations or habits and bring higher, more expanded ways of being and doing into them. Remember that in a place of interconnection with the Universe there can be no-thing outside of yourself – one of the great cosmic jokes of our time!

The best way to practice daily alchemy is to harness the power of choice. When you find yourself triggered by a person or situation, stop and take one deep alchemical breath. From here you access your power of choice: the choice to transcend the lower realms of human relating and move into a more refined state of consciousness.

Dr Hawkins[41] in his book *Power Vs Force* describes the different measurable frequencies that each emotional state holds and creates both within the human body and in the world around you. Of course, enlightenment, love and forgiveness are some of the highest vibrational emotions, whereas hate, fear and anger are some of the lowest. Choosing to restory your emotional reactions is one of the highest forms of alchemy there is. It is a matter of choice; the choice to alchemise your thinking, feeling and acting; a powerful process indeed!

CHOOSING TO RESTORY YOUR EMOTIONAL REACTIONS IS ONE OF THE HIGHEST FORMS OF ALCHEMY THERE IS

AUGUST STORYHACK

GENEVIEVE GUIDES YOU IN THE GENTLE ART OF
RESTORYING YOUR LIFE...

WIPING YOUR LENS CLEAN

A NARRATIVE CLEANSING OF YOUR CORE VALUES

For a long time, I have been using a powerful storyhack exercise known as 'Cleaning Your Narrative Lens'. It is one of the fastest ways I know to immediately change the story that you find yourself living in, by bringing your attention to the characters, environments and choices that create your reality. It's fast, it's powerful, and it transforms.

Imagine for a moment that you find yourself sitting or standing within a circular field of energy or light. This can be flat or spherical; it can be wide or small and expands and contracts depending on the thoughts you think and the feelings you feel moment to moment... just like your breath.

This circle is your intimate, unique human story lens. It is the filter through which you view and manifest the stories and experiences in your world.

It contains:

- ❋ Your beliefs (both childhood and adult)

- ❋ Your thought patterns (the neural networks that govern and operate according to your beliefs)

- ❋ Your senses and emotions that are the results of your beliefs and thoughts

✳   The memories that form as a result of the choices you have made and the actions you have taken

Phew… is it feeling crowded in your story lens yet? Or perhaps your lens is somewhat grimy with years of accumulated beliefs you inherited from other people?

But the good news is that you can choose what stays and what goes. You can wipe your inner story lens clean of other people's beliefs and thinking. You can let go of any narrative keys that restrict you and keep you trapped in old habits. Do you want to detox your story?

Stop for a moment and imagine that you can wipe your lens clean; that you can remove any old beliefs, thoughts and feelings that no longer serve you. It doesn't have to be everything at once. Just go with the things that immediately spring to the front of your awareness, then imagine that you can take them (be they words, pictures or energies) and throw them outside of the boundary of your narrative lens.

Yes – it can be that fast and that easy! By throwing them 'out' you immediately create space within. Now look around at the world once again. How do you feel? Keep doing this until you reach a space inside your lens where you feel clean and clear.

Now examine your lens once again and notice what remains. What is left after a narrative cleansing of your core values? Examine your remaining values. How do they make you feel? How different does your life look when you see the world through a clean lens that authentically reflects YOU?

Get to know your real story from the inside out. Choose a life value and walk with it front and centre of your lens for a day or two. Enhance it. Develop it. Or even decide to evolve it to something better fitting to who you are now. Welcome to your unique human ability to restory and transform your narrative landscape in an instant.

YOU CAN LET GO OF ANY NARRATIVE KEYS THAT RESTRICT YOU AND KEEP YOU TRAPPED IN OLD HABITS

This is the first lens – ME. From here you can start to look out at how your ME lens connects to and interacts with other ME lenses in your local ecosystems. This then becomes the collective lens of WE. How does your story interact and engage with the story lenses of your family, your work colleagues and your society?

Once you are practiced at working with your own story lens, why not try joining your lens consciously with another person's in a *vesica piscis* – where two circles overlap to form a mutual space. See what happens in this transformational area in the middle of your two circles. This is the place of co-creation, of communion and sometimes of love.

ME
WE
ALL

Each one a bigger lens in the human and more than human story on Earth. And you get to play in all three lenses as a conscious and aware storymaker.

SEPTEMBER

THANKS IS GIVEN FOR NATURE'S ABUNDANCE
YET AUTUMN IS BITTERSWEET

SEPTEMBER EARTH SIGNS

The season of mists and mellow fruitfulness is upon us, the golden light low enough now to cast long shadows, yet warm enough still to bask in. The nights are colder, a signal for the setting of seed and the final ripening of fruit. All is busy in the countryside as harvest-time gets into full flow. Corn is cut, potatoes are dug, beans are shucked, apples, pears, grapes and plums are picked and preserved, herbs and vegetables are harvested and stored, and thanks is given for the incredible abundance of Mother Nature.

It is Autumn and in the woods the jays gather acorns and squirrels gather hazelnuts, both burying them with precision, yet generously leaving enough to germinate and reclothe the woodlands; the sycamore seeds swirl down from on high like gyroscopes, then twirl into Earth's embrace and a period of dormancy before regeneration. All is focussed on coming to fruition, enabling the cycle of life to begin again after the Mystery Time of Winter.

There is a sense of melancholy too, in Autumn. In September, we know that the time of ease has passed, and that Winter's embrace will soon be upon us. Autumn can be pleasantly warm and golden, clothed in colours that delight the senses and yet there is a feeling of loss that the glorious days of Summer are over for another year, and this is exacerbated as the swallows and martins leave these shores, gathering *en masse* for one final spectacle of aeronautics before they head south for the Winter. September is truly bittersweet.

ALL IS
FOCUSSED ON
COMING TO
FRUITION

SEPTEMBER COSMOLOGICAL SIGNS

VIRGO TO LIBRA

I SERVE (COLLECTIVE)

Service grows in resonance and amplitude as you move into the collective realms of the goddess in Virgo. Your outer world purpose, gifts and acts of service to others can now come from the solid foundations built in Leo and a cup that runneth over and is eternally replenished from the fires of your inner truth.

Authenticity and integrity are watch words here that draw you forward into new systems, structures and opportunities to connect, create and consolidate. You find a current of passion enters into your heart and your soul fire is fanned by experiences that take you out of your comfort zones.

You are called into action on behalf of your community, your culture and your Earth, for this is truly serving life.

AUTHENTICITY AND INTEGRITY ARE WATCH WORDS THAT DRAW YOU FORWARD

Harvest Moon

– full orange and huge as it rises on the Eastern horizon, the Harvest Moon represents the culmination of what was sown. A time of plenty and a time to honour the alchemy of Nature.

SEPTEMBER ARCHETYPES

SOLAR ARCHETYPE: ENERGY

As you walk through Autumn in the Western Quarter of your Soulistic Wheel, you will be feeling a change in your energy as it reflects the urge of the natural world at this time, towards reunion. Now you can enjoy the fruits of your labours and in doing so, you will feel a different Energy to that of high Summer and all its busy-ness. But if you are feeling irritable or have a need to let-off some steam, don't judge that feeling; open up to it, embrace it. Mystery asks that you contemplate how the changing Energy feels for you; do you resist it? Do you try to hold on to busyness and jubilance of summer because it is a convenient distraction? Enjoy contemplating your energetic levels and what they are saying to you.

Energy is omnipresent and also multifaceted: it has changing frequencies and vibrational qualities depending on the season, yet it is infinitely generous and can always be harnessed, transmuted and redirected in myriad ways, yet never destroyed. This is the sheer beauty of Energy: it is ceaseless, immortal, and transcendent, and offers these gifts to humanity unconditionally.

Energy burns with the fire of a great star and accompanies evolution, both personal and planetary. Energy is self-replenishing and radiates a Cosmic force that interacts with every molecule in existence. Energy interconnects us all in a web of dynamic relating. If you ever doubt your interconnectedness with all of creation, look how the sun – the great star that provides our Energy abundance – awakens all kingdoms of Nature into action in the Spring and Summer, and settles us all into rest and recuperation in the Autumn and Winter. We are one with Nature and the Cosmos.

In the field of human endeavour, Energy fuels our passion and creates the precise interactions needed for manifestation to take place. There is always enough Energy to support your creative endeavours – it's bountiful and infinite; suffused within and without you, there for the taking and asking nothing in

ENERGY IS OMINPRESENT AND MULTI-FACETED WITH CHANGING FREQUENCIES DEPENDING ON THE SEASON return. What a gift. In using this gift wisely, you are invited to breathe energetic resonance into the patterns that are aligned to and ignite your Soul Story. In doing so, Energy, moves you into new territory.

> *Do you every hear yourself saying, "I just haven't got the Energy for that"? Your wise soul may well be ushering you towards your true purpose without you realising it. Make a list of all the things you haven't got the Energy for, and all the things you have got Energy for. Pin it to your dreamboard and continue to steer yourself towards your Soul Purpose.*

LUNAR ARCHETYPE: DIVINE LAW

As you navigate the Western Quadrant of your Soulistic Wheel, you will notice abundance everywhere, fulfilling the Divine Law of life's annual cycle of 'coming to be and ceasing to be'. Divine Law is the archetype that constantly reweaves Indra's Net so that all is balanced. This is truly wondrous: that in the great biodiversity of life on Earth, balance prevails. If something tips out of dynamic equilibrium – and there are myriad reasons why this can happen – Divine Law will reweave it. This reweaving can take many forms, sometimes through chaos and confusion and at others through death or natural disaster, but always reweaving into harmony, even if it takes aeons of deep time to do so. This is why the ability to see with symbolic sight is so liberating: because it enables you to glimpse Divine Law in action.

You too are part of the miraculous warp and weft of life and so Divine Law impacts upon you. How could it be otherwise? Remember: As Above, So Below, As Within, So Without – which means in essence that if you are out of balance, Divine Law will also work her alchemy upon you. If you are experiencing chaos and confusion in your life, this is a signal that something is out of balance. Mystery asks you to contemplate where that imbalance is arising. Divine Law will eventually bring all to equilibrium, but Wisdom knows that right action and choice-making can ease the transition. Chaos and destruction are the precursors to creativity. Do not fear them but ask what lessons they offer.

Divine Law is the great synthesiser, keeping cosmological systems in harmony; she destroys that which is out of alignment with the highest laws of the Universe and clears away all that is unnecessary, allowing for new beginnings. Divine Law holds a mirror up to your stories and shows you through the clarity of balance and harmony, or the confusion of chaos and destruction, the realities that you are creating for yourself. In this way, she is the guardian and mirror of your free will, enabling you to redesign your realities.

Come to your altar, or to a place in Nature if you prefer. Sit quietly and bring yourself into a state of contemplation. Can you think of a time in your life when Divine Law emanated in your life? When what you thought was a disaster turned out to be a blessing? Have you seen Divine Law in action in your family or friendships? Write about it in your journal and remember that creation always follows destruction.

UNIFICATION: CO-CREATION

The energies of Above and Below unify and create the most beautiful archetype of Co-creation. Co-creation expresses as an enormous sense of excitement and opportunity when we take full responsibility for our story and its manifestation in the world. Mystery asks you to examine your thoughts. Do you expect good fortune or bad luck? Do you live in fear of what might happen or are you open to any experience? Wisdom reminds you that your thoughts co-create your reality, so be mindful, always. You have ultimate choice and your choice is part of the co-creative Universe.

The archetypal energy of Co-creation encircles diversity in all its complexity and weaves a sparkling web of connectivity that keeps the matrix in perfect

condition for the experiments of life, made manifest in the vast and breath-takingly exquisite cornucopia of existence.

Co-creation happens at multiple levels, multi-dimensionally. We co-create with our inner beliefs and thought patterns through choice and action. We co-create with those around us in choosing which stories we believe and live by in our communities. And, of course, we co-create with the energies of the Universe (all represented in these Solar and Lunar archetypes), through the energy of our hearts, minds and souls. Co-creation gives form to idea.

What is coming to fruition for you right now? Look back over your journey to date and see the golden thread of intention from your dreamtime of Winter, through your seed-sowing back in the Spring, to the germination and growth of ideas in Summer, and now to the Co-creation of your story as it moves into Autumn. Weave your Soulistic Journey into a poem, a song, a painting, a story… What adventures have you been on? What different choices have you made? Take some time to reveal your story of Co-creation to yourself: what at first glance may seem insignificant, can come to be life changing.

SEPTEMBER PRACTICES

WATER PRACTICES

WATER SHAPESHIFTS. IT FEELS AND IT KNOWS

Water came to the Earth from the hearts of exploding stars when our galaxy was first formed 13.8 billion years ago. It clothed the Earth in a fluid cloak of blue and facilitated the emergence of early life in the vast oceans. Now, water is more vital to our bodies, ecosystems and future evolution than ever before, because at last, we have become aware of its omnipotence and omnipresence – a fact that may encourage us to stop fouling it with waste and pollution. A healthful future is dependent on our respect for water.

Water is also one of the Earth's most powerful transformative shapeshifters.

It moves in micro and macro cycles, through every in-formed being on the planet be that a fungus, a maple tree, a grizzly bear, a mountain, a cloud or an ocean. Humans are 60% water – it flows through our veins and out of our bodies, back into the waterways of the planet. Water cycles and spirals through liquid, vapour, ice, snow and back again; through soil and rock, to underground caverns and lakes and then it bursts forth through springs into rivers, creeks and eventually the sea itself. What a beautiful cycle of life.

You were germinated in the watery womb of your mother – and your mother was germinated in the watery womb of her mother and her mother before her, since our species itself began to germinate in the watery wombs of Gaia. We are water as animated life. So, having a 'water practice' in your journey helps you to reconnect to the fundamental place that you came from. It nurtures you and it nurtures life itself when you take the time to feel gratitude for the multifaceted gifts that water brings.

A HEALTHFUL FUTURE IS DEPENDENT ON OUR RESPECT FOR WATER

The ground-breaking work of Japanese researcher Masaru Emoto[42] in his book *The Hidden Messages in Water* shows us that water responds to emotion, intention and frequency. Using photographic imagery, he explains how water molecules that are infused with love and compassion form exquisite fractal ice patterns when frozen and put under a microscope, compared to sludgy, confused and chaotic crystals from water that is subjected to hate, anger and sorrow.

Not only does water respond to your emotions, but water can also hold memory. This is the principle behind homeopathy – that there is an energetic memory of the healing compound 'succussed' (infused) into the remedy, even though materially, the compound is no longer detectable. Scientist, Rupert Sheldrake[43] calls this ability of water to hold memory a 'morphic field'. So, water that we imbibe has a memory of its journey, whether of anger, sorrow, love or joy, as it passes through a human being; it has memory of the restriction of the canalised pipes of a water company as it comes out of our taps; or it has a memory of the love and compassion of a water birth – indeed, all of these things, as water cycles infinitely.

Richard, in his equally ground-breaking book *The Gene Keys*[44] has this to say about water and conscious evolution: "There is a peculiarity in the hydrogen atom that allows it to transfer consciousness as memory. Since our planet and our bodies are made up primarily of water, this is the medium through which our collective consciousness evolves. The water cycle on this planet is actually how we are awakening. Every form that dies releases its water content back into the water cycle which means that every form releases a finite number of more evolved hydrogen atoms back into the world." From these words you can see it is incumbent upon all of us to think, speak and act with love and compassion so that through our deep interconnection with water we can aid the spiritual evolution of humanity.

If you honour water and show appreciation and love to the waters you consume and bathe in, then that will cleanse and re-energise the water as it flows through you. Ask any gardener about the quality of rain and they will tell you that you can water a plant all summer with tap water and it will survive, but when it is rained on, it will thrive. This is because water that runs through pipes is restricted and de-energised, whereas water that has been through its natural cycle and has evaporated back up to the clouds is rejuvenated, recharged and energised with negative ions and is massively more healthful for plants. Similarly, you can recharge water by treating it with respect and love, as you would any other living being.

Years ago, when I (Genevieve) realised the hidden power of water in all its forms, I decided to create a series of water practices that would allow me to form a strong, loving alliance with the waters both in my body and in the body of the planet. Therefore, whether I am drinking, bathing or honouring water, I bring a level of conscious gratitude to the essence of life that it contains.

We really encourage everyone undertaking a Soulistic Journey to develop your own practices with water, however, to get you started here are some of our favourites to inspire you:

VIBRATIONAL WATER

As Masaru Emoto discovered, water changes shape and form when exposed to different words and vibrations. To give your drinking water extra healing potential, purchase a glass water bottle or carafe and decorate it (using pens specifically made for glass art) with high frequency words, sacred geometry and images that bring you joy, healing and vitality. As you do this, contemplate the meaning of the words and images you are creating and imbue them with that energy. The water you drink from this container will be infused with the same levels of frequency.

CRYSTAL WATER

The vibrational quality of crystals can infuse water and create a healing, nurturing drink. We asked our friend Donna Byatt[45], from Elements of Avebury to recommend a good crystal for this purpose. She said, "I use all sorts in my water, or at least I did... until I found Shungite Elite which is 90-98% pure carbon. This is an amazing crystal because it is able to purify water from inside and outside. I use a Shungite tile as a coaster on which I put my water jug, but I also place a little net bag of Elite in my water jug. It cleanses and purifies the water and removes any pollutants. This makes sense when you consider some of the top water filters use carbon as their substrate. The other amazing crystal I use in water is rose quartz, which blesses the water with complete love – who wouldn't want a drink of love?"

INTENTIONAL SHOWERS

When you take your morning or evening shower, spend a moment asking the water to clear and cleanse you of any energetic blocks, fears or stagnation. As it flows over your body, allow your mind and emotions to also be cleansed.

SACRED WATERS

Waters from springs and sacred sites, and even the morning dew, have always been revered as highly healing and transformative. Start to carry a small glass vial with you in your gifting bag whenever you make a pilgrimage or quest to a special place. If there are waters, ask permission, offer gratitude and gather some water to create your own sacred water infusion. This can be used in ceremony or a drop can be placed in your drinking water to infuse it with the healing vibration memory in the water. **It's worth checking the source of the water for information on safety and purity, especially if you want to drink the water you gather.

WATER ACTIVISM

Water is one of the most precious elements on our planet and there are many who still lack access to safe drinking water. Therefore, the more of us who undertake sacred activism to protect and heal water, the faster we will come into balance once again. Whether this is cleaning up the oceans, protesting against large corporations who are poisoning or profiteering from water sources, volunteering to clean up your local river, or simply re-using your own washing-up or bathing water on the plants in your garden, water will thank you for anything you feel called to do to protect it[46].

When you choose to work with water in a sacred way, it will bring massive benefits to your life and your journey. Even a simple thanks every time you pour a glass of water or acknowledge the gift that you have instant access to safe, clean drinking water will create a mutually conscious relationship between you and waters of our Earth.

SACRED SOUND

MUSIC ACTS DIRECTLY ON THE SOUL

Have you ever noticed that when you are happy, you spontaneously burst into song or whistle a tune? That is sacred sound – it is an irrepressible utterance that wells-up from somewhere deep within; an energy that needs to be given voice. Voicing an energy in this way – singing in a choir for example – can be joyful and give you peace of mind. One of the most ancient practices of sacred sound is the art of mantra, the voiced repetition or chanting of words or tones to aid healing and meditation.

Many cultures use the practice of mantra to bring about a blissful, spiritual state. Have you ever tried it? Repeating the same phrase over and over again quietens your mind and deepens your breath – but the most well-known mantras are often associated with spiritual traditions that you may not be familiar with and therefore may not resonate with. To most Westerners, the beautiful and ancient mantra, 'Om Mani Padme Hum' – Praise to the Jewel in the Lotus – doesn't really mean anything to them and is difficult to say. But have you ever thought about creating your own mantra?

Sacred sound[47] is a science in its own right and in this book, we can only briefly

"MUSICAL SOUND ACTS DIRECTLY ON THE SOUL AND FINDS AN ECHO THERE, SINCE MUSIC IS INNATE IN HUMANS."
– WASSILY KANDINSKY

touch upon music as medicine, so for our purposes, let us focus on energising our bodily chakra centres with some simple sounds. There is a wonderful exercise (taken from the book *Sounding the Inner Landscape* by Kay Gardner) that uses the vowel sounds in certain words to awaken the chakras, the unseen medicine wheels of your body. Here it is:

Ooo   – as in 'soothe': awakens the root chakra

Oh   – as in 'awoke': awakens the sacral chakra

Aw   – as in 'awe': awakens the solar plexus chakra

Ah   – as in 'karma': awakens the heart chakra

Eh   – as in 'echo': awakens the throat chakra

Ih   – as in 'inspire': awakens the third eye chakra

Eee   – as in 'feel': awakens the crown chakra

Now chant these vowel sounds slowly, enjoying the vibrational feel of them in your body, opening and moving your mouth to accommodate the sounds.

Ooooooooooooooo, Ooooooohhhhhhhhhh, Aaaaaawwwwww, Aaaaaahhhhhh, Eeeeeehhhhh, Iiiiiihhhhhh, Eeeeeeeeee… Ooooooooooooooo, Ooooooohhhhhhhhhh, Aaaaaawwwwww, Aaaaaahhhhhh, Eeeeeehhhhh, Iiiiiihhhhhh, Eeeeeeeeee

You might feel a bit daft doing this, so find a quiet room or do it when the kids are at school! You may also like to move through an octave from one note up through the scale and then back down again. If you are feeling a bit emotional one day, you might just give the heart chakra a bit of a spin by chanting Ahhhhhhhhhhhhhhhhhhh, Ahhhhhhhhhhhhhhhhh, Ahhhhhhhhhhhhhh for a few minutes. Do it and see if you feel better.

Or perhaps you can create a mantra out of these words or similar words with the same vowel sounds, something you can chant or sing when you're washing up or weeding the garden. "I am soothed, awoke and in awe. My karma is an echo that inspires the way I feel. I am soothed, awoke and in awe. My karma is an echo that inspires the way I feel…"

Be playful with this exercise and don't take it too seriously, smile and dance as you pronounce these vowel sounds, in the knowledge that you are awakening and refreshing your chakra centres. That said, in the first century AD, Demetrius is credited as saying that, "In Egypt the priests 'hymn' the gods by means of the seven vowels which they utter in due order" – the order we have denoted above – so though you can be playful with this, it is actually powerful, healing sacred sound.

The human soul, according to the ancient sage, Hildegard von Bingen, is 'symphonic'; the soul relates to harmony, tone, and the inner accord of music. We cannot walk a Soulistic Journey without the accompaniment of sacred sound. So, sing when you feel moved to sing; find a chant or mantra that is meaningful to you, beat out a rhythm on a drum or dance to the pulse and splendour of music whenever you can. You will always, without fail, feel better for it.

"THE HUMAN SOUL IS SYMPHONIC"
– HILDEGARD VON BINGEN

SEPTEMBER STORYHACK

GENEVIEVE GUIDES YOU IN THE GENTLE ART OF RESTORYING YOUR LIFE...

THE DOORWAY OF DOUBT

RELEASING YOUR SABOTAGING STORIES

THE MORE AWARE YOU ARE OF YOUR 'WORRY NARRATIVES' THE FASTER YOU CAN TRANSFORM THEM

This has been quite a tough year for me one way or another, and it has made me reflect that perhaps I should be more careful of what I wish for! Yet these tough times always pass and often lead to epiphanies, new relationships, opportunities and grace if you have the courage to ride their waves.

Deliberately courting new experiences and life adventures brings challenges that you will have likely never dealt with before. These new situations ultimately help you to grow but take a lot of focus whilst you learn to acclimatise to them. There is no avoiding the amount of mental, emotional and physical energy that you are called to expend when you jump outside of your comfort zone and paddle into new waters.

Of course, anything new (or old for that matter) comes with a degree of risk to it. Stories rarely unfold the way you wish them to. This is part of the magic and mystery of adventure but often causes stress to the human part of you that likes to feel in control of your destiny. Risk creates one of the biggest destabilising energies in the Universe: doubt – but doubt is not bad.

Doubt can be a healthy sign that you are transforming. When you doubt things, you enter into a state of 'unknowing'. You seek answers because you can't see clearly how things are going to turn out. This process can result in a healthy openness, where you allow your doubt to lead you into new ideas, options and circumstances. Alternatively, it can become unhealthy, leading to worry, anxiety and an eventual shut down to opportunities through fear and perpetual uncertainty of which way to go next.

The reality is that we all experience a spectrum of doubt on a daily basis and are asked to fall back on our fundamental beliefs and stories in order to lead us through the confusion. I split my daily dose of doubt into two categories that help me to make empowering choices. These are:

1. Distracting Doubt

2. Divine Doubt

Distracting doubt is the kind that brings low (and high) levels of worry with it. This is the kind of doubt where my inner voice loops around in stories of fear and doom, creating technicolor movies of what might (that 'might' word again!) happen if I fail. I entertain this for a while and then come to an 'enough's enough' moment where I call an inner timeout. A deep conscious breath, a visualised image of burning up my worries or simply calling in angelic assistance to release the sabotaging stories. The more aware you are of these 'worry narratives', the faster you can release them and the less they can distract from your purpose.

The other form of doubt can be more useful to you if you can discern its more refined frequency. I call this 'divine doubt' and its qualities are that of epiph-any, revelation and consideration. Divine doubt sneaks into your established narratives and worldview, showing you where you might be limiting how you are choosing to see your current situation. It comes in the quiet moments of 'pause' when you are called to challenge your own established beliefs about something and see if there is a wider pattern at play that will help you to grow. Divine doubt asks you to question your patterns of thinking and behaviour, loosening them a degree to allow space for something new to emerge.

Divine doubt leads you to a doorway; an entry point that you can step through into a whole new worldview if you choose. It leads you down the path of

DIVINE DOUBT SNEAKS IN TO YOUR ESTABLISHED NARRATIVES SHOWING YOU WHERE YOU MIGHT BE LIMITING YOUR CURRENT SITUATION conscious evolution and beyond your current stage of development into the process of alchemy. On an inner level, you know that there is gold waiting to be revealed from within. You have to be courageous enough to let go of everything that is getting in its way; everything that is distracting you from the process of living the adventure of your lifetime.

Where are you distracting yourself with worry? Can your doubt be transformed into divine discernment? Perhaps it's time to let go of distraction and step through the doorway?

OCTOBER

A FINAL CRESCENDO OF BRILLIANCE
HERALDS A TIME OF DEEP INNER
AND OUTER REUNION

OCTOBER EARTH SIGNS

All is fiery red in October. The leaves of the cherry turn scarlet and fall to Earth like embers from a fire, and orange rowanberries braid the tree fleetingly before the thrushes gorge on them. Light withdraws and as it does so, the colours of Autumn intensify – yellows, oranges, reds and ochres light up the landscape in one final crescendo of brilliance before the cold sets in.

October is a time of reunion and transformation: from life to death and rebirth. The grasses and flowers have set seed, and whilst their bodies wither and reunite with the Earth, their seed scatters to the four winds and will bring forth new life. Before our eyes, the verdance of Summer is replaced by the crispness of Autumn, where husks of once lush vegetation have succumbed to the inevitable turning of the seasons, their forms eventually unifying back into the soil. But this change brings its own gifts.

Animals that are preparing to hibernate for winter do so with the embryos of new life in their wombs; birds migrate to reunite with their Winter feeding grounds that will sustain them before they return next Spring; the leaves and detritus of this year's growth will rot and turn to mulch and nourish next year's emergence. Truly, October is the time of reunification.

This year's burgeoning is coming to an end; but as the Soulistic Wheel turns, you can rest assured that next year, you'll watch the emergence once again. It will be so familiar, but so utterly different.

OCTOBER COSMOLOGICAL SIGNS

LIBRA TO SCORPIO

I PARTNER

Co-creation is the essence of evolution. Yet in order for birth to be joyful and healthy it is necessary to choose very carefully the seed and womb essences that are used for gestation.

In reality you are 'partnering' with the molecules of life constantly. Your beliefs, stories and emotions co-create with the world around you and manifest the experiences that you have chosen to give birth to. You are Nature and Nature is you – so you can never be isolated or out of relationship with anyone and anything around you.

Partnering becomes a sacred act of choice and conscious co-creation in this month, as Libra reminds you to create balance and harmony in every aspect of your life, as much as you are able. This involves embracing the light and the dark and all the shades of grey in between in order for you to transcend seeming polarities and enter into the alchemy of the Middle Way.

PARTNERING BECOMES A SACRED ACT OF CHOICE AND CONSCIOUS CO-CREATION

FIRE MOON

– life trans-forms; creating the seedbed for rebirth.
The Fire Moon destroys and unifies, ready to create
another cycle of the Wheel of the Year.
Blessed is the Fire Moon.

OCTOBER SOULISTIC ARCHETYPES

SOLAR ARCHETYPE: MICROCOSM

You are now taking your final steps in the Western Quadrant of the Soulistic Wheel, at a time when the natural world is relinquishing its form and returning to the bosom of the Earth to prepare for reunification, transformation and rebirth. This cycle is reflected throughout the Universe; even stars and planets disintegrate and are reborn in the great cosmological cauldron of life. We are part of the Microcosm and the Macrocosm, because it is one holographic reflection. Everything you see echoes the fractal essence of the Universe.

The maxim 'As above, so below; As within, so without' gives great succour to those who can see with mythic eyes, for it reveals Infinity and Unity and the omnipresence of Spirit in all things. The first few lines of William Blake's *Auguries of Innocence*[48] express this Microcosmic perspective perfectly:

> 'To see a world in a grain of sand
> And a Heaven in a wild flower
> Hold Infinity in the palm of your hand
> And Eternity in an hour.'

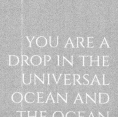

YOU ARE A DROP IN THE UNIVERSAL OCEAN AND THE OCEAN ITSELF

Imagine that, like cosmic mycelium, the archetype of Microcosm reveals to you the vast and awe-inspiring web of interconnection between all beings. Imagine Microcosm weaving his magic in sacred geometric patterns throughout the Universe, connecting everything and no-thing. Then you will see that you are a drop in the Universal ocean and also the ocean itself. That is a mind-blowing concept but like Blake's poem, it takes imagination to see the truth of it. Microcosm is all-encompassing and humans are the mid-way point between the smallest thing in the Universe and the largest thing in the Universe. Therefore, you are Microcosm's fulcrum: if you are in balance, the Universe is in balance.

It is possible to intellectually understand this exquisite archetype, yet still feel separate from the Universe, doubting that life is anything more than a fleeting existence on planet Earth, where you have no feelings of faith or connection to anyone or anything. If this is how you feel, then it is likely that you have been wounded on a deep level either through illness, family conflict or abuse, or you have a personal story that you have so far been unable to rewrite; or perhaps your childhood was so full of rules and regulations that there was no place for the imagination to flourish? Do not despair: most wounds can heal but the deeper they are, the longer it takes. Yet eternity unfolds before you and if this lifetime is not long enough, know that any intentions you make and the choices you sow now to facilitate your healing, you *will* reap in deep time. Remember 'Restorying 101'; that through changing your thoughts and intentions you can create a new reality. Mystery asks you to trust that one step at a time is enough.

Take it easy on yourself. Life is not meant to be taken too seriously! The Soulistic Journey itself is designed to offer you insights into the beautiful sacred geometry of the Universe, and yet it is enough to live simply, to love your family and give selflessly. Your journey need not be hard. Look for simplicity in all things. To paraphrase Einstein, (or was it Woody Guthrie?) 'Any fool can make things complex, but it takes a genius to keep things simple'.

LUNAR ARCHETYPE: SEED

The Western Quadrant of your Soulistic Wheel coincides with the time of Seed; in Nature and in your thoughts, seeds begin to form – seeds of new beginnings, new ideas, new life... In the turning of the season from Autumn to Winter, seed that is formed unites with fertile ground where it will lay cradled by soil until the warmth of Spring triggers germination. Seed can lie dormant for years, and then, for some reason beyond our understanding, the time becomes ripe for germination. Seed always knows when the time is right, for her gift is deep knowledge of time.

Therefore, if your path seems unclear, or if you have walked thus far on your Soulistic Wheel and still feel clothed in the 'old you', Seed asks you to trust and have faith. You may feel impatient or even begin to doubt your commitments, but perhaps the time is not ripe for the germination of your intentions? Perhaps your Seeds need to lay fallow a while longer to fully settle into the seedbed you have prepared. As in horticulture, you may plant the Seed (of an idea), but it will only germinate when it is ready and that is down to many different factors converging to create the perfect conditions. So have the patience of Mother Nature herself.

Seed holds all of diversity in her codons so she is fecund and potent, yet what you thought you had planted may not be quite what germinates, for Seed is always cross-pollinated by cultural and environmental frequencies. Your intention will be in there, but it may be tempered or enhanced by the subtle energies that you were experiencing as you sowed. The key is to trust the flower within the Seed. From a tiny acorn a great oak tree will grow; a being that will nurture and nourish myriad other beings for aeons and that will bear witness to events that are currently beyond our imagination. That is the alchemical mystery of Seed.

Seed holds open a doorway for you to see your beginnings and endings. Just like each Seed in the Earth instinctively knows which way to move through the darkness into the light, Seed reminds you that deep inside, the Seed of your soul knows this too. Your soul knows which path supports your true purpose. Mystery asks you to listen to the voice of Seed, who teaches you that there is a time for rest and dormancy and a time for growth and momentum. Wisdom will help you distinguish one from the other.

SEED HOLDS
ALL OF
DIVERSITY IN
HER CODONS

Can you feel any new Seeds forming in your consciousness? As you walk the Western Quadrant you are nearing the dreamtime of Winter where these Seeds can take shape. It's time to do some Soulistic Doodling! Just doodle – with your non-dominant hand if you find it hard to connect with your heart centre – and see what transpires. Pin your doodle to your dreamboard.

**TEMPO
IS YOUR
INFALLIBLE
GUIDE IN
BOTH LIFE
AND DEATH**

UNIFICATION: TEMPO

The Solar and Lunar archetypes of Microcosm and Seed pair to give birth to Tempo – a child of time and outside of time. Tempo is the synthesis of persistence and desistance. The essence of precision and patience. Tempo knows when to move and when to stay still, both needed in the exquisite interplay of creation.

A most magical and mysterious archetype, Tempo holds the key to the rhythms and patterns of the Universal heartbeat. We owe our lives to Tempo, who knows the perfect rhythm of how to dance through evolution, leading you forward in your own unfolding story. Tempo accesses the movement keys that create momentum and moments of still integration. Both are needed to remember, rejuvenate, restory and reunify with your Soul Story again and again and again.

Tempo can be accessed through music and dance; wherein she resides and transcends time. Tempo offers her great gift of timelessness, when you surrender yourself to her and dance in her ecstatic frequencies. Tempo is a time-traveller, and will journey with you, reminding you to listen to your own heartbeat, to tune in to your unique Tempo. Tempo is your infallible guide in both life and death.

It's time to dance! Kick off your shoes, put on some music that energises you and dance, feeling Tempo in your body and soul. Can you engage with the transcendent quality that music and dance create in your body? Where do you go in that ecstasy of dance? That feeling is transcendence. Tempo guides you and fills you with energy. Call on her often for she is one of the Universe's greatest gifts to humanity.

OCTOBER PRACTICES

LEAF CEREMONY (LETTING GO AND COMPOSTING)

RELEASING PRECONCEPTIONS ABOUT YOURSELF AND YOUR STORY

At this time of year, the trees are relinquishing their leaves. They flutter to the ground to nourish and fertilise the soil in forthcoming years – the great gift of reunion. The leaves have turned golden-red, a sign that they have served their purpose and are no longer necessary for the health of the tree. During the Winter months, the tree's buds swell with the promise of new leaves that will open in the Spring and begin the cycle again.

Like the trees, we all carry 'excess baggage' – things that no longer nourish us, and we too can use the seasonal pause in activity to reflect on what we might like to let go of. Are you carrying personal stories, grudges or anxieties about anything that no longer serves your greater good? If you are, then you can choose to release them. Does it really help your wellbeing not to forgive a slight against you? Do you really need to hold on to stress about situations over which you have no control? Can you relinquish your anger over a past hurt?

You have a choice to let go of any story you are telling yourself about who you are. This simple fact is a revelation to many people, but the truth is, you don't have to live that narrative – you can change it. Often, by holding on to anger or hurt about a given situation, the only person you are affecting is yourself. But 'letting go' of these emotions can be difficult – you think you've done so, and then suddenly the spectre of anxiety arises from nowhere to confront you all over again. One thing you can do, however, is to compost those stories; relinquish them to the Earth for transformation, and here's how.

DOES IT HELP YOUR WELLBEING NOT TO FORGIVE A SLIGHT AGAINST YOU?

�֎ Find some card or beautiful paper and draw the shape of some leaves on it. If the card or paper is coloured yellow or orange to echo the colours of the Autumn leaves, so much the better. Make the leaves big enough that you can write a few words on them.

✖ Cut out the leaves.

✖ On each leaf, write a word or brief sentence that encapsulates something you would like to let go of in your life. For example, if you wish to bury the hatchet between yourself and a friend who you feel betrayed you in some way, then write: 'I forgive 'Lucy' for what I perceived as a betrayal. I realise she may not see things as I do.' Or, if you wish to move on from a past narrative, do the same. For example: 'I no longer see myself as lacking motivation. I accept that I can change my world for the better.'

✖ You can write anything – be creative; think deeply about what you would like to change and determine what it is you need to let go of in order for that to happen. Then write it down on your leaves.

✖ When you have a pile of leaves representing all the emotions, thoughts, opinions and narratives that you want to let go of, gather them up and take your pile of leaves into the garden. Dig a hole deep enough to put all the leaves into and place them in it. Cover with earth and then say a few words: "May the healing power of the Earth transform these energies; let them become the fertile soil of new, healthful beginnings." If you feel so moved, make an offering from your gifting bag on the place where you have buried your 'letting-go leaves'.

✖ If you don't have a garden, or anywhere to compost the leaves then you can discretely scatter them to the four winds when you are on a walk. Remember to say a few words as you let them go; they will decompose in time.

This is an act of alchemy. By releasing preconceptions about yourself and your story, you are clearing space for new energetic emergence. You are making a choice to move on from that which may have held back your personal growth, sometimes, for years. This is a big step to take, and one that will leave you feeling cleansed and refreshed. You will also be less likely in future to hold-on to any negative thoughts and emotions having done this practice, as you will be aware that in doing so, you are not serving your greater good.

DEATH PRACTICES

BEAR WITNESS TO STORIES THAT NEED TO BE SPOKEN

As I (Genevieve) sit here to write this practice, I am reflecting on the life of my grandfather who recently passed away. His 85-year old physical body has reunited with the Earth from whence it came, and his soul is undertaking its next adventure.

Am I sad? To a degree, yes. But I am also celebrating his life and celebrating his liberation beyond form. I was lucky enough to spend time with him before he passed, and to see the light shine through another's skin when they prepare themselves to depart is a grace-filled honour. One that, if done consciously and with presence, is full of gifts for both the dying and the living.

For truly these days, it seems to me as I walk hand in hand with more souls up to this gateway, I am convinced by the fact that we have our conventional 'death story' all mixed up. Death is also birth into a new form of being. Perhaps even more of a birth than coming into physical form as a baby would be, given when we 'die' we remember who we actually are beyond form. If you believe so, that is.

DEATH IS ALSO BIRTH INTO A NEW FORM OF BEING

Beliefs create stories and stories create experiences. So choose your beliefs carefully.

All of us will eventually die

All of us will also be reborn

So, how can we approach this threshold experience with honour, honesty and awareness? By practicing it. There are many 'death practices' in different wisdom traditions and almost all of them relate to rites of passage or initiatory challenges that we must journey through in order to release our fear.

WE HAVE SHIELDED OURSELVES FROM THE REALITY OF DEATH FOR TOO LONG

Death in the Western cultures is often shrouded in fear, which is the primary reason we have turned our backs on its gifts, hidden it away in hospitals and hospices and handed over our watch to the medical profession, who whilst always taking a vital and caring role, often cannot bear witness to the stories that need to be spoken at this time. Culturally, we have shielded ourselves from the reality of death for too long. It is also one of the primary reasons why many people come to their threshold of physical death with so many unresolved stories. They have never allowed themselves the gift of resolution whilst still alive and vibrant in their bodies.

Don't deny yourself this gift. For death can come when we least expect it, even though it always bears a gift. Death may not relate to something physical, like the leaving of a loved one from this physical plane of existence. Death can come to help us release old, worn-out emotional patterns, relationships that have run their course or stories and habits that are ready to be transformed. For death always transforms. Nothing is lost in this Universe.

Often, when I come to the end of a project or a client relationship, I will hold a ceremony to honour the death and transformation that has occurred through this relationship over time. Just as we would have a funeral to celebrate a life, I will hold a ceremony to celebrate the lessons and blessings I have gathered throughout the course of a relationship.

What if divorce could become a conscious celebration of a teaching shared by two people, ready to move on? What if, instead of grieving when someone or something dies in our lives, we could instead honour them and the gifts that this interaction brought to our evolution? What if death, instead of inspiring fear, could catalyse love and gratitude? Afterall, death is simply a doorway beyond this particular lifetime.

So, we offer you these death practices in honour of this powerful transitional initiation:

❀ Practice recognising all the mini-deaths that occur in your life each day. Whether this is a death of a project, the loss of a friendship, or the passing of a thought pattern or habit. Honour it as it leaves for the lessons it has brought you.

❀ Imagine your own passing (pain-free and in your sleep is fine!) What is left unresolved at this moment in time that needs to be reconciled before you go? What would you like to say to your loved ones: what legacy do you bequeath? This is not a morbid exercise in any way: none of us know when it is our time to pass over. The time for reconciliation and reunion is now; the time to be honest with ourselves and our loved ones is now. This death practice allows you to live in the moment without regrets.

❀ Set aside a day or a weekend to go into your own personalised 'death lodge' ceremony. This is a much more intensive way of honouring something or someone who is dying or who has died, by setting aside sacred time to speak your memories of them, and share your stories (good, bad and ugly) to the Universe; to cry, to mourn, to rejoice and to remember the gifts this one brought to you. Then, to let them go.

❀ You may wish to invite other members of your family to this ceremony, or you may wish to go it alone. The person you are honouring may have passed recently or many years ago. Use your altar and any elements

PRACTICE RECOGNISING ALL THE MINI-DEATHS THAT OCCUR IN YOUR LIFE EACH DAY from your gifting bag to sanctify your space. This is a profound and deep process and one that can be adapted to whatever your needs are in the moment. Be creative, design your death ceremony however you feel it is appropriate, and then allow yourself time to move all the way through it until you feel 'cleaned out' and purified.

For death purifies and rarefies us. It is one of the most powerfully creative and destructive forces of change on our planet. To deny it seems foolhardy.

To embrace it, in order to understand it, seems wise.

OCTOBER STORYHACK

GENEVIEVE GUIDES YOU IN THE GENTLE ART OF RESTORYING YOUR LIFE...

THE ETERNAL CYCLE OF DEATH AND RESURRECTION

WITHOUT LETTING GO, WE CANNOT LET IN

I was compelled to get up this morning, come down to my kitchen table and start writing, because I realised that this is the story of my life. Your life too I believe. It is the time of the Coronavirus, and I am reflecting on death.

The saying that, 'Life is full of death' may sound like a cliché, but let's stop for a moment and consider those words. Without death, there could be no life – life is an eternal cycle of coming into being, and then ceasing to be, but this does not just apply to life forms; it applies to ideas, organisations and even social systems. So, perhaps for the purposes of this storyhack, it's more accurate to say, 'Life evolves through a series of mini-deaths,' each one a shedding of an old way of living, an outworn belief, or even a global system that is long past the time of it being useful to ALL. And ALL is the watch word of our time.

For some months now, something has been happening inside me. Something I have been listening to in a deeper way than ever before. This 'thing' has been reflected back to me through the mirror of my life in almost every form...

※ through the fears of friends and family about what is happening in the world

※ through the global voice of Nature as she has flooded, burned and shook

※ and through the soft voices of beings on multiple planes of reality beyond this one, who have been speaking to me

Each has told me that the change isn't coming – it's here. And this 'thing' is death. Not death in the way that I would have traditionally thought of it, though of course, the death of physical beings is always here; but more the death of a way of life; of a system of social, economic and environmental constructs that are ready to be reborn. These thoughts are not new. Those of us working in sustainability have been using them for decades – but now it feels that change is finally here. As the Universe has been saying to those who have ears to hear, 'The time is now'.

The main challenge humans have always had with any form of death is our massive resistance to change. We struggle (if not flat-out refuse) to let go, until the decision is taken beyond our hands, beyond our mind and into our hearts. Our hearts know how to let go. And the letting go, always like an outbreath, allows the space for pause – before the new thing can be born. Without letting go, we cannot let anything new in. There is simply no space for it.

LIFE EVOLVES
THROUGH
A SERIES OF
MINI-DEATHS

Right now, there is very little space anywhere on Earth because humanity has filled it with things. There is very little space in our minds because we have filled them with excuses. There is very little space in our communities because we have filled them with distractions. In our current situation of overcrowding, death – both physical and metaphysical – becomes our friend, as it always has been. We have just become desperately afraid of the transformation death brings. But death brings new life. Death is a new birth. Death makes way for resurrection.

I invite you to contemplate resurrection, no matter what faith or cultural context you find yourself living in. Resurrection. The etymology of the word comes from the Latin *resurgere*, meaning to 'rise again'. And what is so scary about rising again? Perhaps it's because when we let go of the old, we are also making a monumental leap outside of our comfort (dis-comfort) zones and are asked to surrender to the mystery of new territory. Perhaps it's because we know that a new adventure into unknown lands will leave us stripped bare, challenged to the limits of our inner capability and forever changed? Or perhaps it's because we don't believe that we will survive the ordeal? Perhaps it is all of these things.

But the reality is, if we don't change and we refuse death itself in whatever form, then we will definitely not survive. Any of us. I sense that in this moment of time, we are being asked individually (ME) and collectively (WE) to embark on a global adventure where we ALL survive and flourish in new forms. Our species is being asked to metamorphosise from ME to WE to ALL; to take into account the bigger story of the Earth, of all beings. We are being asked to die and resurrect into a vast evolutionary adventure where ALL of us transform into something far more beautiful than our current mythology can even conceive of.

I know this still sounds scary – but to ME at least, it is starting to sound like an adventure worth taking. Contemplate the resurrection. See whether your fear transforms too.

THE NEXT ALCHEMICAL SPIRAL

THE DEEPENING JOURNEY

AS WE MOVE TOWARDS THE END OF ONE JOURNEY, WE NATURALLY APPROACH THE BEGINNING OF ANOTHER

THIS IS AN OPEN-ENDED ENQUIRY – A PILGRIMAGE WITHOUT DESTINATION

One of the unexpected gifts of the Soulistic Journey, as we – Genevieve and Lorna – prepare to enter our next 'spiral' of adventuring, is how the process continues to evolve, deepen and expand before our very eyes. The beauty of walking this path with fellow seekers means that we share our epiphanies, insights and synchronicities, and of course, our doubts, anxieties and struggles – so that we all learn from each other's experiences and co-create the ongoing adventure together. We have found that the journey is never linear, but like a river, it meanders, and is joined by other streams and flows of energy so that it becomes ever more dynamic and fluid. This is the beauty of an open-ended enquiry: it is a pilgrimage without destination.

The next 'octave' of this alchemical spiral is now beckoning us to open up the journey to more seekers, hence the writing of this book, and the formation of The Soulistic Journey Mentoring Programme (see The Soulistic Library for more details). We certainly could not have foretold that this would be the outcome as we set out on our adventure, but this is the beauty of the Soulistic Journey being a year and a day in duration: the shamans knew what they were doing using this magical time-frame in their own healing work, because that extra day makes all the difference; it facilitates your next step on the spiral. We just kept putting one foot in front of the other, and here we are, and here this book is!

Hopefully, as you have worked your way through this book, you will have engaged with us and other Wisdom Weavers through our Mentoring Programme – and will have experienced first-hand, the powerful alchemy of choice and sovereignty. Hopefully, your life will have changed for the better in so many ways as you embraced the adventures presented in this book. Our sole aim in writing it is to facilitate joyfulness, empowerment and purpose in your life!

What is fundamental to this book and the Soulistic Journey itself is that it is a self-led enquiry. We have written about our journey, but yours will have been exhilaratingly different, albeit similar in certain ways. You will have adventured as deeply or as lightly as you felt necessary. There is no judgement, just exploration. We hope you enjoyed the ride and invite you to consider in what direction your next steps will take you forward from this moment on.

WE JUST KEPT PUTTING ONE FOOT IN FRONT OF THE OTHER – AND HERE THIS BOOK IS!

THE SOULISTIC LIBRARY

THE SOULISTIC JOURNEY MENTORING PROGRAMME

THE WORLD IS TRANSFORMING NOW AND THIS BOOK IS PERFECTLY TIMED TO SUPPORT THOSE IN TRANSITION

As those who walked previous spirals of the Soulistic Journey with us wished to continue deepening their journey within the container of our Soulitsic Community, a group of wise souls formed, who meet online and on-life to share their own unique gifts and insights. Over the course of the last few years, during our Soulistic Journey retreats, many 'graduates' were called to offer creative workshops to the community to explore what was arising for them on a more experiential level. These workshops have ranged from 'Writing from the Heart' to 'Sacred Movement'; 'Art and Soul' to 'Crystal Alchemy', 'Poetry in the Raw' to 'Your Evolved Archetypes' and much more.

What has become clear to us as we completed the first draft of this book, and as Covid-19 forced our gatherings online, was that the world is transforming NOW, before our very eyes and so this book is perfectly timed to support those in transition, and Zoom offers a perfect mechanism for us to share our experiences more widely.

So, we have evolved The Soulistic Journey Mentoring Programme for all those who are reading this book and feel moved to connect with our community on a deeper level. When you become a 'Member' of the Mentoring Programme, you will enter into a guided and facilitated version of the journey outlined in this book, with monthly Zoom calls, Quarterly Zoom Ceremonies and a wide variety of supplemental classes offered by members of our community that allow you to tailor your Soulistic Journey to your specific and unique needs throughout the year. These will range from one-to-one mentoring sessions with either Genevieve or Lorna, writing workshops, Sacred Numerology, Chakra Movement, Art of the Soul, Beauty in Photography, Archetype Mapping, online retreats and much more.

To keep in touch with the Soulistic Community and register for our Mentoring Programme, visit: www.beyondhumanstories.com/soulistic-journey

THE SOLAR AND LUNAR ARCHETYPES OVERVIEW

JANUARY SOULISTIC ARCHETYPES

SOLAR ARCHETYPE: FLOW

He of Flow comes from Source and permeates our Galaxy. He of Flow is the energy of light, the enlivening quality of life. Flow is powerful and creative yet can be diverted by barriers and boundaries. He of Flow desires to run without restriction. He streams forth in the molecules of winter sunlight, caressing you and inviting you to open to the potential of new opportunities and ways of being. He takes you by the hand and leads you into the forest of your life story, inviting you to journey into the heart of your adventure.

Will you accept his challenge and take your first few steps into unknown territory? Know that if and when you do, He of Flow will be right there with you, guiding the way with the magic of synchronicity.

Solar Wisdom: *a new challenge, unknown territory, a sense of opportunity, adventurousness, synchronicity, new beginnings*

Solar Mystery: *feeling stuck or impeded by daily duties, restriction or complication, lack of momentum, diversions and distractions*

LUNAR ARCHETYPE: COMPLEMENTARITY

She of Complementarity unites parts into the whole; She sees beauty in completion. Complementarity shows her face in opposites and contradictions, finding synthesis. Complementarity is divinely paradoxical and playful, presenting you with a mirror image of yourself. She steps forth from the frosty moonlit nights, to lovingly show you where you have choice. She of Complementarity can guide you to right thought, right feeling and right action if you allow her to. For She is your sister and knows you well. She of Complementarity understands that we are all mirrors of each other and are therefore able to remind each other when we have strayed off the path of our true destiny.

Lunar Wisdom: awareness of choice and synergy, feelings of playfulness, the completion of something, destiny, the cosmic joke of separation

Lunar Mystery: experiencing contradictions or paradoxes, mirroring and projection on to others, opposition or conflict

UNIFICATION: CLARITY

They of Flow and Complementarity merge to form pure potential. The child of their mystical union is called Clarity. Clarity illuminates the path you knew you came here to walk and have been seeking ever since you were born. The child Clarity calls to you as the light of your soul, the star of aspiration, the centre of your story. Will you follow Clarity, leaving behind outworn beliefs and stories? Of course you will – when, is up to you.

Unification Keys: fulfilling your potential, owning your vision, bathing in the illumination of awareness, seeking clarity beyond human stories

FEBRUARY SOULISTIC ARCHETYPES

SOLAR ARCHETYPE: BALANCE

He of Balance is fine-tuned and represents the divine mind, coming straight from source essence and coding. He is the exquisite precision of ultimate Universal purity. He of Balance is the foundation of epiphany and revelation: the light of understanding in the darkness of illusion. He will find you in unexpected moments of reflection; he will shake your story by its foundations, allowing you to come to a new equilibrium should you accept his path to wisdom.

To choose what is offered by He of Balance, you must first surrender that which no longer serves you. Balance is a barometer of change, indicative of forces at play and at rest. Tune in to your inner sense of Balance when guidance is needed.

Solar Wisdom: unequivocal acceptance, surrender and transformation, experience of epiphany or revelation, dynamic rebalancing of life's elements

Solar Mystery: chaos leading to a new state of creation, the collapse of old stories, disillusionment, change and uncertainty, a feeling of being unravelled

LUNAR ARCHETYPE: PEACE

She of Peace is flirtatious and exquisite. She resides in the heart and is nourished by Love. Peace wanes when conflict, anger or animosity arise, and at times it is difficult to find her, especially if you are distracted by outer noise. She of Peace needs compassion in order to flourish.

She of Peace embraces us in the never-ending spiral of life and death. She resolves conflicts and reminds us that all life is interconnected and related; she shows us our eternal spiral through the Universe, smiling with empathy when we forget that we are eternal beings, playing in form.

She of Peace reminds us to take deep breaths and relax into the perfect rhythm and tempo of our soul journey. There is no need to rush forwards, only to dream and choose the future that we wish to create.

Lunar Wisdom: *a sense of tranquillity amid the chaos, nurturing your relationships, recognising the interconnectedness of all beings, the truth of eternity, surrender, grace*

Lunar Mystery: *being distracted from your path, conflicting emotions, fear of punishment or death, resentment and the need for revenge*

UNIFICATION: BLISS

When fused, Balance and Peace create the child called Bliss. Bliss brings the inner gnosis that all ever has been and always will be perfect in the Universal story of life. Bliss comes to sit beside us when we are ready to stop long enough to drink in the joy and elation of simply being alive.

Bliss asks us to release our judgements of right and wrong, so that we can rest in the field of acceptance, acknowledging that our story can be heaven on earth if we choose it to be. Bliss is the precursor to heightened awareness and a divine gnosis of inter-being.

Unification Keys: *upwelling of joyfulness, a sense of elation, acceptance without judgement, knowing Heaven is on Earth*

MARCH SOULISTIC ARCHETYPES

SOLAR ARCHETYPE: FREEDOM

He of Freedom flies like a bird on high, unfettered. He breaks the chains of conditioning, and shoots arrow-like towards an unknown destination. The energy Freedom brings makes all things possible. Freedom is a pioneer, a courageous out-rider, a harbinger of new worlds.

He of Freedom is the ancient seer of truth beyond all story. Flying above the noise of the lower worlds, He views the vast expanse of all horizons and rests upon the currents of Universal energy. If you choose to look up, this guardian of the bird tribes will lead you out of your current story and into new beginnings. He of Freedom, exists to remind you of your own ability to fly beyond any restrictions you may believe you are limited by. Freedom is a guide to your future.

Solar Wisdom: making courageous decisions, a shifting of perception, a sense of liberty and possibility, conscious rebellion

Solar Mystery: choosing to stay within existing comfort zones, feeling trapped, limited imagination, accepting others' narratives or truths

LUNAR ARCHETYPE: KNOWING

She of Knowing is a consistent inner voice. She has alchemical powers, enabling the retelling of personal narratives in a new light. Knowing presents you with the threefold path of your lifetime – the past, present and future – all are her domains and indeed, she moves simultaneously through them, facilitating your evolution.

She of Knowing is the keeper of life lessons, hard won through your childhood, adulthood and elderhood. She reminds you when you are about to repeat the same patterns and offers you the potential for rebirth from her cauldron of time. Knowing is ancient and wise. Listen to her as she whispers from your core.

Lunar Wisdom: awareness of unfolding patterns, ability to define your life lessons, sensing into your heart wisdom, a strong connection with your intuition or instinct, accessing your inner truth

Lunar Mystery: confusion or uncertainty in life, living in the past, fear of the future, inability to appreciate the present moment

UNIFICATION: FUTURE

Freedom and Knowing synthesise to give birth to the child called Future. Future teaches you that when you combine self-knowledge and wisdom with inspiration and courage, you create your dreams in the present moment.

Future waits for you at the threshold of new life, beckoning you forward with a smile, knowing that when you choose to follow, Future becomes your Now.

Unification Keys: recognising the potentiality in all things, ability to make dreams into reality, acceptance of the non-linearity of time, infinity, manifestation through choice and sovereignty

APRIL SOULISTIC ARCHETYPES

SOLAR ARCHETYPE: ABUNDANCE

He of Abundance is everlasting and fills your cup to overflowing, but in ways that are often unseen or unacknowledged. Abundance shape-shifts presenting what is needed with perfect timing. He holds in his hands the Cauldron of Plenty and will fulfil your every wish – just be careful you know what you are asking for.

He of Abundance lives by Creation's laws and will turn your world upside down if you try to control things too tightly. After all, life itself cannot be controlled, only respected. Abundance reminds us that we are all creators and that our thoughts and feelings give birth to our realities. Open your heart and receive Abundance with gratitude and with absolute self-responsibility.

Solar Wisdom: an arising respect for the 'other-than-human' worlds where all life is created, a sense of plenitude and bounteousness, upwelling gratitude, Universal plenty

Solar Mystery: needing to be in control, a fear of lack or scarcity, inability to see wealth beyond money, greed, a need to hoard

LUNARY ARCHETYPE: HARMONY

She of Harmony sings you into empowerment. She of Harmony resonates with the sacred tones of creation, the Universe, and with your own personal soul vibration, weaving her song with yours, creating a state of grace. Harmony channels joy; she operates on the inner realms of life, harmonising everything that calls her name. She is the great stabiliser, bringing exactly the right energy, at exactly the right time to create new levels of evolution.

Invite Harmony into your life and expect both destruction of old stories that no longer serve and creation of new, more empowering narratives of healing. She of Harmony reminds you that life involves a constant cycle of rebirth and surrender. Once you are aware of the harmonious state of grace, you will want to reside there always.

Lunar Wisdom: integrity with divine essence, acceptance with grace of all that befalls you, healing on all levels, development of symbolic sight

Lunar Mystery: imbalanced relationships, feelings of low-energy and fatigue, joylessness, breakdown of existing systems creating a sense of chaos

UNIFICATION: EVOLUTION

When Abundance and Harmony pair, they co-create the child called Evolution. Evolution lives within you – within your very genes – ready to move you forward in the direction of your dreams and your destiny. Evolution is patient and indulges your foibles, never retracting any benefaction or gifts, because Evolution is ever-unfolding, dancing in the cells of every being, compelling us all to keep moving towards new life, new stories and new adventures.

Unification Keys: cellular reprogramming, dynamic choice-making, stepping into your destiny

MAY SOULISTIC ARCHETYPES

SOLAR ARCHETYPE: LIFEFORCE

He of Lifeforce is your animating Spirit; the energy that makes you unique, the rising impetus of transformation. Lifeforce is unstoppable yet unpredictable: he comes to be and he ceases to be, and your fate resides with him. He inspires new growth in the Spring and is the energy behind every relationship and connective force.

He of Lifeforce reminds us that being consciously alive is a privilege – one that, if we take for granted, will depart – allowing dis-ease to ensue. He of Lifeforce asks but one thing from us: that we feel gratitude each day for the blessing of our unique life and demonstrate that through our actions in the world.

Solar Wisdom: rekindling energy through embracing life, awakening to a sense of aliveness, gratitude for life's blessings, learning how to surf the waves of creative energy

Solar Mystery: the lessons of ill health, feeling uncomfortable in your own skin, wishing you were different, unable to accept opportunities when they arise, repression

LUNAR ARCHETYPE: TRAJECTORY

She of Trajectory establishes the direction of your life path and orientates your soul's journey. Trajectory is the muse who inspires your dreams; the one who excites you when you are on the verge of a new path or opportunity. It is She of Trajectory who energises you with potential pathways for your journey.

She of Trajectory weaves your lifeforce into a web of possibility asking that you practice conscious choice to activate that energy. Trajectory turbo-charges your creative projects and also nudges you back onto your path if you become distracted on your journey.

Lunar Wisdom: *harnessing of potential energy, feeling excited and motivated, fearless choice-making, expressing yourself creatively*

Lunar Mystery: *feeling lost and uncertain, lacking interest in life, apathy, distraction via addictive behaviours*

UNIFICATION: INTUITION

Lifeforce and Trajectory combine to form the child, Intuition. This child is a way-finder, a cosmic tracker and Universal guide through the dream-weave of life. Intuition beckons to you, showing you the way to your own inner wisdom, sense of integrity and self-knowledge. Intuition shows us where to go when all seems lost or if there are too many options to choose from. This child lives within you, reminding you of your ability to practice discernment and decision.

Unification Keys: *remembering to ask for guidance, listening to the quiet voice of inner wisdom, acting with integrity, ability to discern the right path for your evolution*

JUNE SOULISTIC ARCHETYPES

SOLAR ARCHETYPE: LEAP

He of Leap is a playful energy, encouraging you to take a chance, to move beyond complacency. He of Leap is the exhilaration of change in action, the passion of dreams looming into reality. Leap is an act of faith; Leap is a heart-stopping moment in time.

He of Leap is likened to the Cosmic archetype of The Fool – he leaps off the cliffs of the known into the ocean of possibility. He reminds you that everything you need is outside your current comfort zone and asks you to be courageous in moving towards new realities.

He of Leap reminds you to trust that all is always well when you follow your inner sense of destiny and adventure.

Solar Wisdom: a sense of playfulness – not taking life too seriously, inquisitiveness, enjoyment from courageous action, passionate but not over-zealous, divine trust

Solar Mystery: loss of faith in your decision-making, self-sabotaging behaviour, being overly cautious, inability to take risks, fear that leads to stagnation

LUNAR ARCHETYPE: SPARK

She of Spark ignites the imagination and kindles the fires of inspiration; she fans the flames of courage and illuminates instinct. She instigates – she fires you up at precisely the right moment and fans your passion for life.

She of Spark is the energy that was with you before you were born, catalysing your entry into human form. She is the lightning rod that fertilises the soil of your dreams and causes the seeds of your imagination to germinate before your very eyes. Spark jolts you awake when you have been dallying too long in the illusion of the world. She of Spark is unique for each of us but is easily diminished by ill-health, or if you are out of balance.

Lunar Wisdom: *Epiphany, catalytic energy, lucid dreaming, nurturing the germination of ideas, being inspired and inspiring*

Lunar Mystery: *holding on to cultural illusions, impotence, laziness, unable to generate a sense of excitement or interest in anything*

UNIFICATION: BLAZE

They of Leap and Spark enter the Cosmic dance as equal partners and merge to create the child called Blaze. Blaze takes the volatile energy of its parents and transforms it into the very stuff that miracles are made of. This child, creates synchronicity, magic and forward momentum once you have said 'yes' to the adventure of your life and harnessed the power of courage – it literally 'blazes a trail. Blaze takes your hand and leads you forward in the dance of inspired action.

Unification Keys: *knowing magic when you see it, opening up to the miracle of synchronicity, aligning with the path of momentum, taking inspired action*

JULY SOULISTIC ARCHETYPES

SOLAR ARCHETYPE: FREQUENCY

He of Frequency pulsates with the Universal rhythm of life. He can be heard in the beat of a heart, the breath of a loved one, the flap of an eagle's wing. Frequency is a fractal pattern that pervades the Universe and connects the molecular with the Cosmic.

He of Frequency is powerful and subtle, an energetic quality that supports the entraining of molecules in the sacred harmonics of life and death. He is the great connector, the great weaver of notes into a symphony of creation. He brings you out of mind and into body, so that you can feel life pulsing through you, especially at this time – the height of the Summer.

He shows us how to listen to the different frequencies of every being on Earth, speaking in a language beyond words. He of Frequency sings you awake at dawn, ready for a new day.

Solar Wisdom: deep listening, harmonising with the pulsing energies of the days and seasons, singing your life into being, the power of words used wisely knowing they all carry frequency

Solar Mystery: deafness to life and its call, negative thoughts and behaviour patterns, nerves on edge, inability to listen

LUNAR ARCHETYPE: BLOSSOM

She of Blossom has perfect timing; she emerges when conditions are ripe and potent. She of Blossom is the key to manifestation; the point at which all things flourish. Blossom delights in beauty – she opens her loving arms and welcomes you into the erotic dance of plenty. She flaunts her full, voluptuous exquisite form, tempting you to forget your inhibitions and do the same.

Blossom is the celebration of Summer and of the fullness of Earth's everlasting generosity. She is the high noon sun and the blessed full moon. She is the flowering of love. When you look to her, you rise in love for yourself. Blossom reminds us of our Divine heritage; she is a multidimensional blessing.

Lunar Wisdom: appreciation and celebration of the sensual world, communicating with love and generosity, an ability to see the multi-dimensional facets of all life, finds life seductive, eros as creation

Lunar Mystery: self-sabotage, self-deprecation, cannot see the beauty in the world, cynicism and judgementalism, feeling like a victim to fortune

UNIFICATION: ECSTASY

They of Frequency and Blossom, make love to create the child, Ecstasy. Ecstasy reminds you that anything in your wildest imaginings is possible, if you have the courage to allow Ecstasy to manifest in your life; for Ecstasy is also mischievous and can bring chaos in her wake. Ecstasy is the child of the Summer sun and the warm Earth being sung alive in beauty.

Ecstasy leads us out of our habitual rights and wrongs and into spontaneous mischief and celebration – for this child lives among the 'other-than-human' – the fairies and the devas and the transcendental beings. Ecstasy encourages you to frolic with the hidden ones and stop being so serious! Relax into the joy of Summer. Fall in love with yourself.

Unification Keys: bringing dreams to fruition, enjoying the energy that comes from playfulness, giving yourself permission to relax and take pleasure in life without guilt, innocent sensuality

AUGUST SOULISTIC ARCHETYPES

SOLAR ARCHETYPE: CHOICE

He of Choice comes masked, disguised, so often you think he is not there at all, but Choice is a trickster; he empowers and distracts depending on how you choose to engage with him. He presents you with a cornucopia of options and it is up to you to find your truth amongst the distraction of variety. Once you remember your power of focus and soulful discernment however, He of Choice becomes a powerful ally.

Choice reminds you of your authentic path through the vast Cosmos and empowers you to choose only that which leads you back to your Soul Story. Choice is multifaceted and omnipresent, and it is incumbent upon you to choose wisely.

Solar Wisdom: learning how to seize opportunity, recognising what feels authentic to you, living with integrity and honesty, non-judgementalism, soulful integrity

Solar Mystery: feeling like you have no choice, inability to see a different way is possible, distracted by the minutiae of life, victimhood and the giving away of your power

LUNAR ARCHETYPE: INFINITY

She of Infinity embodies timeless wisdom, where time is not linear but cyclical and revealing; the eternal and endless loop of creation. She of Infinity invites us to see with mythic eyes in deep time, a practice both enlightening and nurturing.

She persists when everything else transforms. She is the constant keeper of eternal wisdom and power. She of Infinity is the silent space behind all things, showing us deep time and Cosmic law. She brings balance and integration to chaos and dissolves them again paradoxically when right time and right action calls. She of Infinity unites you with your Self, who you will come to know intimately.

Lunar Wisdom: *learning to interpret what is unsaid or symbolic, experiencing time as cyclical rather than linear, practicing a deep time perspective, knowing all is well in the long cycles of evolution*

Lunar Mystery: *linear sense of life and time, fear of death, breakdown and chaos, inability to perceive on a metaphysical level, bitterness and lack of forgiveness*

UNIFICATION: COSMOS

They of Choice and Infinity give birth to the child called Cosmos, who conveys multidimensional realities. This is the child of holographic in-form-ation; the DNA that creates and evolves. Cosmos creates new potentialities through imagination, choosing life in alignment with the biggest story there is. The child called Cosmos, weaves the world around you through Universal law and shows you how to do the same; a powerful ally in your evolutionary journey.

Unification Keys: *celebrating the potentiality of life, knowing evolution is continual and boundless, engaging imaginatively with the other-than-human realms, remembering you are a child of a miraculous Universe, holographic Cosmic law.*

SEPTEMBER SOULISTIC ARCHETYPES

SOLAR ARCHETYPE: ENERGY

He of Energy is omnipresent and can be harnessed, transmuted and redirected in myriad ways, but never destroyed. He of Energy is ceaseless, immortal, transcendent, yet offers his gifts to humanity unconditionally. He of Energy burns with the fire of a great star. Self-replenishing, he radiates cosmic impulse that interacts with every molecule in existence.

He of Energy fuels your passion and creates the precise interaction needed for manifestation to take place. He supports your creative endeavours and breathes energetic resonance into patterns aligned to your Soul Story. He of Energy, co-creates your vision.

Solar Wisdom: learning how to energise yourself, opening to the magic of manifestation, awareness of your interaction with Universal energy on a molecular level

Solar Mystery: low energy and exhaustion, needing to let-off steam, inability to relax, always needing to be busy or occupied with something, need for external stimulants

LUNAR ARCHETYPE: DIVINE LAW

She of Divine Law constantly reweaves Indra's Net so that all is balanced and evolving. She is the great synthesiser; she destroys that which is out of alignment to the highest laws of the Universe and enables that which needs to express. She clears away all that is unnecessary in order for new beginnings to occur.

She of Divine Law represents purity and precision and holds a mirror up to your stories and shows you the realities that you are creating with them. She is the guardian of free will and life design.

Lunar Wisdom: taking action with purity of spirit, enjoying harmonious relationships and relinquishing those that are not aligned to your truth, understanding the power of free will, both creatively and destructively

Lunar Mystery: resisting life, unable to bring projects to fruition, relationships seem to unravel easily, friction and frustration

UNIFICATION: CO-CREATION

They of Energy and Divine Law encircle diversity in all its complexity and weave a sparkling web of connectivity that keeps the matrix in perfect condition for the experiments of life. Their fusion creates the child, Co-creation.

Co-creation represents the vast cornucopia of Universal existence. This child opens its arms to the lessons of the past and the potential of the future, catalysing the metamorphosis of each. Co-creation reminds us that we have ultimate choice and that our choices create our worlds. Co-creation teaches us to be mindful of our thoughts, feelings and actions as all combine to create experience.

Unification Keys: diversity as a state of mind, living in the eternal now, your thoughts create your world, conscious co-creation with others, the Earth and all of life

OCTOBER SOULISTIC ARCHETYPES

SOLAR ARCHETYPE: MICROCOSM

He of Microcosm is holographic and reflects the greatest story there is. He expresses the fractal essence of the Universe: 'As above, so below; As within, so without'. Like cosmic mycelium, He of Microcosm reveals the vast web of interconnection between all beings, both animate and inanimate.

He is the dreamweave in living essence, connecting everything and no-thing, showing that indeed you are a drop in the Universal ocean and also the ocean itself. He of Microcosm is all-encompassing.

Humans are the mid-way point between the smallest thing in the Universe and the largest thing in the Universe. Therefore, you are Microcosm's fulcrum: if you are in balance, the Universe is in balance.

Solar Wisdom: deepening awareness of the holographic nature of life, feeling the omnipresence of spirit, able to reflect and express metaphysical concepts in thought and deed

Solar Mystery: feeling insignificant and alone in the Universe, cynical and pessimistic, having no faith or feelings of connection with anything

LUNAR ARCHETYPE: SEED

She of Seed can lie dormant for years, but always knows when the time is ripe for germination. Her gift is deep knowledge of time. You may plant the seed of an idea, but it will only germinate when it is time.

She of Seed holds potential in her codons; she is fecund and fertile. Seed holds open a doorway for you to see your beginnings and endings. Just like each seed in the Earth instinctively knows which way to move through the darkness into the light, She of Seed reminds us that deep inside, the seed of your soul knows this too. Seed teaches us that there is a time for rest and dormancy and a time for growth and momentum. The trick is learning to distinguish one from the other.

Lunar Wisdom: loves the process of ideas and projects germinating, goes with an instinctive or 'gut-feeling' for decision-making, is relaxed and able to act with right timing, understands (on a metaphysical level) that we cannot have Spring without Winter

Lunar Mystery: feelings of impatience and frustration, pushy and impetuous, unable to engage with people on a deeper level beyond the current story

UNIFICATION: TEMPO

He of Microcosm and She of Seed pair to give birth to the Child called Tempo. This is a child of time and outside of time. The Child called Tempo holds the key to rhythm and the patterns of the Universal heartbeat.

This child knows exactly how to dance through evolution, leading you forward in your own unfolding. Tempo reminds you to listen to your own heartbeat, your guide in life and death, and trust the dance of your soul.

Unification Keys: an innate awareness of rhythm and pattern, seeing the evolutionary perspective in all things, letting go of fear, finding your own rhythm

NOVEMBER SOULISTIC ARCHETYPES

SOLAR ARCHETYPE: PURITY

He of Purity is the essence of impeccability according to Universal principles. Purity is a quality of being, a way of seeing, a state of heart-mind. He of Purity brings perspective and higher insight to any situation you call him into.

Omniscient and all seeing, He of Purity will show you ultimate Universal truth. He will also clear out and clean your narrative cupboards, allowing you to move beyond old stories, beliefs and habits into clean pure territory. Essential and whole, He of Purity rests in the silence of source.

Solar Wisdom: has a clarity of perspective that is insightful yet creative, communicates beyond words through action and intention, a person who embodies purity is one who radiates light and love

Solar Mystery: unwillingness to change habits or self-limiting behaviour, dislikes uncertainty, can create confusion and interference with gossip or partial truths

LUNAR ARCHETYPE: VIBRATION

She of Vibration is the gateway to elevation, a key to other worlds. She of Vibration is the dynamic force that resides in every cell of your being. She is the guardian of sacred sound and communicates your dreams, visions and thoughts to the molecules of the quantum realm for actualisation.

All things manifest in Vibration and like the dial on a radio, you can tune-in to your own vibrational qualities, and with commitment and patience, you can tune-up and connect with new dimensions and realities.

She of Vibration shows you that the music of your life is completely determined by your will. You can create disharmony and noise, or you can tune-in to exquisite symphonies on the wind. The choice is up to you.

Lunar Wisdom: *ability to attune to the highest potential in everyday life, bringing forth the actualisation of dreams and visions, having the ability to access and contemplate your inner wisdom, choosing your vibration and harmonics at will*

Lunar Mystery: *inability to remember dreams, prioritising the needs of others before yourself, feelings of anxiety, foreboding or disquiet, overwhelm with the noise of the external world*

UNIFICATION: TRANSCENDENCE

They of Purity and Vibration merge to create the magical child called Transcendence; a being who shows you how to move beyond the boundaries of everything you thought and believed possible, into the mystical, metaphysical realms of miracles.

This is the child of transmutation; the child who shows you how to pupate from your 'caterpillar' state into a soulful butterfly. The path of Transcendence is a path less travelled, but it is open to you if you choose it.

Unification Keys: *understanding the metaphysical perspective, a mystical worldview, seeing transformation at work, embracing metamorphosis*

DECEMBER SOULISTIC ARCHETYPES

SOLAR ARCHETYPE: UNITY

He of Unity makes love to the world. He is the Divine Lover. With love in your heart you are kin to all life. He of Unity is omnipotent and omnipresent. Like the warp and weft of a loom, completion of the whole creates inherent unity in diversity.

He of Unity is the force that sits in the centre of the Universe, in the Great Silence. He is source creation. He is all form and all manifestation. He smiles at you when you forget this truth; then He wraps you in the embrace of home-coming. He of Unity is the end of your journey and is the light in the eyes of your soul.

Solar Wisdom: feeling the omnipresence of spirit, understanding that the principles of holism apply to all things, a wonderful sense of homecoming

Solar Mystery: lack of compassion or love for self and others, eluded by creativity or passion, dullness and lacking in vitality, a sense of separateness

LUNAR ARCHETYPE: ALCHEMY

She of Alchemy is the Divine Flame that catalyses spiritual transformation from one state of being to another; the animating process that creates Unity from separation. She transforms all the archetypal energies through the fire of creation and destruction. She of Alchemy births new life forms from old. She breathes the sacred breath and moves the Earth through her evolutionary cycles.

She of Alchemy fans the flame of your heart's longings and moves you to begin again when you feel like giving up. She is hope. She is light. She is grace and grit. She creates infinity in her vessel of transformation.

Lunar Wisdom: birthing new ideas and challenges into being, surrendering to the fires of transformation, knowing that life always follows death, a sense of destiny in the changes life brings

Lunar Mystery: resistance to change, stuck in old stories and ways of living, happy in your (dis)comfort zones

UNIFICATION: TRUTH

They of Unity and Alchemy are our oldest ancestors; the Wise Ones who prevail and bring all into being. It is no coincidence that they reside in the darkest month of the year, for here they give light to the mystery; here the spiral takes another turn. They of Unity and Alchemy form the child called Truth.

Truth resides at the very core of every story and eventually calls you home to your wisdom after a long journey well-travelled. The child called Truth comes to you when you are ready to know who you are at the core of every story you hold dear, and to let them all go, dying to who you have been so that you can live as unadulterated Spirit.

Unification Keys: a sense of completion and homecoming, knowing that matter is animated by spirit, accepting your innate wisdom and destiny in evolution

BOOKSHELF

A NEW SCIENCE OF LIFE, RUPERT SHELDRAKE

A WORLD WAITING TO BE BORN, M. SCOTT PECK

A MORE BEAUTIFUL WORLD THAT WE KNOW IS POSSIBLE,
CHARLES EISENSTEIN

ACTIVE HOPE, JOANNA MACY & CHRIS JOHNSTONE

ANIMATE EARTH, STEPHAN HARDING

ARCHETYPES AND THE COLLECTIVE UNCONSCIOUS, CARL JUNG

ARCHETYPES AT WORK, RICHARD OLIVIER

BECOMING ANIMAL, DAVID ABRAM

BREATHE: SEASONAL REFLECTIONS, PAUL CLARKE

BUTTERFLY'S CHILDREN, ANNIE MARCH

CLARE SELECTED POEMS AND PROSE, JOHN CLARE

COMFORTABLE WITH UNCERTAINTY, PEMA CHÖDRÖN

LIVING THE WISDOM OF THE TAO, DR WAYNE DYER

LOVE & THE DIVINE FEMININE, DAVID CADMAN

MOON MOTHER, ROWENA PATTEE KRYDER

NATURE AND THE HUMAN SOUL, BILL PLOTKIN

NEW COLLECTED POEMS, WENDELL BERRY

ONE HUNDRED YEARS OF SOLITUDE, GABRIEL GARCIA MARQUEZ

PARZIVAL AND THE STONE FROM HEAVEN, LINDSAY CLARKE

PERMACULTURE: A DESIGNERS' MANUAL, BILL MOLLISON

PLANT INTELLIGENCE & THE IMAGINAL REALM,
STEPHEN HARROD BUHNER

PONDER ON THIS, ALICE BAILEY

REGENERATIVE LEADERSHIP, GILES HUTCHINS AND LAURA STORM

RESTORING BALANCE, DR IAN TENNANT

SACRED ECONOMICS, CHARLES EISENSTEIN

SACRED EARTH CELEBRATIONS, GLENNIE KINDRED

SACRED GROUND OF SACRED SPACE, ROWENA PATTEE KRYDER

SPELL OF THE SENSUOUS, DAVID ABRAM

SOPHIA'S BODY, ROWENA PATTEE KRYDER

SOULCRAFT, BILL PLOTKIN

THE BIOLOGY OF BELIEF, BRUCE LIPTON

THE CHILDREN'S FIRE, MAC MCCARTNEY

THE COSMIC HOLOGRAM, JUDE CURRIVAN

THE EARTH'S CYCLE OF CELEBRATION, GLENNIE KINDRED

THE GENE KEYS, RICHARD RUDD

THE HERO WITH A THOUSAND FACES, JOSEPH CAMPBELL

THE ILLUSION OF SEPARATION, GILES HUTCHINS

THE KEY TO THE SECRET OF THE ANCIENTS, RORY DUFF

THE LAST GHOST DANCE, BROOKE MEDICINE EAGLE

THE LOVE POEMS OF RUMI, RUMI

THE PERENNIAL PHILOSOPHY, ALDOUS HUXLEY

THE PILGRIMAGE, PAULO COELHO

THE POWER OF MYTH, JOSEPH CAMPBELL

THE PROPHET, KAHLIL GIBRAN

THE RED BOOK, CARL JUNG

THE ROAD LESS TRAVELLED, M. SCOTT PECK

THE SPIRAL DANCE, STAR HAWK

THE SPIRIT OF THE HEDGEROW, JO DUNBAR

THE SUFI BOOK OF LIFE, NEIL DOUGLAS KLOTZ

THE THOTH TAROT, ALEISTER CROWLEY

THE WILDWOOD TAROT, MARY RYAN

TOUGH BLISS: RESTORYING LIFE, GENEVIEVE BOAST

UNCOMMON WISDOM, FRITJOF CAPRA

WEEDS AND WILD FLOWERS, ALICE OSWALD

WHITE BUFFALO WOMAN COMES SINGING, BROOKE MEDICINE EAGLE

WILD GEESE, MARY OLIVER

WILDMIND: A FIELD GUIDE TO THE HUMAN PSYCHE, BILL PLOTKIN

WILDWOOD, ROGER DEAKIN

WORLD AS LOVER WORLD AS SELF, JOANNA MACY

YOU ARE THEREFORE I AM, SATISH KUMAR

ENDNOTES

[1] See page 325 for more information on The Soulistic Journey Mentoring Programme, or visit www.beyondhumanstories.com/soulistic-journey

[2] Permaculture (from 'permanent agriculture') was a concept first mooted by Australian scientists Bill Mollison and David Holmgren in the 1970s. Initially the concept of permaculture was applied to organic growing systems that imitated natural ecosystems, but as the idea became more popular, proponents realised that permaculture design principles, which centre on whole systems thinking, could be applied to all areas of life, including regenerative agriculture, rewilding, architecture and community resilience. For more details on the principles of Permaculture, visit: https://permacultureprinciples.com/

[3] *The Cosmic Hologram* by Jude Currivan Ph.D. examines the latest research across many fields of study to show how our Universe is in-formed and holographically manifested. Currivan explains how the fractal in-formational patterns that guide behaviour at the atomic level also guide the structure of galactic clusters in space, and how the in-formational relationships that underlie earthquakes are the same as those that play out during human conflicts. These patterns are reflected in how cities grow in the same ways that galaxies evolve, and how the dynamic forms that pervade ecosystems are identical to the in-formational structures of the Internet and our social and cultural behaviours. The author explores how consciousness connects us to the many interconnected layers of universal in-formation, making us both manifestations and co-creators

of the Cosmic hologram of reality. *The Cosmic Hologram* by Jude Currivan is published by Inner Traditions.

[4] Jamie Sams is a Native American Holy person with ancestors from the Cherokee, Seneca, Chocktaw and Mohawk tribes. She is a member of the Wolf Clan Teaching Lodge and is an author, healer and keynote speaker. She founded Children of the Earth Foundation which focuses on the needs of children to help ease the suffering of all humanity. Her books include *Earth Medicine: Ancestors' Ways of Harmony* and *The Thirteen Original Clan Mothers.*

[5] In 2008, international best-selling author, Lynne McTaggart published a book called *The Intention Experiment* to prove, once and for all, that our intentions, thoughts, prayers and wishes do have a real, calculable effect on the world. In her book she recounts scientific investigations and real case histories with evidence that we are all connected, and our intentions can be harnessed as a collective force for good.

For the last 40 years, scientists experimenting with the limits of quantum physics, have made seemingly impossible discoveries: in 1966 a lie-detector expert accidentally discovers that plants can read thoughts; in 1982 meditating Buddhist monks in the Himalayas turn their bodies into a human furnace; in 1994 a psychologist's experiments reveal a stream of light flowing from healers during healing. These events form part of an extraordinary scientific breakthrough: that thought is powerful and can affect that which it is focused upon; and that thought can change our lives for the better, cure our illnesses, transform our communities and even heal our impoverished planet – if that is our intention. In his review of the book, Deepak Chopra states, "*The Intention Experiment* is an extraordinary advance in our understanding of consciousness as a field of all possibilities where intention orchestrates fulfilment." For more information on how intention can change the outcome of events, visit: https://bit.ly/3cAqNxU

[6] This translation comes from *Original Meditation* written by Neil Douglas Klotz. In this book, Klotz investigates the ancient tradition of creation mysticism and shows how Western culture became side-tracked into an increasingly narrow, apocalyptic world view. The author suggests that we can recover an authentic meditation on our shared beginnings, a meditation that can bring us into a more embodied and compassionate present. To help us on our way, Neil Douglas-Klotz offers us a living anthology of voices, from a mystical view of the first chapters of Genesis, to the Aramaic words of Jesus, to translations of voices like Jelaluddin Rumi, Ibn Arabi, Meister Eckhart and the Jewish Kabbalists.

[7] Silvio Gesell (born 1862, died 1930) was a German theoretical economist, social activist, anarchist and libertarian socialist. This quote from fellow economist John Maynard Keynes puts his endeavours in a nutshell: "Gesell's chief work is written in cool and scientific terms, although it is run through by a more passionate and charged devotion to social justice than many think fit for a scholar. I believe that the future will learn more from Gesell's than from Marx's spirit."

[8] A brief search online will give you plenty of links to FreeForm Writing resources. They all have useful ideas and suggestions to get you started, but really, the only thing to do is to just write, without judgement and without editing or spell-checking; simply allow your stream of consciousness to flow onto the page like a waterfall for a set amount of time or number of pages. If you don't know what to write, just write, "I don't know what to write," until a thought comes into your mind, then follow that thought. It is a process that flourishes with practice. Here's a reflection on the value of FreeForm Writing (or Reflective Writing) from the University of Edinburgh: https://bit.ly/31t7LFP

[9] This feeling of 'Everything bad is happening TO me from outside forces I can't control,' is a theme that is discussed at length in Victor Frankl's seminal book, *Man's Search for Meaning*. Holocaust survivor, Frankl, a neurologist and psychiatrist, was interred in a Nazi concentration camp in the Second World

War. In the midst of great suffering and grief, Frankl made a startling discovery about the human spirit: 'But what about human liberty? Is there no spiritual freedom in regard to behaviour and reaction to any given surroundings? … Most important, do the prisoners' reactions to the singular world of the concentration camp prove that man cannot escape the influences of his surroundings? Does man have no choice of action in the face of such circumstances? We can answer these questions from experience as well as on principle. The experiences of camp life show that man does have a choice of action. … Man can preserve a vestige of spiritual freedom, of independence of mind, even in such terrible conditions of psychic and physical stress. [...] Everything can be taken from a man but one thing: the last of the human freedoms — to choose one's attitude in any given set of circumstances, to choose one's own way.'

[10] Entrainment: In essence, entrainment refers to a natural phenomenon in which one entity resonates synchronously with another in response to its dominant frequency of vibration. And whether this resonance occurs on a gross or subtle level, it invariably involves rhythm. We tend to associate rhythm and entrainment with music and sound, ignoring just how pervasive they are in the world around us and within us. Indeed, the human heart's rhythms play a vital role in producing waves of blood, sound and electromagnetism, all of which either entrain or influence every cell in the body to varying degrees. Researchers at the University of Arizona have discovered evidence that the heart's energetic field exerts an entrainment effect upon the brain. They also showed that 'heart-focused attention' increased this heart-brain entrainment. See: https://bit.ly/32rM48p. See also, *Plant Intelligence and the Imaginal Realm* by Stephen Harrod Buhner, published by Bear & Co., page 387 on 'The Miracle of Entrainment.'

[11] The Wildwood Tarot deck is inspired by Celtic mythology and a belief system steeped in shamanic tradition and forest lore. It is rooted in the seasonal rhythms and glorious festivals of the ancient year, reconnecting you to a long-lost world that embodies deep yet forgotten wisdom. When you delve into the

symbolism and mythology contained within the cards, new and insightful levels of understanding are unveiled, that enable you to make sense of your own world. The deck is easy to use and beautifully illustrated. It is a good starting point to reconnect you with the natural world and your own inner knowledge. (http://thewildwoodtarot.com/).

[12] To listen to the Soulistic Wheel Mentor Meditations for North, East, South and West visit www.beyondhumanstories.com/soulistic-journey-meditations and follow on screen instructions.

[13] Sandy Brown is a world-renowned ceramicist whose work is playful, joyful and spontaneous. She puts great emphasis on 'play' and believes our innate creativity is as natural to us as breathing, yet it is often stifled by well-meaning but critical teachers and the education system itself which does not value true creativity. She runs her acclaimed 'Creativity is Play' courses – listed by the Crafts Council UK as being among the best creative courses in the world – on a regular basis at her ceramics studio in Appledore, North Devon. http://www.sandybrownarts.com/courses.htm

[14] Johann Wolfgang von Goethe (pronounced Ger-ter) is an oft-quoted German writer and statesman, who died in 1832. Such were his spiritual, scientific, literary, artistic and poetic insights that he remains very much in the collective consciousness to this day. Just Google 'Goethe Quotes' and you will see what we mean. Here are two of our favourites:

"A man sees in the world what he carries in his heart."

"I have come to the frightening conclusion that I am the decisive element. It is my personal approach that creates the climate. It is my daily mood that makes the weather."

His seminal novel, which inspired both Liszt and Mahler to pen a symphony based on the book, is entitled, *Wilhelm Meister's Apprenticeship*.

[15] There are many and varied Tarot decks available. Why not ask your friends what Tarot deck they recommend? Alternatively, here are some suggestions from the Wisdom Weavers: Rowena Pattee Kryder's Co-Creation Card Deck or Gaia Matrix Oracle Cards; Diana Cooper's Angels of Light Cards, or Ascension Cards; The Wildwood Tarot by Mark Ryan or The Thoth Tarot by the famed Aleister Crowley. Explore and see what deck calls to you.

[16] Carl Jung's work on Archetypes is the subject of numerous books, and the foundation of many developmental theories, yet Jung's own interpretation was based in part on Plato's Forms – the theory that the physical world is not as real or true as timeless, absolute, unchangeable ideas (later conceived as archetypes). These non-physical 'ideas' are the essence of all things, from which objects and matter in the physical world are mere imitations. As Jung said, "An archetypal content expresses itself, first and foremost, in metaphors." Jung suggests that in the human realm, there are 12 foundational archetypes all seeking different outcomes in life. Put simply:

The Ruler seeks Control; the Artist seeks Innovation; the Innocent seeks Safety; the Sage seeks Knowledge; the Explorer seeks Freedom; the Outlaw seeks Liberation; the Magician seeks Power; the Hero seeks Mastery; the Lover seeks Intimacy; the Jester seeks Pleasure; the Everyman seeks Belonging; the Caregiver seeks Service.

Within this concept there are also 4 Cardinal Ordinations within which we operate:

Ego wants to leave a mark on the world; Order wants to provide structure to the world; Social wants to connect with others; Freedom yearns for Paradise.

Within this construct Jung then dives deeply into the core desire, motto, goal, fear, weakness, and talent of each archetype.

It is absolutely fascinating to determine where you fit within this context and Jung's book, *The Archetypes and the Collective Unconscious* is an excellent (if somewhat dense and academic) starting point if you wish to delve further into the concept of Archetypes. See also the work of Caroline Myss, detailed below under Point 18, who develops Jung's theories further.

[17] From *Plant Intelligence and the Imaginal Realm*, by Stephen Harrod Buhner, published by Bear & Co., page 369. Whilst Buhner's book only touches on archetypes, he does – in great depth – discuss the 'imaginal realm' wherein archetypes form. His subjects, from the plant kingdom, inhabit this realm, have a sense of 'I and not I' and have the capacity to dream. Buhner show us how, by 'un-gating' our sensory perception, we can 'feel' into this realm of meaning-filled communication and forever change our perception of what is real.

[18] Caroline Myss' book *Sacred Contracts* is really thought-provoking. Its premise is that before we were born, we all agreed to come into incarnation in this lifetime to experience certain aspects of our Soul Purpose. Caroline believes that as young children, we can still remember our purpose, but we gradually forget it as cultural mores, family life and education condition us to think analytically, not imaginatively. Myss has synthesised Jung's archetypes further and believes that by working to ascertain which archetypes are dominant or inactive in our lives, we can begin to decipher our Sacred Contract. *Sacred Contracts* by Caroline Myss is published by Bantam Books.

[19] Richard Olivier has developed a concept called 'Mythodrama' which uses the magic of storytelling to uncover our archetypes and help us make sense of the world. His work focuses on enabling leaders of the future to connect with

their leadership archetypes and their hidden power. His book, *Archetypes at Work* is available from oliviermythodrama.com

[20] In this short video, Genevieve introduces a useful tool for interpreting the patterns in your life story – the 'Storywave'. Find out how to draw your unique life Storywave here: https://bit.ly/3jJFH6R

[21] From, *Drawing on the Artist Within*, by Betty Edwards. The book is touted as 'the most effective programme ever created for tapping into your creative powers.' It certainly allowed us to see doodling in another light – one that reveals patterns of emotion and insight (our pattern language) that can open up a different perspective on how we interpret our creativity. Never again will doodling be meaningless!

[22] To connect with the inspiring work of the Indigenous Elders who have founded Wisdom Weavers of the World, and to hear their important message for human-kind, visit: www.wisdomweavers.world

[23] Tufts University website has a detailed explanation of how wolves can change an ecosystem. Visit: https://bit.ly/3lnzShg

[24] On the investigative journalist George Monbiot's website, there is a fascinating video, written and narrated by George, that shows how whales can, and do, affect the climate: https://bit.ly/3jkYPYT

[25] WordClouds can be used to create a visual image of motivational words. Some words will appear more distinct to you on certain days, then others will come to the fore and catch your eye. WordClouds are great for a visual

boost of encouragement. For the best free online WordCloud generators, visit: https://bit.ly/35cno6L

[26] Yoga is an ancient practice that can be found in various different cultural traditions, primarily that of India. The word 'yoga' can be translated to mean 'union' or to 'yoke ourselves' to a committed practice that involves breath, movement and meditation. Its wisdom is far reaching and has been adapted into myriad variations (especially in the West). If you already have a yoga practice or have tried it at various times in your life, then we invite you to deepen and perhaps explore a different aspect of this ancient system such as Pranayama (breath) or Dhyana (contemplation & meditation). If yoga is completely new to you then we recommend that you begin by searching the 'inner net' and seeing where the mystery takes you. Beware – yoga is far, far more than simply a form of exercise and meditation and each soul's yoga journey is different. The adventure is to find the practice that suits you best, much like the other practices we present you with in this book!

[27] Ana Forrest's yoga technique 'Forrest Yoga' is internationally renowned and introduces practitioners to 'a new way to move'. Her work developed as a response to her perceived void in traditional yoga forms. On her website she states, "Traditional forms of yoga did not address my deeper injuries; my lost Soul, the addictions – the helplessness around the addictions – and the ongoing suffering. The blend of Ceremonies, the poses I've created, the sequencing and the infusion of Medicine I learned from the First Peoples of this planet are what healed the suffering and the anguish from having been disconnected from my Spirit. Through that sacred blend, I learned how to reconnect to my Spirit." Visit her website for more information: www.forrest.yoga

[28] We first became aware of the work of Buddhist nun, Pema Chödrön, through her book, *Comfortable with Uncertainty* which has the wonderful subtitle: *108 ways of cultivating fearlessness and compassion*. It really is a highly

recommended book, as is the work of her Foundation. Pema has inspired millions of people across the globe with her simple message from the Buddhist contemplative tradition of practising loving kindness and compassion in these troubled times. She says, "We work on ourselves in order to help others, but also, we help others in order to work on ourselves." This is wisdom speaking.: https://pemachodronfoundation.org/

[29] A random act of kindness is a non-premeditated, one-off action that is offered to friends, family or complete strangers without expectation of anything in return. It is a gift designed to open people's hearts to the possibility of miracles. The phrase was first coined by Anne Herbert and M. Palova Pavel in their book, *Random Kindness and Senseless Acts of Beauty*, which was first published in 1993. Now, people all over the world practice this act of gifting. Visit: Random Acts of Kindness on https://www.randomactsofkindness.org/

[30] Bruce Lipton is an American developmental biologist, noted for his work on epigenetics. His seminal book *The Biology of Belief* unveils incredible new scientific discoveries that prove your thoughts have direct effects on the cells in your body, and Lipton describes the precise molecular pathways through which this occurs. This link between mind and matter explains how, rather than being a victim of our genetic inheritance, we have unlimited capacity to transform our personal lives and our collective future. For more details of the evolutionary scope of Lipton's work, visit https://www.brucelipton.com/

[31] Walking meditation (also known as kinhin) is practiced in many Buddhist traditions, where practitioners walk very slowly clockwise around a room, simply putting one foot in front of the other after each in-breath. There is no destination, there is simply the act of walking; there is no point to it other than the act of walking. In the act of walking slowly, the mind and body cohere and become one; thoughts settle and then disappear, and the body relaxes into a state of slow motion. More recently, walking meditation has been taken out

of the monastery and into the woodland or forest so that there is also a direct connection with Nature. Many practitioners like to walk barefoot and will often walk in this sacred way on their own as well as in community. Here is a lovely Walking Meditation poem by Thich Nhat Hahn: https://bit.ly/32JSQX4

32 'Neural washing' is a relatively new concept that likens the processes of meditation, relaxation and sleep to the cleansing action of the tides, as twice a day they wash through the coastline and estuaries flushing out impurities and bringing a change of energy and ecology to the landscape. Similarly, it is thought that meditation, relaxation and sleep can do the same for your physical body. A report published in Scientific American (https://bit.ly/34WUeID), noted, "Researchers think cerebrospinal fluid may 'flush out' toxic waste, 'cleaning' the brain and studies show that this garbage clearance is hugely improved during sleep." This process of 'neural washing' especially whilst asleep is discussed on page 97 of *Restoring Balance*, by Dr Ian Tennant. https://restoringbalance.life/

33 Dr Jude Currivan PhD is a writer, healer, cosmologist and futurist. Her work has greatly inspired both authors of this book, especially the mind-expanding concepts she presents in *The Cosmic Hologram*. Jude has experienced multidimensional realities from childhood and has worked with wisdom keepers, both incarnate and discarnate, from many traditions. Yet, perhaps her greatest gift is to be able to translate these 'other-worldly' experiences into scientific language so that they can be taken seriously by even the most sceptical. https://www.judecurrivan.com/

34 Vision Quests or Nature Immersions are one of the most ancient practices known to the human species and have been utilised in various forms by many different cultures to induce a 'vision experience' outside of our current story, comfort zone and identity. There are many wonderful individuals and organisations that offer these kinds of journeys (including Genevieve in the Summer months in the UK -https://bit.ly/3cDV5zG). We also recommend The Animas

Valley Institute in Colorado, USA (https://animas.org/) as well as The Way of Nature in the UK (https://bit.ly/3icsp1X).

[35] Genevieve Boast, co-author of *The Soulistic Journey*, is founder of Beyond Human Stories (www.beyondhumanstories.com), a vocation that allows her innate storytelling ability to help us transcend 'old paradigm' limitations – about who we are and what we can achieve – into a new story; one where humans are reinitiated into the natural ecosystems of Mother Earth and our place in the vast web of Universal life. She facilitates deep human transformations using myriad tools, most especially her unique and potent method of 'storyhacking' – which we have presented in detail in this book. Genevieve's first book, *Tough Bliss: Restorying Life* is an account of her own journey of transformation, through the cycles of remembering, rejuvenation, restorying and reunion.

[36] Pulitzer nominee, and Writer in Residence for the Chickasaw Nation, Linda Hogan is an internationally renowned speaker, writer and poet. Much of her work focuses on the limitations of human language; in her book, *The Bond Between Women and Animals*, she writes, "It is clear that there is a vocabulary of the senses, a grammar beyond that of human making." She believes that we live in a world of many intelligences and that human language is not all that is spoken in our world. Here is an insightful interview with Linda Hogan from *Superstition Review*: https://bit.ly/32KC36e

[37] Interbeing is a term first used by Vietnamese Buddhist monk Thich Nhat Hanh, who sums-up its meaning very simply: "Everything relies on everything else in order to manifest." In his book, *The Art of Living* Thich Nhat Hanh discusses the work of biologist Lewis Thomas who posited that human bodies are "shared, rented and occupied" by countless other tiny organisms, without which we could not function. Our bodies are a community of trillions of non-human cells all of which 'inter-be' with us. Interbeing is at the heart of who we are and

the heart of the Universe. A short extract from this book called 'The Insight of Interbeing' is available here: https://bit.ly/2QPvppS

[38] The benefits of wild swimming are well documented. A cold-water plunge is said to improve circulation and heart health, boost the immune system by increasing your white blood cell count and helps you to lose weight – but this is as nothing to the mental health benefits that have been attributed to swimming in wild watercourses. Wild swimmers talk of getting a 'natural high' from the practice, attributed to endorphins which are natural painkillers that are released to ease the sting of cold water. A quick browse online will detail wild swimming groups in your area and even give water quality guidance and safety advice. It is a practice not to be missed!

[39] Nick Polizzi's book and film of the same name – *The Sacred Science* – is a true story of a journey into the heart of Shamanic healing. With a pioneering spirit of adventure, Polizzi taps into the ancient roots of healing, and he reveals not only the incredible medicine of 'grandmother and grandfather plants', but also some ingrained psychological blind-spots that prevent true wellbeing in the modern world. There is deep wisdom still to be found among the indigenous peoples of this planet; *The Sacred Science* honours that wisdom whilst bringing it to the attention of a new generation of seekers. https://bit.ly/2Z2ojTw

[40] Little Gidding is No. 4 of *Four Quartets* by T S Eliot, a series of poems, that have beguiled scholars and readers since they were first published in 1943. All the Quartets deserve to be read and contemplated, but it is Little Gidding that continues to inspire us most. Indeed, Eliot's response to the season of winter most eloquently reflects the initiatory conversation Genevieve and Lorna had as this book began to evolve; about how one cannot conceive of the abundance of summer in the depths of winter, and whether it is possible to trust, as Nature demonstrates, that all will unfold in its own good time, without pushing, achieving, goal-setting and all the restless stress of contemporary culture.

'In the dark time of the year. Between melting and freezing
The soul's sap quivers. There is no earth smell
Or smell of living thing. This is the spring time
But not in time's covenant. Now the hedgerow
Is blanched for an hour with transitory blossom
Of snow, a bloom more sudden
Than that of summer, neither budding nor fading,
Not in the scheme of generation.
Where is the summer, the unimaginable
Zero summer?'

Use this link to read Little Gidding by T S Eliot in full: https://bit.ly/2F5HHaI

[41] What if there could be a 'calibration of consciousness' based on the positive/ negative responses of applied kinesiology? This is the work that Dr David R. Hawkins is undertaking and details in his book, *Power Vs Force*. If consciousness is calibrated on a scale of 1-1000, 'Courage' comes in at 200 and is the fulcrum between the lower less enlightened states that Hawkins considers are 'destructive of life both in the individual and society at large', and the higher 'constructive expressions of power'. His Map of Consciousness shows feelings of shame, guilt, apathy, grief, fear, desire, anger and pride as all coming in below the 200 fulcrum, thereby being destructive to self and others; whereas neutrality, willingness, acceptance, reason, love, joy and peace come in between 200 and 700 and are constructive expressions of power. Above 700 is enlightenment itself. He calls these aspect of consciousness the 'hidden determinants in human behaviour'. It is up to us as individuals to work on transcending those aspects of ourselves that express in the lower levels, thereby freeing ourselves to align with our unique expressions of power. https://bit.ly/2QNLBIb

[42] Masaru Emoto's research into the crystalline structure of frozen water first came to light in his New York Times best-selling book, *The Hidden Messages in Water*, first published in 2004. Using detailed electron micrographs, Emoto

showed how the structure of water changes when it is subjected to different emotional frequencies, and he hypothesised that water can hold 'memory' in its form. The micrographs showed how water that is exposed to angry vibrations (for example) and then frozen and viewed under an electron microscope, has jagged, broken patterns in the crystalline structure, whereas love or joy or other high-frequency vibrations create beautiful, harmonious patterns. Although Emoto died in 2014 his colleagues continue his work, calling it 'The New Science of Water' (see https://www.masaru-emoto.net/). Nonetheless, Emoto's work is considered by some as 'pseudo-science' with critics stating that his experiments had insufficient 'controls' and were therefore prone to manipulation and human error. Continuing development in our understanding of how observation and thought can affect the behaviour of particles (see The Double Slit Experiment, for example and the work of Jacques Benveniste) is opening up this field of enquiry to further investigation.

The purported ability of water to hold the memory of a substance, even when that substance has been diluted to the point that it cannot be traced physically, is the mechanism by which homeopathy works. Again, homeopathy is derided by the scientific community, because when subjected to analysis, no molecule of the original substance remains, only the 'memory' of it. Despite this, I (Lorna) have seen the miraculous effects of homeopathy with my own eyes, both in humans and in animals (who cannot be subject to 'the placebo effect'). My own raging tinnitus subsided significantly after I took a homeopathic remedy; I once saw a seriously ill cow who had lain prone with milk fever for several hours get to her feet ten minutes after a dose of homeopathy; and just recently our dog, who suffers from a degenerative spinal condition bounced back to something akin to his puppy-like former self after the vet gave him a homeopathic remedy. Homeopathy can work like a miracle.

It is worth noting that when a scientist (whether qualified or a layperson) presents theories that challenge the status quo in any given field, there will be an outcry of 'heresy'. When Gallileo championed 'heliocentrism' (that the Earth and planets revolve around the sun, rather than the sun and planets revolving around the Earth, as was previously believed), his work was considered to be 'foolish and absurd'. He was tried by the Inquisition and found to be 'vehemently suspect of heresy' and spent the rest of his life under house arrest. Of course, he was later found to be right. Those who think 'outside the box' are still subjected to an inquisition of sorts (see Point 43 below), and yet it was Einstein himself who said, "We cannot solve our problems with the same kind of thinking that created them." Perhaps the lesson here is to remain open-minded about our Universe, for one thing is certain: humanity is like an infant in its understanding of the magnitude of the Cosmos. Who are we to be so sure we are right?

[43] Rupert Sheldrake is a contemporary scientist who has been called, "the most heretical scientist of our time". The late Sir John Maddox, editor of the journal *Nature* was so incensed at the favourable reviews of Sheldrake's book, *A New Science of Life*, that he published an editorial denouncing it as a 'book for burning'. Perhaps this fact alone proves that Sheldrake is onto something important! Sheldrake's work is multifaceted, but for us, his theory of 'morphic resonance' is one that really resonates (if you'll pardon the pun). On his website, Sheldrake states, "Morphic resonance is a process whereby self-organising systems inherit a memory from previous similar systems. In its most general formulation, morphic resonance means that the so-called laws of nature are more like habits. The hypothesis of morphic resonance also leads to a radically new interpretation of memory storage in the brain and of biological inheritance. Memory need not be stored in material traces inside brains, which are more like TV receivers than video recorders, tuning into influences from the past. And biological inheritance need not all be coded in the genes, or in epigenetic modifications of the genes; much of it depends on morphic resonance from previous members of the species. Thus, each individual inherits a collective memory from past members of the species, and also contributes to the collective memory, affecting other members of the species in the future."

[44] Richard Rudd, the author of *The Gene Keys* has married the 64 ancient hexagrams from the I Ching with the 64 genetic codons, and together with a

deep dive into his own personal journey of transformation he has synthesised this into The Gene Keys. By working with your own Hologenetic Profile and the Keys that are predetermined at your birth, it is possible to divine the true higher purpose of your life. Not for the faint-hearted, for once embarked upon, this could be a lifetime's work, The Gene Keys is both complex and simple, profound and yet practical on a daily basis. For more information on the Gene Keys, visit: https://genekeys.com/

[45] Our good friend, Donna Byatt, is a Crystal Alchemist who divines the healing qualities of crystals that can help any journey of transformation. Her shop is at the centre of the Avebury stone circle and she is a Guardian of the Stones, keeping the energy clear and the ley lines vibrant. See her work at: element-sofavebury.co.uk

[46] The World Water Law is the first initiative towards the adoption and implementation of Codes for a Healthy Earth, because, "the water of life, the first medicine of the world, is so precious to everything that grows, breathes and lives." The aim of Codes for a Healthy Earth is, "towards a radical, whole-system healing". As David Attenborough says, "We cannot be radical enough in dealing with the issues that press us at the moment." To find out more about Water Activism, visit: https://www.codes.earth/waterlaw

[47] Music has been an integral part of our culture for millennia and has a transcendental quality that can take us to other worlds in an instant – the sound of a sitar transports us to India as an oud does to the Middle East; an old song on the radio can transport us in time to our childhood like nothing else can. We live in a vibratory universe and the word 'harmony' underpins both the resonance of these vibrations and the state of our own health. The basic principle of sound healing is this concept of 'resonance' (the vibratory frequency of an object.) Every organ, cell, bone, tissue and liquid in the human body, and the electromagnetic fields which surround the body, have a vibratory frequency. If we are not resonating with some part of ourselves or our surroundings harmoniously,

we become dissonant and therefore unhealthy. Sound healing can help to correct this dissonance through the application of healing frequencies to the physical and subtle energy fields around the body. These healing or therapeutic frequencies come in myriad forms: from live sound therapy sessions, to using your voice in overtone chanting, for example, and via a variety of sound healing tools such as tuning forks, Tibetan singing bowls, quartz crystal bowls, as well as instruments from shamanic sound healing traditions, such as digeridoo, Native drum, Native flute, rattles and so on. Kay Gardner's inspirational book on the subject of sound healing, *Sounding the Inner Landscape: Music as Medicine*, is a seminal work on the healing power of music. The book is now out of print and hard to find, but Sound Healing itself is a concept that has taken off and a brief search online will appraise you of practitioners in your area.

[48] William Blake's beautiful poem, The Auguries of Innocence is perhaps best known for its first stanza:

> To see a World in a Grain of Sand
> And a Heaven in a Wild Flower
> Hold Infinity in the palm of your hand
> And Eternity in an hour

This ability to see a world in a grain of sand (or heaven in a wild flower), is the epitome of the macrocosm in the microcosm; the very essence of interbeing – something the genius Blake intuited over a century ago before quantum physics was able to confirm the interconnectedness of all life. It is said that poetry predates the written word and is a form of communication that embodies 'genius' for it allows an imaginative force – or as Blake suggests, 'God' – to speak through the poet. You can read the complete version of The Auguries of Innocence here: https://bit.ly/2Dpq8C7

MY INSIGHTS AND ILLUMINATIONS

THESE NEXT PAGES ARE FOR YOU TO MAKE NOTES AND COMMENTS AS YOU EMBARK UPON YOUR OWN JOURNEY OF DISCOVERY

Made in the USA
Middletown, DE
03 January 2021

28347753R00230